US Power and the Internet in International Relations

US Power and the Internet in International Relations

The Irony of the Information Age

Madeline Carr

Senior Lecturer in International Politics and the Cyber Dimension, Aberystwyth University, UK

First published 2016 by
PALGRAVE MACMILLAN

Palgrave Macmillan in the UK is an imprint of Macmillan Publishers Limited, registered in England, company number 785998, of Houndmills, Basingstoke, Hampshire RG21 6XS.

Palgrave Macmillan in the US is a division of St Martin's Press LLC, 175 Fifth Avenue, New York, NY 10010.

Palgrave Macmillan is the global academic imprint of the above companies and has companies and representatives throughout the world.

Palgrave® and Macmillan® are registered trademarks in the United States, the United Kingdom, Europe and other countries.

ISBN 978–1–137–55023–1

This book is printed on paper suitable for recycling and made from fully managed and sustained forest sources. Logging, pulping and manufacturing processes are expected to conform to the environmental regulations of the country of origin.

A catalogue record for this book is available from the British Library.

A catalog record for this book is available from the Library of Congress.

For my family, Joan, Reg and all the Francis women – you know who you are

Contents

Acknowledgements   viii

1 Introduction   1
2 International Relations Meets Technology Theory   16
3 A (Select) Political History of the Internet   45
4 Cyber Security   77
5 Internet Governance   117
6 Network Neutrality   149
7 Conclusion   182

Notes   191
Bibliography   197
Index   218

Acknowledgements

I take this opportunity to thank Professor Lorraine Elliott for her guidance, intellectual input and continuing friendship. She has fundamentally shaped me as a scholar and I am fortunate to know her. I also thank Christian Reus-Smit for setting an excellent example of collaboration, intellectual risk taking and making work fun.

1
Introduction

Over the course of the past two decades, much of the world has developed a dependence upon an unsecured, open computer network for communications, financial transactions, military weapons systems, critical infrastructure, commerce and diplomacy. Despite the pervasiveness of the Internet and its importance to a wide range of state functions, we still have little understanding of the implications of this technology for power in the context of international relations (IR). How does Internet technology relate to other material elements of state power like the economy and the military? What are the implications for social power factors like legitimacy and authority? Why do states adopt different approaches to Internet technology? And does the Internet produce universal outcomes or does its impact on state power differ depending on context? Answers to questions like these are essential to the analysis of what this dynamic technology means for our understanding of state power in the information age. However, the complex ways that Internet technology is embedded in civil, political, economic and military systems in developed states mean that this has proven extremely difficult to analyse with any clarity in a generalizable way.

Existing IR theories of power, developed in the context of industrial technology, have struggled to incorporate the Internet and address these questions. For much of the 20th century, scholars of IR have approached the relationship between power and technology in a relatively stable and consistent manner. Technology has been largely understood as a constitutive and material element of state power. Its military and economic relevance has led to an understanding of technology as a mechanism through which power (or security)-seeking states pursue relative advantage by the development of more efficient production methods (economic power) as well as advanced weaponry (military power) (Morgenthau, 1978, p. 322). This has been the predominant view through major technological shifts including the industrial revolution and the emergence of nuclear technology. Even as IR power theories broadened to incorporate social elements as well as material factors, a singular, narrow approach to technology has prevailed. This approach is manifestly inadequate for the study of the relationship between state power and new technology like the Internet.

In a unique way, information and communications technology (ICT) more, broadly, and the Internet, specifically, have led to a power paradox which forms the central focus around which this book emerged. President Obama has referred to the fact that those states which have most successfully adopted and exploited the opportunities afforded by the Internet are also the most vulnerable to the range of threats which accompany it as 'the great irony of our Information Age' (Obama, 2009b). Power-enhancing outcomes such as economic growth, advances in public diplomacy and the revolution in military affairs have to be balanced against the theft of intellectual property, attacks on critical infrastructure and the circumvention of conventional military force by asymmetric actors. No previous technology has been regarded concurrently as a source of power and vulnerability in quite the way that the Internet has.

In addition, Internet technology affects many diverse state systems and functions which make it difficult for analysts to sort through the implications to arrive at any kind of definitive answer about what the Internet means for state power. Technological developments which are beneficial for the online economy may be detrimental to cyber security. Those which enhance cyber security may undermine norms and values such as human rights or civil liberties. Technology policies that the telecommunications sector regards as essential may stifle innovation in software and applications development. Misaligned legal frameworks for dealing with online crime coupled with the capacity for actors to remain anonymous over the Internet undermine the state's monopoly on violence and make distinctions between crime, terrorism and state belligerence difficult or impossible.[1] These factors combine to render conventional approaches to understanding the relationship between technology and power in IR less useful than they may have been in the context of industrial technology.

Polarized literature

Viktor Mayer-Schöenberger and Gernot Brodnig write that the information age is 'opening a new chapter in defining and understanding international affairs' (Mayer-Schöenberger and Gernot Brodnig, 2001). Much of the literature which has sought to engage with this 'new chapter' has done so through existing theory which is not able to accommodate the distinctive features of ICT. Johan Eriksson and Giampiero Giacomello have observed this suggesting that too much work in this field had been primarily policy-oriented with 'little or no ambition to apply or contribute to theory' (Eriksson and Giacomello, 2006, p. 235).

Existing literature on the relationship between power and new technology in IR tends to fall into two broad categories. Some scholars regard ICT as simply an extension or enhancement of existing technology and therefore reinforcing existing power structures. Many studies which take this view are conducted with a rigid adherence to conventional military concepts such as 'deterrence' and 'arms control' – neither of which have particular relevance to ICT. The vocabulary employed to discuss issues of 'cyberwar', 'cyber-terror' or 'information warfare' is a product of Cold War military concepts blended with computer gaming terminology and leads to the commodification of information.

Mary Kaldor elaborates on this in the context of the revolution in military affairs which she argues is conceived of within the 'inherited institutional structures of war and the military' (Kaldor, 2007, p. 3). She argues that within this structure, new techniques are perceived of as developing in a more or less linear extension from the past. ICT becomes another 'artefact' of power to be understood in the same way we have previously regarded new missile technology or energy sources (Rothkopf, 1998, p. 325). This literature ignores important and unique aspects of emerging technology which impact on its relationship to power in IR in diverse ways. These include the integration of the technology into civil society which broadens the range of interests that politicians must take into account, the decentralized drivers of innovation which make future developments of the technology somewhat unpredictable, and the complexities of states sharing and relying upon a central, unified system.

The second broad category of literature concerned with the relationship between power and new technology in IR regards this technology as a transformative force. This is particularly evident in the literature on the democratizing nature of the Internet and changes to state sovereignty – both of which have attracted significant scholarly attention (Berman and Weitzner, 1997; Katznelson, 1997; Barney, 2000). Many studies have concentrated on the manner in which technology like the Internet has impacted on state power by eroding the institution of sovereignty. The general emphasis in these debates is that information technology is undermining state power in a variety of ways. Prominent among these are the proliferation and organization of non-state actors which compete for power with states and the challenges of state control over extraterritorial issues which stem from interconnected networked systems. This literature is predominantly concerned with the way that the Internet affects the state's changing relationship with individuals and the non-governmental and private sectors. Of these, amendments to the domestic power dynamics between civil society and the state have been most thoroughly investigated – as demonstrated by the response to the 2011 revolutions in the Middle East. While many felt that social networking tools had been instrumental in the success of the protest movements, others remained unconvinced, arguing that the same technology had been used by the repressive regimes to track the protests (Shane, 2011; Ward, 2011). This debate was epitomized in the 'Shirky/Morozov' debate which pitted a utopian view of the Internet which regarded these tools as liberating and democratizing against a dystopian view which regarded them as tools of state surveillance and repression.[2]

This particular debate was specific to the Middle East revolutions, but it is indicative of these two broad approaches in the literature: one that regards Internet technology as an extension of industrial age technology with regard to state power and the other that regards it as transformative. Both sides of this debate adopt a 'universal effects' approach to Internet technology. If one focuses on the Internet as a new realm or commons in which technologically advanced states may exercise power – through highly sophisticated surveillance, through information and cyber warfare strategies, through the efficiencies and advantages which the Internet offers the state economic apparatus and through the promotion of particular values – one might conclude that the Internet reinforces existing power structures (Mussington, 1997; Hughes and Wacker, 2003, pp. 139–61). Conversely, if one focuses on the many ways in which the Internet undermines state power – by turning those same surveillance techniques against the state, by empowering non-state actors, by reassigning the functions of the state and (through anonymity) by affording individuals access to the same 'weapons' as the state – one might conclude that the Internet is a democratizing or liberating technology (Smith and Naim, 2000; Deibert, 2002; pp. 143–59; Litfin, 2002). In fact, both of these approaches instil agency in the technology, and this leaves us only to argue over which view we find more compelling. Do those factors that reinforce state power outweigh those factors that undermine it, or the reverse? How would we begin to assess that?

Examining state intentions

When we acknowledge the wide range of variables at play in calculations about power and the Internet, it becomes clear that approaches that refer to the Internet as either 'empowering' states or as 'devolving power' from the state have skipped an important analytic step – one in which they examine closely the specific ways in which actors intend or expect this technology to enhance their power. An alternative approach (and the one which drives this study) observes that Internet technology is not discriminating – it can be used to enhance or undermine state power, in a multitude of ways and simultaneously. The Internet then is neither empowering nor disempowering. The Internet does not have a set of values or a purpose – those emanate from our interaction with the technology. In this view, the Internet is an *expression* of the interests and values of those who engage with it.

Just as international political economy would be regarded as theoretically impoverished without the incorporation of economic theory, understanding power in the information age requires engagement with theories and concepts applied to the relationship between society and technology. The philosophy of technology provides just such a mechanism as it focuses on human interaction with technology. This literature asks questions like 'how does technology impact upon power and how does power shape technology?', 'does technology follow a pre-ordained developmental path?' and 'if so, are we powerless to stop it?' These are important questions for IR because understanding power relations in the information age necessarily involves understanding the relationship between new technology and state power.

Scholars working in the philosophy of technology have developed a range of conceptual approaches and methodological tools to aid the investigation of these questions. One of these, the social construction of technology, forms the basis of the conceptual framework developed in this thesis for the analysis of the case studies. This cross-disciplinary approach retains a connection with the big questions in IR (in this case, power) while introducing a much more nuanced and sophisticated theoretical approach to technology which allows the analysis to move beyond the long-held assumptions that technology is an *artefact* which *impacts* upon power.

This approach shifts the analysis from a focus on 'what technology *does to* state power' – which, as the previous pages have indicated, can vary widely from state to state and even from issue to issue – to a more holistic approach which investigates 'how states *engage with* technology' in the context of conceptions of power. The advantage of looking at how conceptions of power influence and shape technology rather than focusing on the outcomes is that it moves the debate away from assumptions that technology has a universally applicable impact. In fact, politicians have to decide which elements of state power are most important when making Internet policy. They sometimes have to choose between privileging one conception of power over another. Therefore, looking closely at the drivers of Internet policy can tell us not only about *technology* but about *power*. As will be established in Chapter 2, the ways in which a given technology develops can provide insight into the locus of power as the interests of some actors are inevitably privileged over others. This approach provides insight into how different conceptions of power compete in these debates and why certain conceptions prevail in some cases and not in others.

This book relies upon three essential elements of the conceptual framework which is fully developed in the following chapter. First, IR theory provides a starting point for the analysis of power. There is no single theory of power which proved most suitable or helpful for this study. Because the research dealt with *conceptions* of power, it was necessary to remain open to a range of views. The case studies demonstrated the utility of this approach as politicians expressed multiple conceptions of power – sometimes in the context of a single issue – and this allowed the research findings to be guided by politicians' conceptualizations rather than a particular approach to power.

The second element of the conceptual framework is the philosophy of technology literature that identifies the range of *approaches* to technology. This is essential first to illustrate the long-held assumptions about technology which are endemic in IR literature which deals with the relationship between power and technology. In addition, it provides a conceptual language for engaging with how politicians approach Internet technology. These are not self-consciously expressed positions; they are assumed just as approaches to power are assumed. However, it is important to remain aware that these approaches to technology carry with them a whole set of assumptions that inform political decisions about technology. The philosophy of technology provided a means to identify these as they emerged in the case studies.

The third element of the conceptual framework developed in this thesis is a set of methodological tools borrowed from the social construction of technology – one of several philosophical approaches to technology. Specifically employed in this study are the 'reverse salient' and the 'relevant social group'. These are used in the research design to set the parameters and to generate the case studies. They also proved useful within those case studies when it became clear that there was not one single conception of power and/or approach to technology which was driving the political decisions about that particular aspect of Internet technology.

The 'reverse salient' can be understood as a perceived problem or point of lag in a technological system – something which prevents it from fulfilling its 'potential' (Hughes, 1989, p. 73). Social constructivists have found that identifying an actor's normative assumptions about technology – particularly what they regard as the 'problem' or reverse salient of a given technology – can lead to insights into how they conceptualize a whole range of other elements of social life. Wiebe Bijker uses the example of bicycle chain guards to illustrate the utility of the reverse salient (Bijker, 1995). Bicycles in the 19th century did not have guards over the chain running between the pedals and rear wheel. They were not found necessary because only men rode bicycles and trouser legs were not prone to being caught in the chain. In the late 1800s, women began to ride bicycles and, finding their long skirts became easily entangled, the exposed chain came to be regarded as a 'problem' resulting in the development of a chain guard.

Bijker points out that the reverse salient of the bicycle chain emerged for social reasons rather than technological (or design) reasons. Furthermore, an analysis of the way this reverse salient prompted innovation in bicycle design reveals much more about how social systems (in particular, perceptions of gender restrictions) were changing at that time, than it does about technology. This example serves to illustrate the important point that social constructivists make about technology, that is, that technological change reflects wider social, cultural and political change and for this reason, its analysis can provide insight into important issues including understanding power in IR.

In this study, the reverse salient has been applied for two purposes. First, it has been used to identify three empirical case studies (to be discussed more fully in the next section). The reverse salient has also been used *within* the case studies to provide a lens through which to examine the empirical data. Each of these three case studies was analysed to determine how politicians perceived the issue as a problem relating to

US power. This included identifying which conception (or conceptions) of power they employed in the debates, which approach to technology they engaged with and how these conceptions and approaches impacted on the development of the technology. The research revealed that politicians engage with multiple conceptions of power in these case studies and so the reverse salient was useful at this level to help distinguish the (sometimes competing) ideas driving policy decisions about the specific aspect of Internet technology.

In addition to these two ways in which the reverse salient contributes to the methodology of this thesis, there is a second important tool drawn from the social construction of technology employed in this methodology. The 'relevant social group' is a mechanism for focusing on whose needs or preferences are being privileged in decisions about technology. MacKenzie (1996, p. 6) stresses that although it may seem that a decision about technology is 'best', we must ask the question 'best for whom?' Different actors or groups of actors may have very different responses to a particular technology as did men and women to the bicycle chain.

Certainly these distinctions need not be this stark. Factors like gender and class are obvious examples for illustrating this point but any two people of similar circumstances may have different responses to technology. Scholars from the social construction of technology argue that it is necessary to be clear about this in any study because in the context of technology, priorities and values can vary widely from one group or actor to another. Within the case studies, the concept of the relevant social group sometimes proves to be a useful mechanism for understanding how politicians regard the Internet as linked to US power through the way they privilege the needs or priorities of one section of US society over another. A focus on the relevant social group in these instances helps to clarify how politicians conceptualize US power and which factors they regard as most significant when formulating Internet policy.

Scope and focus

In seeking to understand the relationship between the Internet and state power, the United States offers a unique opportunity for an historical study. The United States has played a seminal role in the evolution of the Internet and with over four decades of history in the development, implementation and management of Internet technology, it continues to globally influence key sectors of it. How the United States has dealt with the rapid development and implementation of the Internet and how it has sought to shape it in such a way as to enhance US power need to be understood not only through a snapshot of current circumstances, but through the analysis of the ideas and intentions of those politicians who facilitated or instigated the initial research phase as well as those who have continued to influence and shape the implementation and the development of Internet technology.

Conceptions of US power have intersected with the Internet's growth at many stages and over many issues over the past two and a half decades. Initially funded by the US Department of Defense (DoD), the Internet evolved as a joint military/academic project before being made available for commercial activity. The ideas and values of the early developers of the Internet are fundamental to its structure and design and are therefore constantly reinforced through its use (Lessig, 2006a; Zittrain, 2008). Based on 'rough consensus' and bottom-up development guided predominantly by highly regarded technicians, the Internet consists of agreed standards and code which provide its structure and functionality. Paradoxically, considering the role of the DoD, this technical evolution has come to be regarded as quite separate from state concerns. Consequently, the fact that these ideas arguably run counter to IR norms and institutions such as state control, sovereignty or hierarchical rule has been of little concern in the dynamics of the technical community. However, the rapid 'informatization' of the past two decades has made it very clear that Internet code and architecture *is* deeply political and how it is conceptualized and shaped has very real implications for states and the international system. This is significant for understanding the political implications of Internet technology and demonstrates that there already exists a 'political history of the Internet' worthy of scholarly attention.

The second reason why this study takes an historical approach is because there is a persistent focus in the relevant IR literature on contemporary issues. This provides valuable insight into the particular concerns of a given social context and time. However, without engaging with the debates, perceptions and decisions which accompanied the emergence of these issues, the arguments they put forward remain suspended in time with no connection to the past and no capacity to envisage a future. Mackenzie argues for an historical approach to studies of this nature because rather than a linear, predetermined path, he argues that looking at the history of technology demonstrates that there were a number of options all along the way – what he refers to as a 'constant turmoil of concepts, plans and projects' (MacKenzie, 1996, p. 6).

In bringing together the political history of the Internet, it becomes evident that many key decisions have been made by US politicians about how the Internet could or should function. In addition, a close analysis reveals how normative ideas about the relationship between US power and the Internet have influenced those decisions.

Finally, technology is frequently studied in an historical context because the history of technology can tell us much about what people wanted and how they viewed the future. It can also reveal much about how their perception of 'problems' with technology changed over time. Marita Sturken, Douglas Thomas and Ball-Rokeach (2004, p. 1) write that 'the meanings attributed to new technologies are some of the most important evidence we can find of the visions, both optimistic and anxious, through which modern societies cohere'. By taking an historical approach, it is possible to encounter change, continuity and patterns – all of which not only better equip us for understanding the current state of the relationship between power and new technology in IR but provide the basis for studying future change and continuity. This book argues that states can and do shape Internet technology. Therefore, understanding how they have done so in the past is essential to conceiving of how they may do so in the future.

A range of material has been examined in the research of these case studies. A major component of the empirical material for this study has been Congressional hearings and because they may be less familiar to readers than more conventional sources like speeches or policy papers, it is useful here to elaborate briefly on how these hearings function.

Congressional Committees are formed in order to create a body of expertise within Congress which is then able to offer broader advice. Committees are able to commission reports, to call hearings and to summon and interrogate witnesses so as to gain the knowledge and expertise they feel they need in order to formulate and vote on policy. They then report back to Congress, and these reports are often submitted alongside a proposed Bill as supporting documentation. As politicians have to vote on many issues about which they may have limited practical knowledge, they rely to an extent on the advice of their colleagues who sit on relevant committees. These Committee assignments change over time sometimes as a consequence of restructuring and sometimes as relevant issues rise or recede in importance.

Hearings are called by Congressional committees for a number of reasons including the investigation of pertinent issues, the need to gather information on or debate a piece of proposed legislation, or as a means of conducting oversight of a government body or department. Prior to the hearing, a list of witnesses is drawn up. These can include government employees, experts and people affected by the issue. Generally, the hearings call witnesses from a range of views but it can happen that the witness list is biased in a particular direction.

Hearings open with a statement by the chair followed by statements by a number of committee members. These statements are often used to frame the concerns each member has about the subject of the hearing and often how they frame those concerns is as relevant for this research as the concern itself. Once these opening statements are concluded, the hearing moves to testimony by the witnesses followed by a question and answer session. During this time, committee members are free to ask candid questions of the witnesses either about their testimony or about related issues. Due to its unscripted format, these exchanges between committee members and witnesses can be extremely enlightening. They provide a means of accessing the conceptions, concerns and priorities of politicians in a way that formal speech does not always allow.

Policy documents and speeches, though less frank, serve two purposes for this research. First, they provide an 'outcome' to the debates which transpire in Congressional hearings. Linking policy outcomes to debates can help to illuminate which approaches to power and technology prevail. In addition, policy documents often become the loci of further debate which is one of the benefits of adopting an historical approach to this study, discussed briefly below and at more length in the following chapter.

A third source of empirical material is the legislative record. This includes Bills proposed as well as Bills passed into law. Legislative proposals are very complex and the reasons behind the failure of a particular bill can be varied and, in many cases, external to the issue at hand. However, an analysis of how politicians propose law is very useful in working to understand how they normatively approach issues of technology in the context of US power.

Finally, as part of this research, a small number of interviews were conducted, particularly with senior policymakers who worked on Internet-related policy in the late 1980s and early 1990s when documentary material was somewhat less readily available.

The case studies

Given that Internet technology has implications for so many aspects of state power and in diverse ways, an ordered approach to generating the case studies was necessary. Through the examination of Congressional hearings, policy documents, speeches and debates over the past 25 years, a number of Internet policy issues emerge as key 'problems' for US politicians – in that, they generated significant and complex debates. Of these problems, some had no clear implications for state power. Examples of these are the use of the Internet for primary school education, the use of the Internet for medical records and protecting children from obscene material or predatory behaviour on the Internet.

Of the problems which politicians perceived as having clear links to US power, three stood out as issues which have been consistently regarded as a significant problem for state power. These were cyber security, Internet governance and network neutrality. These issues were also identified through an assessment of the technology itself. Some technological issues have quite obvious implications for power in IR while others are more obscure or still evolving. The case studies have all been consistently referred to by politicians as having significant relationship to US power through a mix of material and social factors. In addition, they are issues acknowledged by the technical community to have very serious implications for how the Internet develops.

One of the obvious areas of concern was the consistent political anxiety about security. Although politicians had been aware of security threats to DoD systems from the 1980s, the adoption of the technology by the commercial sector and by private individuals introduced a whole range of evolving cyber security problems. Successive administrations have struggled to find a balance between the demands of cyber security which compete with norms and values such as privacy, freedom of information and more recently, human rights. The long-standing conviction of politicians that cyber security has implications for US power on a number of levels led to the generation of the case study on cyber security.

A second consequence of the rapid uptake of Internet technology was the need to implement governance structures without fully understanding their implications. The notion that the Internet should be linked to US economic power rather than military power was promoted by the 'Atari Democrats' including Senator Albert Gore Jr., who would prove to be a key figure in political approaches to Internet technology. In the mid-1990s, the Clinton–Gore administration commercialized and privatized the Internet leading to an exponential increase in the number of people accessing it and the amount of data travelling across it. This introduced a range of problems, one of which was how to effectively and efficiently govern the names and numbers database – the Domain Name System (DNS). The debates around this and the problems associated with US power led to Internet governance being selected as one of the case studies for this thesis.

Finally, changes in telecommunications legislation which directly impacts on how the Internet continues to develop not only in terms of technology but also in terms of our interaction with it have prompted a series of debates about how the Internet *is* and how it *should* be. These normative debates are linked to concepts of US power through material and social factors. In the United States, there are some factors which have made refining laws to regulate new technology very difficult to resolve. These developments and the contentious views about how best they should be managed in ways that would promote – or at least not undermine – US power resulted in the identification of the case study on network neutrality.

Contribution

This project is able to contribute on both a theoretical level and an empirical level. While IR scholars have taken some steps to incorporate recent technological change into theories of power, it has been done without adequately engaging with either technology theory or emerging and complex technical issues. This work has, therefore, tended towards dystopian or utopian conclusions without developing a useful conceptual framework with which to examine these pressing issues. By incorporating the philosophy of technology which provides theory and concepts for engaging with the social implications of technology, and demonstrating its utility in the analysis of state power in IR, this study takes an important step forward. It illustrates how much of the literature has been driven by assumptions about technology – particularly the assumption that technology has a universal effect on power regardless of social or political forces. The conceptual framework developed and employed in this study can contribute to IR scholarship which investigates questions dealing with new technology by moving debates beyond questions about whether technology like the Internet enhances power more than it undermines it.

On an empirical level, this project contributes in a number of ways. First, the analysis of the political debates around Internet technology reveals the multifaceted and contradictory nature of US power in ways that studies which look at power through realist, liberal or constructivist lenses are not able to. Politicians take into account many factors of power when they make critical decisions about Internet technology. These conceptions of power can lead to conflicting policy choices and when they do, politicians privilege one conception of power over another.

Second, the three case studies reveal how conceptions of power have shaped and influenced these three aspects of Internet technology. This is an important shift away from the view that technology has its own path and produces universal effects – a view which pervades much of the academic literature on the Internet and politics. Observing how the Internet has been shaped by political conceptions of power in the United States – sometimes consciously and sometimes unconsciously as a function of ideas and norms about power – provides a model for a similar empirical analysis of other states and other technology issues.

Finally, the empirical material provides a narrative of the 'political' history of three aspects of Internet technology which is absent in other historical accounts. Despite states' increasing dependence upon and interdependence over the Internet, the political history of how this technology was initially conceived, developed, governed and managed over time has not been critically examined. Although 'histories of the Internet' abound, they are almost exclusively concerned with documenting key technicians and developers and attributing their achievements and contributions to the code and architecture now in use. However, the political forces surrounding those developments are rarely referenced in these accounts and given no substantive place in understanding the progression of the Internet from a military project to a global information and communications network. As this thesis shows, early Internet research was largely funded by government research institutions, the infrastructure was owned and operated by government agencies until it could be privatized in the United States, and political decisions continue to shape and influence the development of Internet technology. The empirical material in this book draws out this political history and contributes a significant aspect of the development of this important technology.

This book does three things: it explains how US political leaders' conceptions of power interact with approaches to technology to shape and influence the development of complex technological systems like the Internet. It also builds a conceptual framework for future studies of the relationship between power in IR and ICTs. Finally, it tells a story about the political evolution and development of the Internet in the United States which has been overlooked in the proliferation of technological histories. In doing these three things, this book offers insights into the relationship between state power and technology in the information age.

2
International Relations Meets Technology Theory

As outlined in the Introduction, a central premise of this study is that existing approaches to understanding the relationship between technology and power in international relations (IR) are struggling to deal with the complexities introduced by the information age. While the discipline of IR has a range of theories about power, it does not have an equivalent framework for understanding technology and this is proving to be a limitation for developing a deeper understanding of the relationship between power and new technology. As this chapter reveals, assumptions are made in IR literature about technology without an adequate critical analysis of how scholars and practitioners arrive at those assumptions. Furthermore, existing theories for understanding power in IR were developed within the context of industrial technology and do not take into account the distinctive features of information and communications technology (ICT) which can render the nature and expression of power more complex. This book demonstrates that by engaging with social theories of technology, IR can be better equipped to pursue answers to questions which have thus far proven difficult to grapple with including how we understand the relationship between new technology like the Internet and state power.

This chapter builds a theoretical and conceptual framework which incorporates insights from the philosophy of technology and, more specifically, the social construction of technology (SCoT), in order to explore the manner in which conceptions of US power have influenced the development of the Internet and what implications this has for understanding power in the information age.

This chapter consists of four main parts. The first section introduces the field of the Philosophy of Technology. A full treatment of the Philosophy of Technology is beyond the scope of this chapter nor is it necessary for the development of the conceptual framework that guides this book. Instead, through a discussion of three key debates which feature in the discipline, a number of important and relevant concepts and theoretical approaches to defining technology and to understanding its nature are introduced. These debates revolve around questions of how to define technology, whether technology is a positive, benign or negative force in society, and to what degree society influences the development of technology.

The second section engages further with these debates in the context of an explanation of the theories of the SCoT. This is one approach of several put forward in the philosophy of technology but because it provides scope for the analysis of social factors of technology, it is best suited to the study of power.

The third section of this chapter demonstrates how the concepts and theories from the philosophy of technology can be integrated into IR theories of power. This is achieved by first demonstrating the unacknowledged role that assumptions about technology *already* play in IR literature which seeks to explore questions about the relationship between technology and power. This is illustrated through the articulation of two dominant paradigms within IR literature. Referred to in this book as the 'industrial age' view and 'information age' view, these paradigms are comprised of self-consciously articulated theories of power coupled with (generally) unselfconscious – but clearly evident – approaches to technology. As suggested in the third section, neither the industrial age paradigm nor the information age paradigm is proving effective for understanding the relationship between power and technology in the information age as they both remain embedded in restrictive theories about technology.

The final section of this chapter outlines the conceptual framework which supports and guides this study. This framework provides a way forward for future analysis of the relationship between new technology and power in IR. By contextualizing this study within the philosophy of technology, it becomes clear why and how this methodological approach can ask and answer questions about the relationship between politics and technology that other approaches are unable to.

The philosophy of technology

The philosophy of technology is a body of scholarship which seeks to understand the human relationship with technology. The emergence of the field can be understood as a response to rapid changes in technology and science following the Industrial Revolution particularly from the mid-19th century. Prior to the Industrial Revolution, the pace of technological change was not generally sufficient to significantly affect the wider social fabric during the course of an individual's lifetime. While technology changed, it happened slowly and – more importantly – its impact on the human experience was gradual. However, the past two centuries have been a time of constant, rapid and profound technological development. This development has been implicated in social, cultural, economic and political shifts which have, in some cases, altered the experience of individuals and societies profoundly over a short span of time. Attempts to better comprehend the impact of rapid changes in technology on the human condition emerged predominantly over the course of the latter half of the 20th century into a coherent study now referred to as the philosophy of technology.

There are a number of key debates within the philosophy of technology. Some of these are of particular relevance to this book and provide a means of introducing some key concepts and theoretical approaches which inform the study. The first of these is an ongoing and unresolved debate about how to define technology and there are parallels here with IR debates about how to define power. Both debates are characterized by a spectrum of views, at one end of which is a very tightly focused and parsimonious definition while at the other end of the spectrum is a broader definition which accommodates a range of social factors. Those definitions, as they apply to technology, are explored in more detail later in this chapter.

The second big debate to be discussed here revolves around whether technology is a positive, benign or negative force in society. The purpose of engaging with this debate is that it provides an opportunity to examine a range of *approaches to* technology – as distinct from *definitions of* technology. These approaches have been conceptualized differently by a number of scholars but key themes run through a general and representative survey of the literature. This debate is primarily concerned with the values and norms that technology does or does not promote and the impact of those values and norms on the human condition.

Finally, the third big debate of relevance for this study involves the degree to which society shapes and influences technology. As will be explained, some scholars argue that the answer is 'not at all', others feel that society could, but rarely does shape technology while yet others believe that not only does society shape technology but technology is, in fact, an *expression* of the norms, values and expectations of society. It is this last view, embedded in the SCoT, with which this study engages in order to address questions about how conceptions of US power have influenced the development of Internet technology. However, the broader range of views is essential to understand because they will feature in the analysis of the empirical material. Understanding how these approaches function and what conclusions they lead to is necessary to an informed reading of the case studies.

First big debate: What defines technology?

One of the big epistemological debates within the philosophy of technology is the question of what exactly technology *is*. 'Technology' is a term plagued by definitional ambiguity in a similar manner to other terms from within IR including democracy, terrorism and, indeed, power – a focus of this study. There are a range of approaches to understanding and defining technology with the essential point of difference being the scope and focus. Some approaches take a very narrow and specific view of technology while others argue that technology includes factors such as science, organizational structures and even systems of knowledge.

The most basic definition of technology is that of 'applied science'. This definition is based on the understanding that science is a 'search for new laws of nature' while technology is the application of those scientific laws (Bunge, 1966, p. 329). Norman Vig understands this approach as essentially an Aristotelian concept whereby 'technology refers to a device or method created by man [sic] (and thus external to him) as a secondary means of achieving his primary ends' (Vig, 1988, p. 11). Technology, in this view, is a tool. In this definition, an artefact or object is what it is – regardless of whether anyone observes it or interacts with it, it has meaning and purpose. A computer is a computer – regardless of whether it is used to compute or to prop open a door. The Internet, in this definition, would consist of the physical hardware – the cables, routers and computers but it would not include the World Wide Web which runs over it and certainly not the decisions about how it is used, governed or interacted with. This definition of technology has three defining qualities: technology is distinct from science; its purpose is 'problem-solving'; and it is narrowly conceived of as 'artefacts' or physical tools. This definition is most closely aligned with studies based on an objectivist epistemology but Donald MacKenzie (1999, p. 3) points out that few scholars are content with a simple definition of 'technology as hardware'.

For those who believe an expanded definition of technology is warranted, justifications come in a number of ways. John Staudenmaier

(1985, pp. 95–101) conducted a study which analysed every article published in the *Technology and Culture* journal between 1959 and 1980. One of his focus questions was this issue of defining technology which played a prominent role in the journal's content over two decades. Staudenmaier found that the notion of technology as applied science faced criticism from within that quarter of the discipline on the basis of two arguments. The first was a rebuke to the view of science as somehow more purely connected to the pursuit of true knowledge – Pinch (1988, p. 72) refers to this as an 'over-idealised version of the nature of science'. Proponents of this position argue that science is as constructed as technology – that scientists do not 'discover the truth', rather they construct facts (Staudenmaier, 1985, p. 100). This assertion is based on the acknowledgement that scientific knowledge changes – sometimes, a 'fact' is later found to be an error.

The second argument against a definition of technology as an artefact and as distinct from science is based on an understanding of the inter-relationships between art, technology and science. MacKenzie point out that technology's boundaries with science, art and the economy are unclear and more importantly, our *perceptions* of those boundaries change over time (1999, pp. 2–5). The extension of this is to suggest then that technology also refers to human activity. It is not just the tool (or artefact) itself, but what we *do* with the tool which constitutes technology. This definition would regard the technology of the Internet as including the software and systems like the web as well as the ways in which people interact with it. The processing of data and transfer of files as well as the systems of knowledge about the architecture and use of the Internet comprise technology in this expanded view.

In one sense, this definitional approach seems intuitive – the cables and computers are not the Internet without data flowing through them and without people connecting across the network. However, this view is not without problems. As MacKenzie and Wajcman (1999, pp. 2–5) points out, this definition implies that technology includes what people *do* as well as the tools they *use* and when we start to discuss behaviour, 'it could well be said that we are already talking about society, not about something separate'. Despite the complexity which an expanded definition of technology introduces, many scholars feel that a parsimonious view leaves out too much of relevance. They, therefore, regard the distinction between not only science and technology, but the artefact and the way we use it, as artificial (Pinch, 1988, p. 72).

The purpose of this study is not to refine the definition of technology, nor does it intend to isolate one of these layers of meaning from the others. In the context of this study which seeks to understand the relationship between ideas about US power and Internet technology, all of these layers of meaning are relevant. It is not useful to look only at the physical infrastructure of the Internet because it is how policymakers perceive the relationship between that technology and US power which gives meaning to this study. It is the more abstract (or at least less brutally objectivist) meaning of technology which is of relevance here – including the uses of artefacts and the organization of people and systems of knowledge about the Internet. However, the artefacts themselves have often been the subject of political decisions which have influenced the abstract – material concerns are shown to impact on the social, political and cultural meaning of technology. Therefore, this study accepts the complex nature of this conceptualization of technology (as do many other studies) and argues that the complexity is, in fact, the very essence of why we need to study it so carefully.

Second big debate: What is the nature of technology?

Beyond the debates outlined above about the *definition* of technology, understanding the *nature* of technology is also a key pursuit of scholars working in the philosophy of technology. There is a tendency to employ a dichotomous framework of reference to technology which ascribes positive or negative attributes to it (Sturken et al., 2004, pp. 1–18). Significantly, this permeates not only literature in the philosophy of technology but also (as foreshadowed in the Introduction) IR literature on the relationship between technology and power. This debate engages with questions about whether technology is 'good' for us or 'bad' for us. This obviously raises a set of sub-questions like 'good or bad for whom, exactly?', 'good and bad in which respects?' and 'good or bad in whose opinion?' In the context of this study, these questions may be realigned to ask whether technology such as the Internet enhances or undermines state power, in whose view and in which ways.

At their simplest, approaches to the nature of technology can be understood to see it either as positive and beneficial or as threatening and negative. Challenges like ecological destruction and nuclear war help to focus attention on the risks of technology and raise questions about the ability of humans to live sustainably on the planet. At the same time, advances in technology which can prolong life, more efficiently produce food or enhance our experiences through the ability to travel, communicate and ease many daily tasks are regarded as positive and liberating. In many of the debates which feature in this book, these two approaches can be observed struggling for prominence as politicians' conceptions appear to be largely dependent on the context. The following section clearly outlines the key approaches to the nature of technology which are prominent in the literature and which feature in the analysis of the empirical material in this study.

Instrumentalism

Instrumentalism is an approach which regards technology as a means to address a human-defined problem or need. Innovation is always regarded in this approach as positive if it is 'successful'. If technology works, it is 'good'. Beyond this, technology is morally neutral and disconnected from its social consequences. Human use makes technology 'good' or 'evil' – the technology itself is detached from moral outcomes. Guns are an example of 'good' technology in that they are very effective at killing from a distance. Human use may include killing an animal for food or killing a human for gain but instrumentalists regard either of those ends as separate and distinct from the technology itself.

Dominant in the commercial sector, instrumentalism justifies continuous innovation while also implying that if there were to arise any negative social outcomes, the answer to them probably lies in a technologically based solution. The instrumentalist assumption that science and technology are the means through which social problems should be solved is observed by Hans Morgenthau in *Scientific Man vs Power Politics* (1946, pp. 267–9). Morgenthau notes here that a belief in science 'is the one intellectual trait which sets our age apart from preceding periods of history' (1946, pp. 3–4). He also makes the point that this belief in science and its capacity to 'solve' the problems of society unites us all as it transcends other divergent philosophic, economic and political beliefs we may hold. In this view, the problems of society and nature are essentially identical and the solution of social problems depends upon the quantitative extension of the method of the natural sciences to the social sphere. This, Morgenthau argues, is the 'common ground on which Jeremy Bentham and Karl Marx, Herbert Spencer and John Dewey take their stand' (1946, pp. 3–4).

In a political context, Vig (1988, p. 13) links instrumentalism to liberal political theories in which 'individuals should be free to pursue their own interests without interference from the state'. The empirical research for this study reveals a persistent notion on behalf of the private sector that Internet technology should be developed without reference to normative expectations about how society will engage with it or what kind of impact it might have on those who use it. This tends to emerge most explicitly in Chapter 6 on network neutrality which deals with political expectations of the public sector provision of Internet infrastructure. Innovation is regarded as an end in and of itself and is always a positive outcome in an instrumentalist view.

This is a point strongly refuted by Herbert Marcuse. In *One Dimensional Man*, Marcuse (1971, pp. 156–69) argues that technology is not neutral and the discourse which suggests that it is, in effect, closes off the space for any substantive critical analysis of values and norms. Certainly, in the context of this study, instrumentalism has that effect on some US politicians by reducing their perceptions of the government's mandate to make decisions about Internet technology. The Internet is often portrayed in political debates almost as an actor: one in possession of a specific set of values and destined for a particular trajectory that must not be disturbed. If technology is to be held separate from the outcomes of its use and implementation as well as its relationship with power, debate about it is limited and constrained. This is a recurring theme in the empirical material and will be drawn out in each of the three case studies.

In studying two concepts of a fundamentally social nature like power and the Internet, an approach which disengages from the social implications of technology is not useful. If technology has no values, then values are irrelevant. In this study, an instrumental approach would lead to questions about whether a particular aspect of Internet technology is 'good' – that is, does it address the problem or purpose it was intended for? However, it would fail to engage with important factors for understanding power such as whose perception of the problem or purpose is being privileged in decisions about technology and how a legitimate use of technology is defined. Instrumentalism does not provide an appropriate conceptual framework for this research project as it leaves out too much of relevance for understanding power but because it does play a role in some of the political debates about the Internet, it is important to articulate here.

Technological determinism

In response to instrumentalism, technological determinists argue against a view of technology as 'value neutral'. Instead, they believe that technology is imbued with values like a desire for power, the quest for efficiency and the profit motive – 'over other human needs (including those of future generations) and against the integrity of nature' (Vig, 1988, p. 17). While instrumentalists regard innovation as inherently positive and progressive, technological determinism tends to be an approach which focuses on the negative and dangerous aspects of technology. Indeed, technological determinism can be understood as a response to the negative effects of modern technology. Vig cites as an example the Vietnam War when practices like chemical defoliation and carpet bombing became 'symbols of technological hubris' (Vig, 1988, p. 17). Episodes like this, he argues, periodically prompt a re-evaluation of our relationship with technology and a fundamental questioning of its benign nature.

There are a number of strands of technological determinism but they are united by some overriding principles. One of these is the fact that technological determinists take a social view of technology which engages with the relationship between humans and technology. It is, however, based on a mono-directional relationship. That is, technology has an impact on society – in many cases, a profound impact – but it is an external force over which society has minimal control or influence. Technological determinism regards technology as having its own governing force; it 'advances according to its own logic and shapes human development more than it serves human ends' (Vig, 1988, p. 16; Bimber, 1990, p. 338). It is the story of Frankenstein, of technology running along a predetermined evolutionary path which may or may not be beneficial for society but which is largely unstoppable.

Technological determinists also believe that society adapts to technology in a homogenous manner. They argue that the introduction of technology into different societies will have the same outcome regardless of cultural, political or social factors or influences. Although technology is not considered to be morally neutral, it is understood as autonomous from its context.

Beyond these unifying characteristics, there exist a number of subtle but important distinctions in positions of technological determinism. Towards the end of the following discussion of these distinctions, this second debate about the nature of technology – whether essentially positive, benign or negative – will begin to segue into the third big debate about whether or how societies shape technology.

Variations in technological determinism

One approach to technological determinism can be understood as 'hard determinism' or what Bruce Bimber terms the 'logical sequence' approach (Bimber, 1990, pp. 333–50). This approach suggests that one technological development emerges logically from its predecessors and we are witness to a certain segment of that evolutionary process which will continue to unfold more or less unabated. The logical sequence approach would argue that given the existence of both sailing ships and the steam engine, it was inevitable that steam-powered ocean travel would eventually follow. This is expressed in Robert Heilbroner's idea of a single, predetermined 'grand avenue of advance' (1961, pp. 335–45). Heilbroner doubts, however, that technology can provide society with the means to control it – for he and his fellow scholars who accept this view, technology remains determined and society must adapt accordingly.

Other scholars see the problem of technology and determinism in a slightly different light. For these scholars, the point of focus is not technology itself but rather society's inability to synthesize it with certain social norms and values. Lewis Mumford makes a distinction between technology which is in harmony with the diversity of human aspirations and that which he describes as mono- or authoritarian technology. Authoritarian technology, he argues, is 'based upon scientific intelligence and quantified production, directed mainly toward economic expansion, material repletion, and military superiority' – in short, towards power (Mitcham, 1985, p. 79). The fear of technological determinists like Mumford is that once large technological systems are in place, it becomes very difficult to alter or reverse them – they become so embedded in society that they are not necessarily responsive to changed human perceptions about their value or use. In this context, an elite group of 'technocrats' control what Mumford calls the 'megamachine', which leaves the rest of society vulnerable to its effects but powerless to alter them (Mumford, 1970, pp. 263–300).

Mumford's approach has resonance with questions about power and Internet technology. Certainly, the Internet has become firmly embedded in social, cultural, economic and political aspects of life in industrialized and industrializing states. It could also be argued that decisions made early in the development of the Internet (e.g. governance mechanisms) now have some very serious and binding consequences for any of us who use the Internet. In part, this tendency towards technological 'lock-in' is exactly why examining political decisions about technology is so important (David, 1985, pp. 332–7). However, Mumford's approach is constrained by its focus on 'impact' and 'adaptation' which fails to engage with an analysis of how those decisions were made (or why they were not made) as well as the ways in which society *does* shape and influence technology.

Certainly, in the context of the Internet, there have been many, many choices about how that technology should or would be developed. The Internet did not spring forth fully conceptualized, nor was it 'discovered'. Rather, it was the consequence of many years of competing ideas,

collaboration and – as this book demonstrates – normative political decisions about what the Internet *should* be and how it *should* function.
The case studies highlight this through the analysis of debates about
how Internet governance should be arranged, how security mechanisms
should function and who should have the power to control the flow
of information over the Internet. Mumford's technologically determinist approach offers some important insights into the question driving
this study but it does not offer a framework for analysis of the ways
in which conceptions of US power have influenced and shaped Internet technology. Due to the way that it negates the role of social choice,
a determinist approach in this project would narrow the focus to an
assessment of technology's impact on power which returns us to the
circular debates about whether the Internet enhances state power more
than it undermines it.

The considerable contribution of Jacques Ellul to the philosophy of
technology can also be understood in this context. Ellul believed that
'technique' – not only technology itself but the organizational, political
and social structures which support it (here we see the broader approach
to a definition of technology) – preferences principles of efficiency, logic
and productivity over all else. This, he argues in his seminal work *The
Technological Society,* subsumes the role of more human-centric norms
grounded in social justice (1964). As the framework of beliefs driven
by 'technique' becomes more pervasive, society is in danger of losing
touch with any other set of values which might suggest an alternative
approach to technology.

For scholars like Mumford and Ellul, technology itself is not the problem. Rather, it is the fact that technology is predisposed to promoting a
certain set of values (efficiency, productivity, profit) which they feel has
an alienating force on human relations and overrides the projection of
other values which may be more conducive to the overall health and
well-being of society. Their view differs from that of Heilbroner in that
they do not argue that it is impossible to control technology and shape
its impact on society. They do, however, regard adequate control as very
difficult and generally unsuccessful and they are pessimistic about the
future of technology's impact on society.

In perhaps a slightly more optimistic or self-determined approach,
Jürgen Habermas (1970) argues that technological determinism is a
choice societies make – either to exert some sovereignty over technology or to leave it to develop and evolve along a path uninfluenced by
norms and values. Bimber (1990, p. 337) refers to this view as a 'norm-
based' account of technological determinism. Because societies tend to

privilege norms of efficiency and production in making decisions about technology, they effectively remove technology from political or ethical discourse and instead embed it in a protective coating of determinism. For scholars like Habermas, it is not that technology *embodies* those norms of efficiency and production, rather that society tends to *imbue* technology with them.

Prominent theorist, Langdon Winner takes a position of modified technological determinism – sometimes referred to in the literature as 'soft determinism'. He argues that technology should better be regarded as *shaping* social change rather than *determining* it (1985, pp. 26–38). For him, the hard determinist view which regards 'artefacts' as replete with political meaning is essentially a way of avoiding responsibility for the true sources of freedom and oppression, justice and injustice which are undeniably human. 'Blaming the hardware seems even more foolish than blaming the victim when it comes to judging conditions of public life' (Winner, 1985, pp. 26–38). While he suggests that there is nothing inevitable about the direction of change, Winner warns against a pattern of 'technological drift', that is, a largely random and thoughtless process of technical and social change to which people adapt like 'somnambulists' (Winner, 1977, pp. 88–99). Along these lines, Albert Borgmann (1984, pp. 104–5) suggests that technology's power lies in our disinclination not only to think critically about its social and political implications but to rather accept them as inevitable. For Borgmann, 'living in an advanced industrial country, one is always and already implicated in technology' but because technology is so profoundly integrated into our way of being, our involvement normally remains implicit rather than self-consciously examined (1984, pp. 104–5).

Technological determinism is irreconcilable with an epistemological position of constructivism which underpins the primary question driving this research project. Its assumption that technology and society have a mono-directional relationship and its disregard for the ways in which societies can and do shape technology preclude its usefulness in the exploration of how ideas about US power have shaped and influenced the development of the Internet. An essential starting point for this study is that politicians make decisions about how they believe the Internet should best promote the state's national interest and enhance state power. However, while technological determinism does not provide a conceptual framework for approaching this research project, it is nonetheless relevant here. As MacKenzie writes, while technological determinism may no longer be prevalent in academic work on the history and sociology of technology, 'it still informs the way technology is thought about and discussed in society at large, especially where modern high technologies are concerned' (MacKenzie, 1996, p. 5). As with instrumentalism, technological determinism will be helpful as an analytical tool in identifying the approaches of US politicians as some of them engage with this view while formulating and debating Internet policies. In this way, rather than providing a methodology, it becomes a conceptual tool for making sense of particular points of view.

Third big debate: Does society shape technology?

The most effective way to engage with the third key debate of relevance to this thesis is to introduce the SCoT – another of the approaches from the philosophy of technology – along with instrumentalism and technological determinism. If we were to arrange these approaches to technology on a linear spectrum, we could locate instrumentalism at one end with its positive view of technology detached from any moral or value reading. We might then place the 'hard' determinist view which attributes values and political meaning to technology but regards society as unable to mediate or moderate them. The 'soft' determinists would follow with their focus on the negative impact of technology on society and their views that it is either very difficult to intervene or that societies largely choose not to. As was evident in the preceding pages, these debates about whether technology is a positive, benign or negative force for the human condition segue into questions about whether society *can* shape technology. If technology can promote or express positive or negative norms and values, to what extent is society able to navigate and direct them? Furthermore, how can we understand this process and analyse social behaviour (including political approaches to power) within it? These are some of the questions which animate the SCoT – the next point on this linear spectrum and the focus of the next section of this chapter.

The social construction of technology

A sense that instrumental and determinist approaches were limited in their scope led some scholars, particularly historians and sociologists, to adopt a new approach to technology (Bijker et al., 1989; MacKenzie, 1996; MacKenzie and Wajcman, 1999). These scholars argued that technology is neither a neutral instrument for problem solving (as instrumentalists suggest) nor a value-laden force which threatens human autonomy (the determinist view). Rather, they believe that society shapes and influences technology, and technology must therefore be regarded as an expression of norms and expectations within society. In order to more fully elaborate on the SCoT approach, it is helpful to lay down some parameters for how SCoT differs from the previously discussed approaches to technology and what questions each approach would raise were it to be employed in this study.

In contrast to instrumentalism, SCoT rejects the premise that a particular technology succeeds simply because it was 'superior' to other competing options. As noted earlier, instrumentalists regard technology as the solution to a human-defined problem. The 'best' solution, they argue, will succeed – without acknowledging that the definition of 'best' is itself socially constructed. Social constructivists argue that technological superiority is a subjective concept and dependent in part upon the articulation or preference of stated priorities.

Instrumentalism also holds technology distinct and apart from any social consequences. For Internet technology, which has had such a considerable social impact, separating the threads of consequence for the state as distinct from those of other social groups is very difficult. The technology is so integrated and spans culture, economics, security and politics so comprehensively that studying the Internet in isolation from its social impact leaves out too much of significance for understanding power. An instrumental view would raise questions like 'what security factors can undermine e-commerce?' or 'how much bandwidth is necessary to conduct an effective cyberwar?' These are interesting questions but far too specific to lead to any better understanding of the relationship between power and new technology in IR. Instrumentalism asks the wrong questions for this study though it will emerge many times in the empirical data as it is the prominent approach of industry and is a widely (even if not consciously) held view in IR literature. As with technological determinism, rather than providing a methodology, instrumentalism in this study becomes a conceptual tool for making sense of particular points of view.

SCoT is also distinct from technological determinism in its view of the development of technology. Determinists broadly take one of two views on this. Some subscribe to Heilbroner's 'grand avenue' notion that technological development adheres to what equates to natural law – that is, the discovery of one element leads inevitably to the next in a linear progression. Others take Mumford or Ellul's view that there is an inevitability about technology which is driven by norms arising from the quest for power. SCoT theorists understand technology as an expression of broader social values and interests. They believe that there are many diverse forces at play which contribute to these developments. Not only do new technologies impact on society, but society also helps to shape new technologies. Indeed, they argue that decisions about which technologies are developed and who benefits from them are 'shaped more by cultural preferences and the distribution of financial and political power than by specific problems or technical opportunities' (Vig, 1988, p. 15).

A technological determinist approach to this project would lead to questions about impact and adaptation. 'Does the Internet promote democracy?' 'Will the Internet enhance states' economic power through market access?' Or 'does the Internet facilitate more effective communications during conflict situations?' As demonstrated in the Introduction to this book, the answers to these questions are a complex mix of affirmations tempered by considerable vulnerabilities. Projection of diplomacy is easier with the Internet but the Internet also empowers a range of new actors who previously had little capacity to voice political dissent. The Internet certainly has been an enormous economic boon to states which have adopted it but it is also the source of massively expensive security problems. And while Internet technology can facilitate military communication, it also opens a portal for misinformation and theft of information. These questions – again all interesting and valid – are not able to delve any further into the complexities of the relationship between power and new technology in the information age. They remain tethered to the understanding of technology as a force which acts upon society – the paradigm of adaptation – and therefore cannot engage with questions about how conceptions of power can and do shape technology.

In addition – and particularly relevant for the Internet – SCoT theorists believe that the adoption of technology can also change it. Those who use it, also improve, exploit, adapt and shape technology. In this process, priorities about how technology should continue to change, in what ways and to serve which purposes as well as the means by which success is measured may change. Therefore, SCoT argues that the emergence of any new technology needs to be understood in the context of social and political forces at work which influence choices and preferences about the shaping of technology. Ultimately, a SCoT approach to this project finds that a meaningful understanding of Internet technology cannot be achieved in abstraction from its human context.

In an attempt to move beyond the previously articulated binary views of the Internet's impact on state power (that it enhances or undermines it), this project proposes a deeper engagement with the *relationship* between new technology and power. Rather than assess these issues exclusively through a determination of the positive or negative effects of technology, this study asserts that the Internet both enhances and undermines state power in complex and important ways but it does so, at least in part, as a consequence of decisions by politicians. The SCoT generates a set of questions which move beyond the conceptual and empirical stalemate of whether Internet technology enhances state power more than it undermines it or vice versa. Asserting that there is nothing determined or fixed about either of these outcomes, it moves on to more enlightening questions about how political ideas (in this case, ideas about power) and technology interact.

Scholars working from within the SCoT ask questions like 'how are technological priorities ordered and by whom?' 'What happens to technology when those priorities are altered?' And, fundamentally for this project, 'what role do ideas play in this process of shaping technology?' These questions emerged long before the Internet but they have as much relevance in the context of information technology as they did to industrial era technology. Indeed, it is these questions and others like them which need to be applied to IR literature attempting to understand issues of the complex relationship between international politics, power relations and information technology. In the context of this study, they may be understood as questions about 'which ideas about Internet technology have been adopted and promoted by US politicians?', 'how have decisions about key technical issues been decided and which conceptions of technology and power have been influential in those decision making processes?' and 'how do competing ideas about power and technology play out in political debates about the Internet?'

The SCoT is fundamentally about looking beyond the impact of a particular technology on society in order to understand how society itself (or in this case, politicians) shaped the evolution and adoption of that technology. With the seminal role of the United States in the development of the Internet, exploring ideas and perceptions about how it relates to US power is essential to comprehending the evolution of that technology. The research methodology for this project focuses on the subjective processes which guided US politicians through two and a half decades of rapid development of Internet technology and entailed a range of critical decisions at every point about how it was to evolve and be integrated into state power. By bringing the political context into closer interaction with technological development, it is possible to better understand both the challenges and opportunities which face states in a globally networked environment. It is also possible to better understand how the United States has responded to those factors and how state power interacts with technology in a post-industrial model.

Existing paradigms in international relations

The following analysis will sketch out two dominant paradigms which can be found in IR literature for understanding the relationship between power and technology. They demonstrate how ideas about power within the discipline have changed over time but that understandings of the relationship between power and technology have remained static – despite the emergence of quite distinct technology. This would pose no problem if IR theory retained its explanatory capability; however, there are compelling reasons (explained earlier and elaborated here) to argue that it does not.

The first paradigm, referred to here as the 'industrial age: technology and national power', identifies a propensity to unite realist notions of power with an instrumental approach to technology. This approach has (largely) dominated IR literature from the Second World War to the late 1980s and early 1990s. As noted earlier, a key characteristic of instrumentalism is a view of technology as a morally neutral means to an end. Technology as an 'artefact' is divorced from its use and its social consequences. It is 'good' only if it solves the problem it was designed to address and 'bad' if it does not. Beyond those narrow parameters, technology has no values or political meaning embedded in it. That comes only from the human engagement with technology. This approach dovetails with realist political ideas of the state as morally compelled to survive in a self-help system by any means necessary. In this view, survival of the state is 'good' and as Martin Wight writes, 'morality is the fruit of security' (1986, pp. 296–7).

The second paradigm, referred to in this book as the 'information age: technology and social power' identifies a tendency in much of the recent literature to link changes in approaches to power which have emerged largely since the conclusion of the Cold War, with the information revolution. Much of the literature in this section is characterized by a technologically determinist view which (often due to insufficient technical knowledge) tends to regard new technologies as value laden and autonomous – an exogenous force which exerts its influence upon societies and states and to which they must adapt. This leads to an assumption in the literature that Internet technology has universal implications for state power.

Both of the existing approaches can contribute to understanding certain questions about new technology but, for different reasons, neither provides a comprehensive framework for analysis of the relationship between power and Internet technology. Essentially, these two oppositional paradigms will be exposed as arriving at a stalemate based on competing answers to the question of whether new technology enhances state power more than it undermines it. Part of the rationale for this book is the understanding that the Internet does both – simultaneously and in complex ways – and therefore, it would be more useful to ask some different and more enlightening questions. Those questions include *how do states influence the emergence and management of new technologies to address their conceptions of state power? And what role do ideas (including those about power) play in the political shaping of social technology?* These questions cannot be asked or answered within the two paradigms which currently dominate IR scholarship. The industrial age paradigm does not engage with the social elements of technology and the information age paradigm does not fully account for the role of political influence and shaping of technology. New technology can no longer be explained simply as a constitutive element of state power but no more can it be explained as entirely liberated from state control. In the midst of those polar positions lies a complex and largely unexamined relationship which forms the basis of enquiry of this project. A SCoT approach which focuses on this very issue proves more useful and enlightening.

The industrial age: Technology and national power

> *The healthy functioning of cyberspace is essential to our economy and our national security.*
>
> (Bush, 2003a)

As pointed out in the Introduction, scholars of IR have approached the relationship between power and technology through the dominant lens of realist theory which views the state as a self-interested, power-maximizing (or security maximizing) unit in an anarchical system with technology as a constitutive element of state power.[1] Its military and economic relevance has made technology a mechanism through which power (or security)-seeking states pursue relative advantage by the development of more efficient production methods (economic power) as well as advanced weaponry (military power) (Morgenthau, 1978, p. 322). An instrumental approach to technology coupled with a material view of power has provided a foundation for realist conceptions about the relationship between technology and power. Having explained above something of the philosophy of technology and instrumentalism, it is possible now to explain how that scholarship intersects with realist power theory to produce what is referred to here as the 'industrial age' approach to the relationship between power and technology in IR.

Realist power theory is regarded by some as parsimonious (therefore robust) (Waltz, 1979; Mearsheimer, 2001) and by others as too narrowly defined (and therefore inadequate) (Wendt, 1999; Nye, 2004). However, in this context it is important to state clearly the reasoning which underpins this theory as it has implications for a corresponding approach to technology. There are two important reasons why realist scholars argue that power must be narrowly perceived as reliant primarily on material capabilities – first, their relative importance and second, their quantifiable nature.

The importance of material power is an enduring feature of realist power theories. Although many realist scholars including Hans Morgenthau and E.H. Carr had nuanced approaches to power – approaches which *did* include social factors such as the quality of national leadership and national morale – they generally regarded material resources (particularly military strength) as overwhelmingly important in determining overall national power (Carr, 1964, p. vii; Morgenthau, 1978, p. 31, Schmidt, 2005, pp. 523–49). In *The Tragedy of Great Power Politics,* John Mearsheimer explains that while non-material factors such as intelligence, resolve, weather and disease may impact (decisively in some cases) on the outcome of wars, material capabilities are the most reliable – and consequently the most important – indicator of which state will prevail in a conflict.

The potential to measure capabilities is the second reason why realists adhere to this view of power. While other scholars proposed alternative views on power which equate it with outcomes (Reus-Smit, 2004; Barnett and Duvall, 2005, p. 67), Kenneth Waltz argues that this produces confusion as 'the usefulness of force is mistakenly identified with its use' (1979, p. 191). This approach, Waltz points out, erroneously asserts that 'only power is needed in order to get one's way'. However, the outcome of applying power, he argues, is necessarily uncertain and for that reason power *has* to be defined in terms of the distribution of capabilities including material resources. 'The paradox that some have found in the so-called impotence of American power disappears if power is given a politically sensible definition' (Waltz, 1979, p. 192). Mearsheimer agrees, arguing that in attempting to understand power in IR, conflating material capabilities (the means) with political outcomes (the ends) leads to a circular argument. As a consequence, he continues to define power by capabilities thus avoiding the 'paradox of power' arguments which have risen in part in response to unipolarity (Mearsheimer, 2001, pp. 57–60).

The realist adherence to this view of power coupled with neo-realism's emphasis on the system structure as determining global order has underpinned the importance of technology, as (despite the acknowledgement of other factors) material capabilities continued to be viewed as the most important and decisive element in determining international order. Indeed, the 20th century witnessed a growing emphasis on technology as material capability while other more conventional resources such as population and territory came to be regarded, by some at least, as diminishing in relevance.[2]

A material view of power sits comfortably with an instrumental view of technology – indeed, they complement one another. The combination of an instrumental view of technology as a value-free tool employed to achieve the ends of a state with only one moral end – survival – results in the approach to the relationship between power and technology described here as the industrial age view. In this view, nuclear weapons are neutral – in the hands of a 'rogue state' they are dangerous but in the hands of a 'responsible' state, they are justifiable and valuable. The technology is neutral – human use gives it meaning and value. Qualitative elements like social capital, influence or information as a source of power do not have a more prominent place in realist theories of power – not because they deny their existence or the fact that they may have an impact on power, but because, as scholars like Waltz and Mearsheimer point out, they are unquantifiable and unpredictable (Waltz, 1979, p. 191; Mearsheimer, 2001, pp. 57–60). Thus, in this framework, technology is a mechanism to enhance state power and thereby has implications for world order.

Despite more recent theoretical and empirical challenges, the 'industrial age' view continues to resonate in contemporary international affairs as states persistently attach a high value to advanced technology as it relates to state power. Just as the launch of Sputnik in 1957 was enough to convince many Americans that the Soviet Union was acquiring strategic superiority (Buchan, 1972, p. 162), the 2007 destruction by China of one of its defunct weather satellites led to international conjecture about China's ambition to prevail in a 'space war' (Covault, 2007; Kaufman and Linzer, 2007). America's subsequent decision to shoot down one of its own satellites in March 2008, despite its earlier condemnation of China's successful experiment, reinforces the view that advanced technology continues to be perceived as a key indicator of national power and a key determinant of world order (BBC, 2008; CNN, 2008).

Clearly, the 'industrial age' view of the relationship between technology and power still has considerable currency in IR. However, there arise a range of problems in applying this paradigm to understanding the relationship between power and new technology that stem from the theoretical misfit of the instrumental/material power view with the unique nature of information technology. Perhaps most importantly, this approach continues to treat information technology as an arte-fact and this limits the capacity of such an approach to address the many contradictions in state responses to the impact of this technology. In this view, the vulnerabilities which come hand in hand with the rapid integration of information technology into contemporary state affairs are surmountable. States simply need more – more ICT capabilities, more rapid advances in the development and application of these technologies and more doctrine for their application.

In this context, militaries the world over are rapidly developing 'information warfare' or 'cyberwar' capabilities. Since 2006, US Department of Defense (DoD) has regarded information as a 'realm, a weapon, and a target of warfare' (Wilson, 2006, p. 1). Information and communication in the 'industrial age' view becomes a commodity to be weaponized in the same way that previous industrial age technologies were. There is a general sense that ICT is becoming a significant factor in conflicts and that militaries need to adapt and be prepared to project state power throughout this new sphere. Dominance in 'cyberspace' is equated with dominance in other international commons such as space or sea lanes (Tanji, 2007, pp. 4–11).

However, early attempts at operationalizing these capabilities in a conventional conflict situation such as the air strikes on Kosovo in 1999 or the first Gulf War (1990–1991) highlighted some of the challenges. Partly as a consequence of the profound integration of civilian systems over the Internet, it has proven very difficult to declare 'cyberspace' a war zone. For example, during the second war with Iraq, military officials had to abandon a planned strike against the Iraqi financial and banking network due to the realization that its failure would quite possibly affect European networks with which it is closely integrated (Smith, 2003). In addition, under international law, the determination of what constitutes the use of force in the context of a cyber-attack remains unclear – one of the key problems highlighted in 2007 when Estonia turned unsuccessfully to North Atlantic Treaty Organization

(NATO) for help while undergoing a massive cyber-attack (Grove et al., 2000, pp. 89–103; Deutsche Welle, 2007b). Responding to aggression with reciprocal force over the Internet remains highly problematic from a legal perspective as counter-attacks have to travel through routers which may be located in 'neutral' states (Wilson, 2006, p. 5). While ICT has certainly been applied to enhance existing warfare technologies, regarding information technology as an artefact similar to any other weapon fails to acknowledge its distinct nature and the complexity of operationalizing it.

Finally, the 'industrial age' paradigm for understanding the relationship between technology and power in the information age is reliant on a static platform for conflict which has not proven to be the case in the post 9/11 years. While a material view of power and technology may have been useful in understanding the dynamics at work in conventional conflicts and the nuclear age, ICT lends itself to unconventional conflict characterized by anonymity, geographical dislocation, asymmetry, previously less significant actors on par with states and the interdependence of industrialized states in a vulnerable global network. Just as nuclear technology prompted a shift from wars of destruction to a strategy of deterrence, ICT is being understood more clearly as a technology of 'disruption' (Shimeall et al., 2001, pp. 16–18; Demchak, 2003, pp. 75–112). The impact of disruption is at the heart of a key paradox of ICT referred to in the Introduction to this book – that states which have been most successful in adopting new information age technologies are most vulnerable to disruption.[3] This has implications for how we understand power in the information age as the long-standing assumption in IR that technology only enhances state power no longer holds true.

It is worth noting that there have been technological innovations in the past which have prompted a theoretical reassessment of IR. For example, as noted above, nuclear technology was responsible for a major shift in strategic thinking from wars of destruction to strategies of deterrence. However, the industrial nature of nuclear power and the necessity of a large state apparatus for developing it meant that this particular technological shift did not undermine the coherence of the 'industrial age' view of technology and power and the relationship between the two. Even given the theoretical challenges of nuclear technology (the weapon which cannot be used), it could be understood from within this existing 'industrial age' paradigm. It did not challenge the instrumental view of technology. Nor did it undermine a realist view of power. The notion that technology enhances power was reinforced by the emergence of nuclear weaponry which, even if not deployed, impacted so significantly on IR. This is not however, proving to be the case with ICT.

Unlike the early part of the 20th century which was characterized by a strong realist practice and fundamentally industrial technology, the latter decades saw a growth in theoretical reassessment of power coupled with the emergence of revolutionary information technology. The relationship between information technology and conceptualizations of political institutions like power and sovereignty appears to be distinct from those of industrial technology. By forcing new social technologies like the Internet into existing industrial technology paradigms, the nuance and complexities of how this technology interacts with the political life of states are lost. Not surprisingly, theories predominantly concerned with material power have not easily synthesized emerging information technology. To date, more ideationally inclined theoretical frameworks have generally been used to examine the relationship between new technology and power and it is to these that this chapter turns next.

The information age: Technology and social power

> *The realpolitik of the new era is cyberpolitik, in which the actors are no longer just states, and raw power can be countered or fortified by information power.*
>
> (Rothkopf, 1998, p. 326)

From the beginning of the 1990s, applications for ICT expanded exponentially. Simon Rogerson and Terrell Ward Bynum (1995) describe computer technology as 'the most powerful and most flexible technology ever devised'. Access to the Internet and the World Wide Web rapidly moved from a small band of academic and military clients in the mid-1980s into the public domain. In a very short space of time, ICT has become ubiquitous in advanced industrial states and integral to the delivery of essential public services including national security. Newly industrialized and industrializing states regard ICT as a mechanism to 'leapfrog' generations of technological development and move more quickly towards modernization and competitiveness in the international system (Wilson and Segal, 2005, pp. 889–906; Xiwei and Xiangdong, 2007, pp. 317–25). In addition to the innumerable applications of ICT to enhance essentially industrial technology such as computerized control systems for factories, the social aspect of ICT has impacted significantly on civil, economic and political relations. Coinciding with the advent of ICT as a social technology was a theoretical shift in IR scholarship to considering factors of power as socially constituted rather than primarily material.

The combination of these factors contributed to the emergence of the second dominant paradigm for understanding the relationship between power and technology in IR – referred to here as the 'information age' approach. This approach encompasses a lot of the theoretical shifts which have arisen to challenge realism, material power and the immutability of the state. In addition, this literature often exhibits a determinist approach to technology – one that regards technology as imbued with values (democratization, freedom of speech and transparency of government or, conversely, invasive surveillance); generally user driven and therefore predominantly responsive to user-specified goals; and finally, widely anarchical and beyond the dominance of the state. Essentially, this is a view characterized by change and re-evaluation of power in which ICT is frequently cited as a catalyst or even the driving force for those changes. This view engages with new technology and generally regards it as breaking down old power structures by redefining both the players and the playing field of IR. However, it does so without engaging adequately with technical issues which ultimately leads to utopian or dystopian readings – dependent largely upon the perception of which values, positive or negative, reside in Internet technology.

Two broad questions have preoccupied the academic debate addressing these issues. First, scholars have worked to understand how technological change has impacted on power relations between individuals and the state (or the idea of the state) (Smith and Naim, 2000; Drezner and Farrell, 2004, pp. 32–40, Slaughter, 2004), and second, what implications those changes have for conceptual approaches to state power (Aronson, 2002, pp. 41–58; Hachigian, 2002, pp. 41–58; Nye, 2002, p. 76). As indicated in the Introduction, many studies have concentrated on the manner in which social technology has impacted on state power by eroding or undermining the institution of sovereignty. The general emphasis in these debates is that social technology is dissipating power away from the state in a variety of ways. Prominent among these are the proliferation and organization of non-state actors which compete for power with states and the challenges of state control over extraterritorial issues which stem from interconnected networked systems (Castells, 2000, pp. 693–9; Langman, 2005, pp. 42–74). The following is a brief introduction to theories of social power and an explanation of how these ideas combine with a determinist approach to technology to form this second dominant paradigm for understanding the relationship between technology and power – the 'information age' approach.

A social view of power is less concerned with tangible resources and capabilities and more focused on intersubjective relations and outcomes. Michael Barnett and Raymond Duvall describe power as 'the production, in and through social relations, of effects that shape the capacities of actors to determine their circumstances and fate' (Barnett and Duvall, 2005, p. 39). A dominant concern for theorists of social power is legitimacy. Richard Ned Lebow traces this back to the Greek distinction between power exercised through coercion (which weakened social bonds) and power exercised through persuasion (which strengthened them) (Lebow, 2005, pp. 551–81). Through an analysis of the US neoconservative approach to power, Christian Reus-Smit (2004) concludes that social capital (such as broad consent for action) is an integral element of political power and that effective influence over the decisions of other states relies on social legitimation. Although a social view of power can be understood independently of technology – either old or new – social technology has significant relevance for issues of legitimacy, 'soft power' and social aspects of power in IR. A 24-hour news cycle, unrestricted access to satellite footage and the rapid dissemination of information and images have intensified awareness of state behaviour and made it much more difficult for states to conceal events detrimental to their international standing. As demonstrated by the mobile phone generated images of torture inside Guantanamo Bay, the release of the WikiLeaks cables and the Edward Snowden leaks, states have difficulty escaping scrutiny even in the most remote and guarded situations. Thus, relations between states are heightened by this technology and outcomes are difficult to subvert to capabilities in this context.

Accelerating theoretical debates about power, the constructivist project emerged to challenge orthodox views by arguing that inadequate attention had been given to the socially constituted nature of political concepts and practices. Alexander Wendt (1992, pp. 391–425) cautioned against uncritical adherence to fundamental concepts which had previously underwritten the literature. The social emphasis of constructivism coupled with the social nature of ICT has combined to produce a range of scholarship which re-evaluates the relationship between power and technology.

For some scholars, changing ideas about power and emerging technology combine to bring about a substantially modified system, transforming from one comprised simply of states to one comprised of multiple and diverse actors. Understanding the role of non-state actors in the international system has become increasingly relevant as their numbers expand to include globally oriented terrorist and criminal organizations, civil society interest groups, non-governmental organizations (NGOs), multinational organizations and the media – many of which have been heavily reliant upon new ICT. Jonathon Aronson writes that 'the spread of integrated global networks is accelerating... and reshaping the landscape of politics and IR, transforming global commerce, recasting societies and cultures, and altering policy formulation and implementation' (Aronson, 2002, p. 39). In this view, states are seen to be relinquishing or losing control with obvious implications for the relationship between technology and power.

There is also a significant body of legal scholarship addressing issues surrounding aggression over the Internet which are fundamental to grappling with the challenges posed to state power. As noted above, under international law, the determination of what constitutes the use of force or an armed attack in cyberspace remains unclear – one of the key problems highlighted by the attacks on Estonia in 2007 and a focus of the United Nations Group of Governmental Experts (UNGGE) (Grove et al., 2000, pp. 89–103; UNGGE Report, 2013). Consequently, responding to aggression with reciprocal force over the Internet is highly problematic from a legal perspective. A US congressional report published in 2006 notes that reciprocating against an attack may lead to 'possible accusations of war crimes if offensive military cyberweapons severely disrupt critical civilian computer systems, or the systems of other non-combatant nations' (Wilson, 2006, p. 1). The report concludes that the US DoD believes that it lacks 'sufficient policy and legal analysis for guiding appropriate responses to intrusions or attacks on DOD networks' (Wilson, 2006, p. 5). Even on a criminal level, there are intractable problems. Crimes may be committed in one state by actors located in another where that behaviour may not be illegal.

For actors in the international system for whom legitimacy underpins a conceptual understanding of power, these legal issues impact on the state's power to respond to aggression. An amorphous concept of territory and legal jurisdiction is obviously problematic for conventional approaches to state power. This has been the subject of research conducted by the NATO-commissioned Tallinn Manual that seeks to establish a platform for interpreting international laws in cyberspace (Schmitt, 2009). The problems persist, however, and will be discussed at more length in Chapter 4.

Territory as geographical space has unequivocally become more complex with the advent of ICT and the implications of that for IR theory are yet to be properly understood in either theoretical or practical terms (Ruggie, 1993, pp. 139–74). Certainly, there have been some attempts to regulate this 'space' through treaties, but these are limited in their effectiveness given that, in a networked environment, agreements between two 'nodes' are easily circumvented.[4] Legislation and state agreements to regulate the Internet are regarded as falling within the purview of state power but (as the case studies demonstrate) there are complex reasons why the United States has not moved more aggressively to control Internet traffic and these can only be understood through deep engagement with the conceptions of power driving policy decisions about the Internet.

Information age literature tends to pick up on the 'bottom-up' processes largely ignored by the nation-state framework, but in doing so it disregards the ways in which states can and do exert influence over the development of new technology (Cleaver, 1998, pp. 621–40; Latham, 2007, pp. 295–314). While these studies have plenty of value and make a significant contribution, they do contain impediments to a richer understanding of how new technology interacts with power. Primarily, the lack of engagement with technical debates leads to misunderstandings about the autonomous nature of new technology. As Sassen points out, this literature frequently fails to make informed distinctions between aspects of the technology which are the consequence of state decisions and choices and those which are beyond the immediate control of states (Sassen, 1999). For although there are some intractable technical issues that pose real challenges to state power, there are no natural or scientific laws which make it imperative that Internet function in the way it does. By failing to make accurate distinctions between what states choose and what they have imposed upon them, the information age view relies upon a largely technologically determinist approach even as it ascribes agency to the end-user. These scholars regard the Internet as having its own internal logic and promoting a set of norms and values which are imposed upon the state, leaving little room for influence and only the capacity to adapt – or not.

These studies consistently focus on the impact of technology on politics, but as Marianne Franklin points out, unless we move from an assumption of technology as an 'exogenous, causal agent of change', we continue to ignore the complex social relationship we have with technology and fail to engage with the ways in which we shape and influence the very technology which in turn impacts upon us (Franklin, 2004, p. 4). Of particular relevance for this project is Donald MacKenzie's observation that technological determinism 'focuses our minds on how to *adapt* to technological change, not on how to *shape* it. It removes a vital aspect of how we live from the sphere of public discussion, choice and politics' (MacKenzie and Wajcman, 1999, p. 5). This focus on 'adaptation' has been a dominant feature in work which has thus far attempted to understand political change including the nature and exercise of power in the context of the Internet.

Both an 'industrial age' approach and an 'information age' approach are able to contribute to understanding the relationship of ICT to power in IR. However, although technology infrastructure and the use of ICT applications to enhance industrial power are significant, the complexities of state responses to social technologies such as the Internet necessitate a broader approach which moves beyond the 20th-century conceptualizations of power in IR. A social view, which places the role of information, culture, identity and knowledge at the centre of its analysis, is able to engage with the more complex and compelling issues. Despite this better conceptual fit, the polarizing debates within this literature about whether ICT enhances or diminishes state power are generally lacking in a sound understanding of technical issues and therefore fail to make accurate distinctions between the *loss* of state control and the *relinquishment* of state control. In addition, the prevalence of instrumental or technologically determinist views of technology limits theoretical development.

Moving forward in the study of power and new technology

This chapter demonstrated how the integration of theories and concepts from the philosophy of science with theories about power from IR can provide an enhanced conceptual framework for the study of power and new technology in the information age.

Through a brief analysis of the ways in which IR is currently attempting to deal with questions arising from the emergence of new technology, the chapter identified two paradigms which dominate the literature. The first, the 'industrial age' approach, combines realist power theory with an instrumental view of technology. Through its inability to engage with social elements of either power or technology, this approach leaves out so much of relevance to states and state power that it cannot provide an effective mechanism through which to approach the central research question animating this study: *how have conceptions of US power influenced the development of the Internet?* Nor can it help develop a more nuanced approach to the broader question from which this study emerges: *how does Internet technology relate to power in IR?*

The second paradigm, the 'information age' approach, combines elements of technological determinism with a social view of power. This approach comes closer to providing a means for exploring these questions through its expanded view of power but many studies emerging from this paradigm continue to regard the Internet as having its own internal logic and promoting a set of norms and values which are imposed upon the state leaving little room for influence and only the capacity to adapt – or not. This persistent emphasis on the impact of technology and the general failure to engage with technical debates leads to dystopian and utopian findings and is consequently unable to address with the necessary sophistication questions about the relationship between power and technology in IR.

Being aware of the range of approaches to both power and technology and also of the ways in which they typically interact is necessary in order to approach the empirical material from a robust conceptual and theoretical foundation. The concepts outlined in this chapter provide a means of moving beyond the long-held assumptions about technology which have dominated IR literature – even much of that literature which has sought to explain power in the information age.

3
A (Select) Political History of the Internet

There have been many accounts of the 'history of the Internet' written by participants and observers of the development of this technology. However, they are almost exclusively concerned with documenting key technicians and engineers and attributing their achievements and contributions to the code and architecture now in use (Leiner et al., 1997; Berners Lee, 2000; Ceruzzi, 2000). The political forces surrounding those developments are rarely referenced in these accounts and given no substantive place in understanding the progression of the Internet from a military research project to a global network. Key enabling legislature, ownership and management of the physical infrastructure of the Internet, the role of the state in Internet governance and the influence of governmental perceptions and intentions in shaping the technology are largely absent in these histories. By focusing exclusively on technological 'stepping stones', these accounts suggest the kind of 'grand avenue' approach to technology described in Chapter 2 – that is, that technology evolves in a social and political vacuum without reference to the norms and values of the society in which it is embedded. In fact, political decisions have played an integral role in the development of Internet technology and this chapter lays out some of the key moments, actors and policies which make up the 'political history of the Internet'.

In doing so, this chapter performs a number of functions in the book. By providing some background to the development of Internet technology which engages with political ideas about how that technology might relate to US power, this chapter explains how particular technological issues came to be understood as a problem for those conceptions of power. This background to the Internet is generally traced back to the establishment of the Advanced Research Projects Agency (ARPA) in

1958 which provided essential funding for the development of computer networking technology. This 'prehistory' is followed by an analysis of the political ideas which began to emerge around early incarnations of the Internet in the 1980s.

The second contribution of this chapter is that it provides an opportunity to manage the information more efficiently while, at the same time, demonstrating the interconnected nature of these case studies. In providing this background to the political history of the Internet in the United States, this chapter not only demonstrates how the case studies were generated, it also introduces many of the policies, legislation and actors important to the case studies. There is a substantial amount of background material for each case study but rather than regard this material as isolated according to issues, it is important to observe that there is a cohesive narrative which runs through the material. By dealing with these issues individually, it is possible to lose sight of the interconnections between them. When viewed more cohesively, as in this chapter, both change and continuity in the material are rendered more apparent.

This is important to this project because one of the key findings of the book is that politicians engage with multiple and sometimes conflicting conceptions of power when they debate Internet technology. This has important implications for how we regard the relationship between Internet technology and state power as it interrupts the long-held assumption that technology has universal implications for power, regardless of social or political context. An analysis of the development of Internet technology which is embedded in a social and political context demonstrates the relationship between ideas and the social shaping of technology. It also allows us to contemplate the international relations (IR) implications of the United States being in a position to so substantially shape this technology over the past quarter century. By setting the agenda for how the Internet would develop, expand, be managed and engaged with, the United States was able to establish a kind of global network of values and norms. This chapter illustrates how much breadth and depth there can be in the long-term expression of Gramscian 'hegemonic power'.

Prehistory: ARPAnet

A sense of the importance of technological superiority is deeply embedded in US political views on global power. Adam Segal has argued that US global primacy 'depends in large part on its ability to develop new technologies and industries faster than anyone else' and this is a view which can be detected in much of the empirical material in this study (Segal, 2004, p. 2). In 1957, the Soviet launch of the Sputnik satellite sent shock waves through the United States where scientists were struggling to develop the much less ambitious Vanguard satellite. This technological coup was regarded by many as a clear signal that the United States was falling dangerously behind the Soviet Union and could no longer take for granted its superiority in science and technology – and, by inference – its position in the global order.

There was speculation that the successful launch and orbit of Sputnik may be married together with nuclear weapons. As serious as they were, these material concerns were compounded by disbelief that the US global dominance in technology had come to be under threat. The news of Sputnik prompted Senator Lyndon Johnson to suggest that the Soviets would be 'dropping bombs on us from space like kids dropping rocks onto cars from freeway overpasses' (Kuhn, 2007, p. 12). This event was regarded by politicians as a blow to the prestige and leadership status of the United States – social power themes which re-emerge 50 years later in the debates about network neutrality as US broadband performance and penetration slips behind many other states. At the time, Clare Booth Luce referred to Sputnik's blinking red light that traversed the night sky as 'an intercontinental outer-space raspberry' to US pretensions of assured and sustained technological global pre-eminence (Killian, 1977, p. 6).

In response to the 'Sputnik crisis', the federal government funded and supported a number of initiatives with a view to reclaiming a dominant position in global science and technology. One of these initiatives was the establishment of the ARPA in 1958 which was charged with ensuring that the United States regained a leading edge in the application of state-of-the-art technology to military capability.[1] ARPA identified suitable projects from the research and development community and then provided funding and research support to those projects.

The response to Sputnik and the establishment of ARPA typify an instrumental approach to technology. As explained in Chapter 2, this is an approach which regards innovation as unquestionably positive and progressive and looks for solutions to problems of a technological nature – in technology. In the context of political debates about US power, this approach to technology was combined with a realist approach to power in keeping with the industrial age paradigm also described in Chapter 2. In this view, technology has a direct and positive impact on state power and more technology leads in a fairly direct manner to enhanced power. This is an approach to questions about US power and technology which had been consistently sustained in the context of industrial age technology but, as this study shows, would prove less useful in the information age.

One of the early ARPA research projects was generated by the government's desire to connect large computer systems in order to maximize their capability to support other research. Computers were still extremely expensive and they had far more computational capacity than could be fully exploited by the small number of people who had access to them. By linking these computers together, especially across time zones, it was anticipated that their extensive capacity could be more fully realized. This, it was hoped, would have a positive effect on many other areas of science and technology research which might benefit from access to these facilities. By the late 1950s, ARPA had already begun to fund and support research which would eventually feed into networking protocols both from within its own research institute and also through funded association with key computer scientists working in academia around the United States.

As networking research progressed and connecting computers became more viable, some specific applications for networking technology were conceptualized by these academics and ARPA. Prompted by Cold War political concerns, one of these was the establishment of a secure communications system which was regarded as necessary to enhance the United States' second strike capability in the event of nuclear attack (Abbate, 2000, pp. 10–13).

Existing communications systems such as the telephone and the telegraph had been built upon a strategically vulnerable architecture. Transmissions arrived at a central juncture from which they were redirected and then forwarded to the intended recipient. This architecture can be visualized as a 'hub and spokes' model. A 'hub and spokes' architecture renders the central transmission juncture (or the 'hub') absolutely essential. Failure at that point would result in disruption of the whole system. This vulnerability led to speculation that if a nuclear attack were to take place on US soil, the administration could be prevented from responding effectively simply as a consequence of the failure of the telephone.

The technology that emerged in response to ARPA's requirements was the 'Transmission Control Protocol/Internet Protocol'– or TCP/IP – the foundational technology of the Internet developed by Vinton Cerf and Robert Kahn.[2] The fundamental design concept of TCP/IP involves the replacement of a central transmission juncture (the telephone exchange hub) with a number of 'routers', each one providing a *possible* pathway for the transmission of messages – or 'packets' of data. This architecture can be visualized as a spider's web, with many possible pathways and multiple alternate connections. Within this architecture, packets are programmed to find the fastest possible route to their destination and failure of a router simply results in packets selecting an alternative pathway. Key elements of this architectural design and the TCP/IP protocols are flexibility and redundancy (no reliance on a central hub) as well as openness which was necessary in order to facilitate connecting machines with running different and incompatible operating systems.

By the late 1960s, a small number of computers had been networked using TCP/IP and the resulting 'ARPAnet', as it was then referred to, provided a test bed for further research on networking protocols. During the 1970s, ARPAnet was expanded to incorporate some 200 computers including a number hosted at universities but it remained restricted to government and scientific use.

Throughout this design phase, security of the network and the ability to accurately identify those connecting to ARPAnet (factors which would have considerable implications for cyber security in later years) appear to have been low priorities. This can partly be explained by the fact that access to this network was originally restricted to a small group of researchers working in defence, science and academia, a relatively closed and homogeneous community. In addition though, the qualities of flexibility, redundancy and openness were consciously privileged over other design options. This is an illustration of how certain norms, values and expectations shape technology. TCP/IP was conceptualized from the beginning as an open and flexible architecture which would ultimately provide a rich environment for both innovation and collaboration (Cerf, 2006, p. 9).

This is actually an example of the relationship between technological determinism and the social construction of technology (SCoT). As illustrated in Chapter 2, decisions about technology can lead to 'lock-in' resulting in the narrowing of options and unintended consequences later on – Mumford's 'megamachine'. So, the technology was shaped and developed in large part in response to human-defined ambitions, but once in place it has ongoing and sometimes contentious implications. Chapter 4 on cyber security demonstrates how this preference for flexibility and openness has impacted on how we use the Internet today and generated consequences for cyber security. The same qualities which made TCP/IP the technology of choice for networking computers in the 1970s are at the core of problems with the identification of cyber-attacks, the growth of cyber crime and the ways in which these feed into politicians' concerns about cyber insecurity and US power – a concern which would be exacerbated by the arrival of the personal computer (PC).

1980s: Atari Democrats and the personal computer

Initially, there had been relatively little interest from outside the research and military communities in taking advantage of networking capabilities, but during the 1980s electronic mail (email) and bulletin boards were developed within this community. These grew rapidly in popularity, accompanied by increased interest from researchers in connecting to the ARPAnet as networking came to be understood as a means to communicate and share data in addition to its original function of distributing the processing power of large mainframes. Concurrently, the PC market emerged in the 1980s and also grew quickly. In 1975, there were 40,000 PCs sold in the United States. Ten years later in 1985, there were 6.6 million sold into the same market (Juliussen, n.d.). The relatively low cost of PCs compared to large mainframes led to their rapid adoption by the commercial sector and this shifted the emphasis of those developing networking technology. Rather than focus predominantly on connecting a small number of large institutional mainframes, researchers working on networking technology turned to the infinitely broader market of desktop machines. The expanding demands of the PC market fuelled private sector investment in commercial network services as people sought to connect their PCs – either locally within their organization – or more widely across a national or global network – in order to allow for file sharing, communication and central maintenance.

Concurrently with the rapid developments in PCs, a new technology-focused political tide was gaining momentum in the United States. There had emerged a small group of politicians (typically but not exclusively democrats) who increasingly believed that new technology would be integral to the future of US power. Branded 'Atari Democrats' (a reference to the early computer game console), these were typically 'young liberal[s] trying to push the party toward more involvement with high-tech solutions' (Tynan, 1984, p. C09). The 1984 presidential candidate, Gary Hart self-identified as an Atari Democrat, explaining that he was amongst 'a small group of us to forecast the transition of the economy from industrialized manufacturing to the information age' (Hart in Carlson and Begala, 2003). Another prominent Atari Democrat was Senator Albert Gore Jr., who would go on to play a major role in the development of the Internet (and Web technology) in America as both a Senator and later as the vice president of the United States.

From the mid-1980s, Senator Gore consistently argued that developing computer technology would be integral to the future of US power. Gore wrote of his belief that 'supercomputers' and the networks which connected them would 'soon prove to be the steam engines of the information age' (Gore, 1989b). In 1989, Gore introduced the National High Performance Computer Technology Bill (also known as the 'Gore Bill'), arguing before Congress that the 'nation which most completely assimilates high-performance computing into its economy will very likely emerge as the dominant intellectual, economic, and technological force in the next century' (Gore, 1989a).[3]

This bill is regarded by policymakers today as a landmark piece of legislation which not only had some specific outcomes (to be discussed below) but which set a tone for US politics of taking the initiative and authority to shape and influence Internet technology specifically to re-establish US global leadership in both material and social power terms. This initiative and the belief in the government's authority and responsibility to play a role in the development of Internet technology are illustrated most clearly in the case study on Internet governance but questions about the authority and legitimacy of government policies feature in all case studies.

There were several key outcomes of the 'Gore Bill'. One of the stated objectives of the bill was for the government to invest in a high-speed 'National Research and Education Network' (NREN) which would further expand access to the existing network infrastructure. Gore's speeches about the concept of the NREN provide insight into how concepts of power were beginning to change during this period from the persistent emphasis on military power which dominated the post-WWII period to a broadened view in which economic power and also some sense of social power factors play a more prominent role.

Significantly, Gore appeared to combine his perception of the future of US power with an approach to technology incorporating some aspects of social constructivism. Specifically, he attributed agency to those who used, developed and governed Internet technology. In his speech before Congress on 18 May 1989, Gore made some fairly standard instrumental claims, arguing that 'electronics are to our age what coal and iron were to the Industrial Revolution' (Gore, 1989a). However, Gore made a distinction between natural resources which he argued are 'the natural endowment of nations' and information technology which he regarded as 'an endowment which can be created wherever there is

sufficient talent and determination' (Gore, 1989a). He regarded information technology as a *resource* or a *source* of power – but one which
could be generated through human endeavour. Recalling the injury of
the Sputnik project to American prestige, Gore outlined key developments in Germany and Japan and predicted that unless America took
action to foster and nurture its own 'resources', the information age
would be led by others. 'American technological supremacy, which we
had thought of as a kind of national attribute, will pass' (Gore, 1989a).

This persistence of the view that innovation, technology and the
global hierarchy of power are linked, previously articulated around the
'Sputnik crisis', was a dominant theme during these debates and, as
foreshadowed earlier, attained prominence in the network neutrality
debates in the 2000s. In the late 1980s though, they signalled an important shift in conceptions of US power. The notion of information as a
form of power was emerging and would become increasingly important
in ideas of state power and its relationship to new technology. It forms
a central tenet of the information age paradigm outlined in Chapter 2,
but Gore's ideas provide an early precursor to that.

In addition to the explicit goal of establishing a high-speed national
research network, the introduction of the 'Gore Bill' provided justification for increased government spending on new technology not
directly linked to military power. Gore believed strongly that a national
information infrastructure would greatly benefit private industry and
he envisaged a significant role for the private sector in developing the
Internet. At the same time, he argued that it was necessary for the government to lead the implementation of this infrastructure in order to
demonstrate to the market and to the US public the potential of Internet
technology.

There were two dominant themes which were used to justify this
expenditure to Congress and to the public. The first was the necessity
of government to invest in public infrastructure like roads (the 'information highway' metaphor continues to appear in political discourse
about the Internet today). The second theme was the post-Cold War
diversion of military spending to new technology – to which President Bush was opposed (Bartels, 1994, pp. 479–508; Russett et al., 1994,
pp. 17–21). In his speech introducing the 'Gore Bill', Gore neatly united
these themes by making the point that government investment in
the 'information superhighway' would equate to 'less than one Stealth
bomber' – juxtaposing Bush's 'new/old world' view with a new, hopeful,
innovative and futuristic perspective (Gore, 1989a).

It was in this political and technological context that one of the most
transformative elements of Internet technology emerged. The World

Wide Web (the Web) was invented by Tim Berners Lee, Robert Cailliau and their colleagues who were working at the CERN lab in Switzerland in the late 1980s and early 1990s (Berners Lee, 2000). There was so much information available (even then) on the Internet that navigating through it in a text-based environment was laborious. Information was presented in a linear format – much like on a piece of paper. Berners Lee and Cailliau wanted to make it possible to jump from one page to another based on an individual and unique line of enquiry rather than an imposed format. If one were reading some material which referred to another document, ideally, the reader could click on a link which would take them to the location of that document (functionality which we take for granted today). The development of Hypertext Transfer Protocol (HTTP) facilitated the easy navigation through documents available on the Internet. 'Hypertext links' allow users to click on visible links in order to navigate to additional information (rather than typing in the address of the desired page). This meant that those with minimal computer knowledge or experience were able to much more effectively engage with the Internet.[4] Berners Lee released HTTP in 1991 and in 1993 CERN announced that the Web would be available free of charge.

The release of the Web proved a catalyst for the rapid increase in numbers of people connecting to the Internet. It also prompted another important outcome of the 'Gore Bill' – the injection of funding for the development of Internet software applications. It was this funding programme which resulted in the development of the hugely successful Web browser, *Mosaic*, which was developed within the National Center for Supercomputer Applications (NCSA) at the University of Illinois by Marc Andreessen and Eric Bina (Abbate, 2000, p. 217).

A Web browser is a software application which further facilitates the users' interface with information on the Internet. It is an application for engaging with Hypertext Markup Language (HTML) and HTTP. Dominant browsers today include Apple's *Safari*, Microsoft's *Internet Explorer*, Google's *Chrome* and Mozilla's *Firefox* but these are relatively new and prior to *Mosaic*, browsers were rudimentary. Although Berners Lee had written a Web browser himself, *Mosaic* was much easier to use, with point and click features which allowed for colour graphics to be displayed as part of a web page and, importantly, as a hypertext link. Not only had *Mosaic* been written to operate on most workstations and PCs, but as a consequence of the funding from the 'Gore Bill' which underwrote its development, the NCSA also gave *Mosaic* away free of charge (Abbate, 2000, p. 217). Within one year of *Mosaic's* release in 1993, there were 20 million users of the Web and 95 per cent of them were accessing it through *Mosaic* (Mueller, 2002, p. 107).

The initial, instrumental response to Sputnik which was motivated by concerns about power and resulted in the establishment of ARPA had transformed somewhat over the course of the 1980s. Military power concerns had begun to recede as the Cold War wound down with economic power emerging as a political point of focus in the United States. Computers had also changed from large mainframes with very restricted access to PCs which were selling quickly into the business, education and private markets. In this context, Gore followed up the first *National High Performance Computing Act of 1991* which focused heavily on the NREN as a tool for the research community, with the *National Information Infrastructure Act of 1993* which placed greater emphasis on the general population as users of the network (Bishop, 1993).

The expansion and democratization of computer use resulted in a fundamental shift from regarding the Internet as a tool for elite researchers who would hopefully convert information technology into a source of US military power to an understanding of the Internet as a part of the public infrastructure which might be utilized much more broadly. The Atari Democrats regarded it as an opportunity to revitalize the US economy as well as re-establish the United States as a global leader of this important new technology. They also believed that computers generally and the Internet more specifically could serve to promote important ideas like freedom of information which had come to be understood as important for strategic and social power reasons – particularly in the wake of the Cold War.

These political perspectives were combined with a social constructivist approach to technology which empowered politicians to act and pass legislation like the 'Gore Bill' with significant implications for the development of Internet technology. Interestingly, while Internet technology emerged from concerns about power, some of the unintended consequences of that technology will be found in the case studies to have also undermined US power in a number of ways. Nonetheless, the intervention of politicians (but particularly Al Gore) over these years is often underestimated or even negated in today's reification of the role of the private sector in Internet technology.

1990s: Clinton–Gore team brings it all together

In the 1990s, the political context for decisions about Internet technology was distinct from that of the first phase of Internet technology in the 1960s and 1970s. As noted above, the relationship between military power and technology was no longer the primary driver. With the Cold

War over and America 'victorious', the emphasis for many turned from 'guns' to 'butter' and by that measure, America appeared less sure of its future as the economy struggled. From the early days of his presidential campaign, Bill Clinton's catchphrase was promoted as 'It's the economy, stupid'. This message was intended to counter the extensive foreign policy credentials of his much more experienced opponent George H. Bush and redirect the political focus away from Bush's strengths to issues of a non-military nature (Matalin et al., 1994). In a major campaign speech at the Wharton School of Business at the University of Pennsylvania, Bill Clinton argued provocatively that 'The American dream is slipping away along with the loss of our economic leadership' (Clinton, 1992).

Small government was a bipartisan trend now and economic power was coming to be regarded as an increasingly significant aspect of foreign policy strength. President George H. Bush's foreign policy doctrine was premised on a 'new world order' which projected a period of peace and stability founded upon the predominance of liberalism, free markets and the rule of international law but still essentially tethered to military strength. The Clinton administration followed up by emphasizing American global economic leadership based on free markets and projection of an enlargement policy which actively promoted democratization and human rights.

Clinton's foreign policy and economic policy were to form a close and symbiotic (although not always comfortable) relationship as his ideas about democratic enlargement through trade, the promotion of human rights and globalizing and liberating markets combined to form a kind of ideological/economic *grand strategy*.[5] A view of the world as open and connected through trade was promoted by the Clinton administration as a foreign policy doctrine that reflected a fresh approach to the post-Cold War international climate, clearly articulating democracy and free markets as 'America's core values' (Christopher, 1993; Lake, 1993).

Like Gore, Clinton was in favour of spending the 'peace dividend' (that money no longer needed to sustain the Cold War) and by 1992 he was explicit about how it should be applied. 'Every dollar we take out of military R&D [research and development] in the post Cold War era should go to R&D for commercial technologies, until civilian R&D can match and eventually surpass our Cold War military R&D commitment' (Clinton, 1992). Clinton articulated a form of international competition which decoupled the national interest (and therefore power) from military dominance and instead focused on the links between productivity and technology. 'This is not a Democratic or a Republican issue. It's America against the rest of the world. Every other advanced nation is governed by a body with a strategy for increasing growth' (Clinton, 1992). Leaving no ambiguity about who America's rivals were, he pointed explicitly to the following examples: 'Japan and Germany spend half again as much on civilian R&D as we do, and have the productivity growth rates to show for it' (Clinton, 1992). Although they were referring to different sources of power, both President Bush and President Clinton regarded this as a 'zero-sum' game. Any increase in a competitor's power was a loss of their own.

In addition, there was something of the zeitgeist about Gore's focus on new technology as there was a real sense in the early 1990s that something revolutionary was underway. Policy documents and speeches emanating from the Clinton administration frequently referred to the multiple ways in which new technology would 'change the way we work, live, play' (Clinton and Gore, 1993; Clinton, 1997). In the speech to the Wharton School, Clinton explicitly stated that

> The world has changed dramatically in recent years, and we have to change with it. History has handed us an extraordinary opportunity in the 1990s. The rise of the new economy coincides with the triumph of democracy and the end of the Cold War. At the moment we most need to marshall and reorganize our resources, the greatest collection of high-value talent and assets has become available. With the right plan to convert defense spending to domestic growth, we can catapult America back to the forefront in world economic leadership.
> (Clinton, 1992)

The 'Atari Democrat' ideas about the relationship between new technology and US economic power, exemplified in Gore's presentations to Congress, seamlessly linked into presidential candidate Bill Clinton's approach to global economic affairs when Al Gore was selected as Clinton's vice presidential running mate in the 1992 election campaign. Clearly, Gore's ideas about technology and the future of the US economy and power synergized well with Clinton's approach. There was a general acknowledgement amongst politicians in this set that the world had changed and the United States was going to have to change with it in order to reap the benefits of the new age and restore itself to what many saw as its 'rightful place' as leader of the free world. In a time of rapid political and technological change, the Clinton–Gore team was able to present a united, forward looking strategy for returning the United States to global dominance (and leadership) through an integrated foreign and domestic policy based on new technology and networks – both human and virtual. Many issues which were at least partially acknowledged as problems for US power during this period would be exacerbated by the privatization and commercialization of the Internet in the mid-1990s.

Privatization and commercialization of the Internet

By the mid-1990s, the belief that the Internet should be integrated into economic policies in order to enhance US power was well established in the Clinton–Gore White House. This led to a set of policies intended to manage the transition of the Internet from a federally funded and operated network restricted to research and educational use to a widely accessible, privately owned network open to commercial activity. Despite the expectation that the Internet would enhance US power through economic growth, the Internet remained restricted by US law to non-commercial activity.

This aspect of the political history of the Internet is particularly significant because, as explored below and in Chapter 5, it demonstrates the way in which conceptions of power can and do shape technology. In addition, the outcome of the policies discussed here later led to the debates and problems which generated the Internet governance case study as overwhelming commercial demands on existing governance mechanisms threatened to restrict the commercial potential of the Internet.

The privatization and commercialization of the Internet are sometimes conflated. In fact, the issues are related but separate. *Privatization* refers to the transition of ownership of the network infrastructure – the 'backbone' – from the US government to the private sector. *Commercialization* refers to the decision to allow commercial traffic to flow across that network. The relationship between these two issues is based in the initial reluctance of Congress to allow for commercial gain from a taxpayer-funded project.

By the mid-1980s, the Internet infrastructure was fiscally supported and administered by the federal government through the National Science Foundation (NSF) though this was regarded by the government as an interim measure on the way to full private ownership and management (Kahin, 1990). The *National High-Performance Computing Act of 1990* specified that the NSF support the establishment of a high-speed national network 'in a manner which fosters and maintains competition and private sector investment in high speed data networking' (S.1067, *National High-Performance Computing Act of 1990*, 1990, Federal

Research Internet Coordinating Committee, 1989, pp. 4–5) and that the involvement of the NSF 'be phased out when commercial networks can meet the networking needs of American researchers' (S. 2918, *National High-Performance Computing Act of 1988*, 1988).

Despite the growing belief on the part of politicians like Al Gore in the potential contribution of Internet technology to the future of US economic power, there remained a firm Congressional reticence to permit commercial activity from this ongoing expenditure of tax-payers' dollars. For this reason, it was anticipated that the *commercialization* of activity over the Internet would be conditional on first achieving the *privatization* of the infrastructure. Although the private sector was increasingly eager to make use of the Internet, it appeared reluctant to invest in the infrastructure – particularly while there was potentially a free option available.

Stimulating private sector investment as well as the development of network management capability formed the focus of a number of policy initiatives. One of these was the enforcement of the 'Acceptable Use Policy' (AUP) drawn up by the NSF. This policy dictated that network traffic should be restricted to 'open research and education' specifically prohibiting commercial activity until such time as the infrastructure was privatized. Through this 'carrot and stick' policy approach, the government sought to stimulate necessary private sector investment and indeed, this policy did have the intended effect (Leiner et al., 1997).

The NSF gradually allowed commercial operators to establish their own networks which could connect to the NSF 'backbone' but still relied upon their own privately funded infrastructure. They also increasingly outsourced to the private sector the Internet services they provided, which both nurtured private sector capability and developed the market for the network. Very quickly, Internet service providers (ISPs) grew in number and scope until they were regarded as capable of assuming the role the NSF had previously filled. In April 1995, the NSF 'backbone' was retired and the Internet moved from government to private hands.[6] The Internet was open for business.

The Clinton–Gore administration had very purposefully designed and implemented policies which would guide Internet technology in the direction they felt would most enhance US power. In order to circumvent the Congressional restriction on commercial traffic, it was necessary to prompt the private sector to invest in and develop a privatized information infrastructure. These politicians believed that the Internet, once commercialized and privatized had the potential to generate economic growth which would shore up US economic power –

the primary focus of their strategy to retain a dominant position in the global order. First, this is an illustration of the ways in which government policies can shape and influence the development of technology which has implication well beyond the United States and the evolution of Internet technology. Second, following this phase, commercial imperatives combined with the rapid escalation in demands on governance mechanisms presented a new problem for US power (and consequently generated one of the case studies in this book) – global Internet governance.

Following commercialization, the governance of the Internet became more complex. There was an exponential increase in domain name registrations and as those domain names now carried some commercial value, managing the registrations and enforcement of their use took on new gravity. Existing arrangements (which are addressed in more detail in Chapter 5) were largely informal – managed by a trusted cadre of Internet pioneers – and though these mechanisms had worked well for the much smaller non-commercial Internet, they were ill-equipped to scale upwards to the extent necessary. Governance was perceived in the late 1990s by most stakeholders as a bottleneck which threatened to prevent the Internet from fulfilling its commercial potential. In 1998, as a response to the growing perception that existing Internet governance mechanisms were inadequate, the US government established the Internet Corporation for Assigned Names and Numbers (ICANN).

The circumstances which led to the establishment of ICANN came about as the consequence of inextricably interwoven forces of politics and technology. While they consulted widely with stakeholders, the Clinton–Gore administration's previously articulated vision for the relationship between new technology like the Internet and US power drove the policies which ultimately established ICANN (Mueller, 2007, pp. 166–7). Indeed, as Chapter 5 shows, the structure of Internet governance was very clearly a product of those ideas – in many ways a continuation of the Atari Democrats' vision for how the Internet could best contribute to US power through the economy.

Three significant policy papers were released between July 1997 and June 1998, all of which are discussed at some length in Chapter 5. These were the *Framework for Global Electronic Commerce* (July 1997), *The Green Paper on Internet Governance* (February 1998) and *The White Paper on Management of Internet names and Addresses* (June 1998). Together, these policy papers formally charted a path from the existing Internet governance mechanisms to a future which was based on a US private sector led system for the global governance of the Internet. ICANN was established as a private, not-for-profit incorporated body subject to the legal jurisdiction of the state of California and placed under the purview of the Department of Commerce.

By the latter half of the 1990s, the Internet was a very different entity than it had been at the start of that decade. Within a matter of several years, it had been privatized, opened to commercial traffic, the Web had been invented and the widespread take up of *Mosaic* and PCs had made the Internet widely accessible to those without substantial computer knowledge, money or expertise. From the mid-1990s onwards, political engagement with Internet issues in the United States grew exponentially both in breadth and depth. Regulation and oversight of Internet technology and function became fragmented and expanded to a number of key politicians, Congressional committees and institutions.

Connecting critical infrastructure to the Internet

Understanding how Internet technology came to be perceived as not only enhancing state power (particularly economic power) but also a mechanism for undermining US power is important to engaging with the 'paradox of power' referenced in the Introduction to this book. Technology often has unintended consequences and this has certainly been the case with Internet technology. The widespread integration of Internet technology into so many functions of political and economic significance in the United States was initiated by the drive towards efficiency and productivity which could feed into economic growth. While this was perceived by politicians as enormously successful, it also introduced a range of vulnerabilities which would later feature in debates about cyber security. The following pages illustrate how politicians responded to the growing awareness that productivity and efficiency were accompanied by some very real threats to US power. Essentially, in a very instrumental way, politicians turned to the private sector to resolve problems of national security threats. They consistently expressed confidence that the market would find a solution to the problem of cyber insecurity thereby, to an extent, effectively absolving the government of the responsibility to do so.

The last quarter of the 20th century saw many advanced industrialized states privatize critical infrastructure like water and sewerage, electricity supplies, the financial sector, communications and transport. The United States was no exception and by the new millennium, some 85 per cent of US critical infrastructure was in private hands (Hearing: *Agency Response to Cyberspace Policy Review,* 2009, p. 3). With privatization came an increased discretion on the part of those managing the infrastructure over the systems and technology which were implemented for the control of these utilities and industries.

Computerized control systems had long been a feature of critical infrastructure being used to monitor and adjust the processes of large systems including dams, power supply and sewerage. Over the past two to three decades (roughly concurrent with trends to privatization), many of these systems employed to control critical infrastructure functions were migrated from proprietary control programs (software programs written and coded specifically for an industry or an organization) to more generic computer programs known as 'supervisory control and data acquisition systems' (SCADA systems).

This had significant benefits, as buying readily available software was much more cost effective than paying to have software written specifically for a system. SCADA systems typically ran on a Microsoft Windows platform – an operating system which, though widespread, is notoriously porous and easily penetrated. In addition to the indigenous vulnerability of Windows, SCADA systems add another layer of standards and uniform coding which increase security problems. While SCADA systems boosted productivity and efficiency of many industries and services by allowing critical infrastructure to be controlled centrally and remotely, the combination of private ownership and the vulnerabilities of SCADA systems led to a range of cyber security concerns around critical infrastructure protection (CIP) when these systems began to be connected to the Internet.

SCADA systems connected to the Internet and reliant on a standardized operating system like Microsoft Windows made it possible for hackers to penetrate the systems and interfere with the smooth and safe operation of important infrastructure like dams, traffic systems and energy supplies. One early example emerged from Australia where a former employee of Hunter Watertech was arrested for tampering with the water supply for Maroochy Shire over a period of four months (WebSecure, 2002). At the subsequent trial, it was revealed that using his laptop he had gained entry to the SCADA system that controls the Shire's water treatment plant and set himself up as 'pumping station 4'. After turning off all alarms and giving himself appropriate clearance and authority, he altered the sewerage outfall, deliberately pouring millions of litres of untreated sewerage into the river. Investigations revealed that this individual was in complete control of 300 SCADA nodes and 'could have done anything he liked to the fresh water' (Weimann, 2004, p. 10). It was becoming increasingly clear that illicit attacks on these systems were a very real and viable concern, one not limited to disgruntled employees or adventurous hackers but with potential for global conflict and terrorist acts. This was a precursor to the Stuxnet attack on an Iranian nuclear plant which will be discussed in Chapter 4.

In 1998, President Clinton issued the *Presidential Decision Directive 63 (PDD-63)* which outlined the administration's approach to CIP (Clinton, 1998b). *PDD-63* makes an explicit statement about the Clinton–Gore administration's perception of the relationship between US power and the Internet – one which regards conventional power factors as reliant upon the same technology which increasingly underpins civil functions like commerce, communications and education. 'The United States possesses both the world's strongest military and its largest national economy. Those two aspects of our power are mutually reinforcing and dependent. They are also increasingly reliant upon certain critical infrastructures and upon cyber-based information systems' (Clinton, 1998b).

In addition to this relationship between the state's critical information infrastructure and its capacity to exercise conventional power, the *PDD-63* also introduces the notion that global order and specifically US primacy may be a catalyst for attacks over the Internet. In this sense, the Internet now poses a potential *challenge* to American power.

> Because of our military strength, future enemies, whether nations, groups or individuals, may seek to harm us in non-traditional ways including attacks within the United States. Our economy is increasingly reliant upon interdependent and cyber-supported infrastructures and non-traditional attacks on our infrastructure and information systems may be capable of significantly harming both our military power and our economy.
>
> (Clinton, 1998b)

In addition to these conceptual claims about US power, the *PDD-63* made two important points which would have implications for the US approach to power and cyber security well into the future. First, it argued that market incentives should be the first choice for addressing problems of cyber security in the context of CIP and that regulation should be an option of last resort (Clinton, 1998b). Second, it stated that 'in order to engage the private sector fully, it is preferred that participation by owners and operators in a national infrastructure protection system be voluntary' (Clinton, 1998b). These two principles that the market is the best mechanism through which to pursue national cyber security and that private sector participation should be voluntary form the basis for what came to be regarded as the 'cornerstone' of US cyber security strategies – the 'public/private partnership'. This arrangement is found in the case study on cyber security to undermine the government's authority to act, even in the face of considerable challenges to material power factors.

The outcome from the PDD-63 was the *National Plan for Information Systems Protection* released in 2000. Titled 'Defending America's Cyberspace', it was described in the executive summary as 'the first attempt by any nation to develop a plan to defend its cyberspace' (Clinton, 2000, p. vi). In the introduction, President Clinton reiterates his belief in the 'public/private partnership', again eschewing the path of regulation or Congressional mandate in favour of 'consultation' with industry.

Richard Clarke, who was at that time the National Coordinator for Security, Infrastructure Protection, and Counter Terrorism, writes in the plan that while the military was making progress to secure its networks, and the US government could order federal networks to be secured, they could not and should not dictate solutions for the private sector – which is where significant risks lay (Clinton, 2000, p. vi). This conflicted approach – that substantial national risk lies in unsecured privately owned cyber infrastructure and yet the government did not claim a mandate to ensure that infrastructure was secured – resulted in Clarke's acknowledgement that the *National Plan for Information Systems Protection* did not stipulate what would be done to secure and defend private networks. Rather, it suggested a 'common framework for action' (Clinton, 2000, p. vi). These ideas, of the government having a limited mandate and the private sector essentially being assigned some responsibility for national security, would continue to feature heavily in cyber security policymaking of the future.

In the *National Plan for Information Systems Protection,* President Clinton also established a clear but didactic relationship between cyber security and civil liberties, reassuring the American people that enhanced cyber security 'cannot and will not come at the expense of our civil liberties. We must never undermine the very freedoms we are seeking to protect' (Clinton, 2000, p. iii). This expands over the following years to include human rights and in Chapter 4, a tension emerges between the intelligence community's desire for access to valuable information and politicians' ambitions for the protection and promotion of these norms and values.

Political responses to the threat of disruption

As explained in Chapter 2, perceptions about technology matter. How actors in a position to influence technology regard it as either promoting or challenging their interests (however those may be defined) will guide the ways in which they seek to affect future development of that technology. Just as the absence of a bicycle chain guard posed no problem until women in long skirts began riding, changes in political perceptions of threats to US power generated a shift in approaches to Internet technology. The growing awareness discussed in the previous section of the vulnerabilities associated with critical infrastructure systems connected to the Internet combined over the late 1990s and early 2000s with a new perception of 'disruption' as a threat to security and US power. Initially perceived as a means to enhance military power, then as a means to enhance economic power, the Internet now came to be regarded as a source of vulnerability – a mechanism through which US power could be undermined in a number of important ways.

Several important developments combined to formulate this shift in perceptions about Internet technology and its relationship to US power – particularly with regard to cyber security concerns – and these stimulated a range of legislative and policy responses. The threat of *destruction* which had underpinned conventional approaches to global conflict was being reconceptualized in the context of Internet technology as the threat of *disruption*. Problems like the 'Y2K bug' and events like the September 11 attacks and the 2007 cyber-attacks on Estonia combined to generate new ideas about how Internet technology related to US power.

One of the first major developments to instigate this change in threat perceptions was the looming public anxiety about what was widely referred to as the 'Y2K bug'. Concurrently over the latter half of the 1990s, while Internet governance and CIP were emerging in political debates, a public anxiety arose about how computer systems which were developed in the early decades of computer programming would deal with the date change from 1999 to 2000. There was a genuine fear that programs not originally designed to accommodate the numeric change in the first digit from a 'one' to a 'two' would fail, causing widespread disruption of both public and private infrastructure which now relied upon these systems. Opinions differed on whether this was a valid cause for concern or whether it was a construct of the industry which stood to benefit through the vast expenditure on compliance programs. Nevertheless, the implications were potentially so significant that governments felt compelled to act and a massive Y2K compliance program was implemented in many industrialized states including the United States where legislation was passed that required both public and private sector compliance with standards set to ensure that the date change on 1 January 2000 did not disrupt systems that the public relied upon.[7] Business and government globally spent years (and millions or billions of dollars) ensuring that their systems were Y2K compliant and certainly – on 1 January 2000 – it seemed all the hard work and expense had either paid off or been unnecessary as systems remained intact and carried on as they had the previous day.

The Y2K bug served to focus attention on just how reliant the United States had become on the smooth and reliable function of its information infrastructure but it also illustrated again the way political decisions can and do shape technology. In this case, legislating compliance with standards forced the private sector to meet a level of system resilience or risk prosecution. The Y2K compliance program is sometimes referred to by politicians as an exemplar of the legitimacy of government intervention in the private sector's management of networks (Brock, 2000, p. 23; Clinton, 2000, p. iv). Although the Y2K legislation was widely supported, in other similar cases (cyber security and network neutrality) calls for government intervention generate debates about the merits of adhering to the liberal value of limited government as opposed to the benefits of a 'strong, central hand' in shaping Internet technology.

This raises questions about the US government's authority to shape technology even in cases where it can be seen to be of vital national interest and have implications for enhancing or undermining power. Themes of authority and legitimacy were found to be important in all three issue areas examined in this book and they form the basis of one of the key findings of this study. That is, regarding an aspect of Internet technology as relevant to US power did not always lead directly to a sense of authority to influence and shape the technology. Without this sense of authority, politicians regarded some policy options as lacking in legitimacy even though they would potentially minimize serious challenges to some US power factors. One of the conclusions of this book is that there is a relationship between this sense of authority and a SCoT approach and this will be developed in the empirical chapters. The Y2K bug and Internet governance are two examples in which politicians advocated a strong role for the government and followed it through with targeted policies. This was not the case with other issues – specifically those associated with a technological determinist or instrumental approach to technology.

Fears of a 'disruptive' attack were realized on September 11. Obviously, there was a devastating physical element to the attacks but there were also some enduring factors which fed into this general sense that the United States was vulnerable in a new and ill-defined way. The impact of an attack on the 'homeland' was profound for a nation protected by oceans and friendly states. Pearl Harbour, of course, had also left a deep scar but Americans retained a deep sense of physical security upon their own shores. The jolt of the September 11 attacks awakened in Americans a sense that they were *not* as safe at home as they had assumed and this led to speculation that this conventionally understood advantage of geopolitics no longer afforded the same protection it once did.

A second reason why the September 11 attacks fed into this perception of disruption as a threat was due to the significant cost of suspending some critical functions like the stock exchange and air travel following the attacks (*The Economist*, 2001). The following December, the Senate Committee on Commerce, Science, and Transportation held a hearing into the response of the technology sector in times of crisis in order to ascertain what went right and what went wrong in the wake of the planes hitting the World Trade Center towers. The committee expressed deep concerns about the impact on New York City's telecommunications which were 'flattened by the blow' (Wyden, 2001, p. 1) leading to rescue workers at the site running handwritten messages and instructions from command and control sites around Manhattan to rescue workers inside the wreckage.[8]

Fears about American resilience to a critical infrastructure attack were also exacerbated by the failure of the Federal Emergency Management Agency (FEMA) to respond effectively to Hurricane Katrina. Representative Bill Pascrell's comments at a 2005 hearing highlight this: 'We saw in the recent hurricane ... that the Federal Government was unprepared to respond to a large natural disaster ... Are we prepared for a cyber attack on our control systems?' (Pascrell, 2005, p. 54). The final report from a bipartisan committee investigation into this disaster found that 'the preparation for and response to Hurricane Katrina show we are still an analogue government in a digital age. We must recognize that we are woefully incapable of storing, moving, and accessing information – especially in times of crisis' (*A Failure of Initiative: The Final Report of the Select Bipartisan Committee to Investigate the Preparation for and Response to Hurricane Katrina*, 2006, p. 1). The same report links Katrina to the September 11 attacks finding that 'whatever improvements have been made to our capacity to respond to natural or man-made disasters, four and half years after 9/11, we are still not fully prepared'.

The failure of the response to Hurricane Katrina is frequently referred to by politicians in the context of debates about cyber security – particularly with reference to an attack on critical infrastructure. Hurricane Katrina required a large, coordinated response; it was a chaotic and disorienting environment to work in; and key services and infrastructure were not restored in a timely manner. All of these factors resonate with the scenario of a cyber-attack on critical infrastructure and feed into concerns about how the state would respond in such a case. In a Congressional hearing into cyber security a few months after Katrina, there was a strongly expressed sentiment on the part of committee members that America was unprepared for a large-scale cyber-attack. 'We saw in ... Hurricane Katrina that the Federal Government was unprepared to respond to a large natural disaster ... Are we prepared for a cyber attack on our control systems?' (Pascrell, 2005, p. 54).

The rapid growth in online crime, which escalated over the 2000s, coupled with the growing perception that much of the critical infrastructure of the state was vulnerable to Internet-based attacks led to a growing unease amongst those politicians tasked with oversight of the Internet. It was becoming increasingly apparent that the Internet was not only a means through which attacks could take place on the physical infrastructure, but actually a critical resource itself, which also must be protected (Branscomb and Klausner, 2002, p. 135). Over the course of the 2000s, as American reliance on the smooth functioning of the Internet increased, political concepts of 'critical infrastructure protection' (CIP) expanded to incorporate *information* and 'critical information infrastructure protection' (CIIP) steadily gained traction as a policy issue and a cyber security concern (Burns, 2000, p. 2).

In response to many of the concerns highlighted by the hearings discussed above, the Bush administration released the *2003 National Strategy to Secure Cyberspace* (Bush, 2003a). Despite the new threat perceptions which had evolved during his presidency, this document expressed continuity with the Clinton–Gore emphasis on the public/private partnership as the primary mechanism through which the United States would pursue cyber security. In it, President Bush reasserted that '[t]he cornerstone of America's cyberspace security strategy is and will remain a public-private partnership' (Bush, 2003a, p. iii). The notion that Internet technology now posed a number of challenges to key elements of US power, but that these should be addressed by the private sector in a voluntary arrangement was a view which would become increasingly entrenched in US cyber security policymaking in future years. It is a view deeply rooted in an insistence on the part of policymakers that a distinction can be maintained not only between public and private space on the Internet, but also between crime, terror and warfare. In essence, as cyber security threats develop, US politicians find themselves caught in a policy paradox – the federal government is understood to be responsible for national security and yet in the context of cyber security they perceive that they lack the authority to act. 'Our traditions of federalism and limited government require that organizations outside the federal government take the lead in many of these efforts' (Bush, 2003a, p. 14).

Later that same year, President George W. Bush released *Homeland Security Presidential Directive 7 (HSPD-7)* on 'Critical Infrastructure Identification, Prioritization and Protection' in which the Internet is identified as essential to many important services (Bush, 2003b). This directive was in part a response to the September 11 attacks as it frames the threat almost exclusively in terms of a terrorist attack. Its purpose was to establish a national policy for federal departments and agencies to 'identify and prioritize United States critical infrastructure and key resources and to protect them from terrorist attacks' both in the physical and cyber spheres. The newly created Department of Homeland Security (DHS) was mandated to produce an integrated 'National Plan for Critical Infrastructure and Key Resources Protection' by the end of 2004. Instead, it issued an interim report in February 2005 which was an underdeveloped and generic document that made no significant contribution to either the debates or the practice of CIP (Ridge, 2005).

The completed plan was published in 2006 and this was more comprehensive generally and also with regard to the information infrastructure. In the Introduction, it states that protecting the critical infrastructure of the United States is 'essential to the Nation's security, public health and safety, economic vitality, and way of life' and that an attack on this infrastructure could produce 'catastrophic losses in terms of human casualties, property destruction, and economic effects, as well as profound damage to public morale and confidence' (Chertoff, 2006, p. 7). Yet, as did previous policy documents, this plan is built on the assumption that the public/private partnership remains the most appropriate mechanism through which to pursue this (Chertoff, 2006, p. 26).

By April 2007, concerns about a critical infrastructure attack over the Internet were obviously already well established in US political circles. In this context, a diplomatic stoush with Russia led to Estonian critical infrastructure coming under a massive and sustained cyber-attack. Involving over a million computers around the world, primary targets were the websites of the Estonian president and parliament, three of the country's six news services, two of its largest banks and several communications firms (Deutsche Welle, 2007a; Traynor, 2007). Estonia's Defence Minister Jaak Aaviksoo declared a national security situation which could 'effectively be compared to when your ports are shut to the sea' (Landler and Markoff, 2007). After three weeks of sustained attacks, Estonia was forced to isolate itself from Internet traffic beyond its borders in order to restore its systems and the attacks subsequently died off. North Atlantic Treaty Organization (NATO) then convened a meeting of foreign ministers to discuss a more appropriate response to the problem of cyber aggression.

This was the first public assertion of a state-to-state cyber-attack (though the actual origins of the attack remain unclear) and it inevitably prompted debate and speculation in the United States about the consequences for America if such an attack were successfully launched there. This type of attack, which targeted critical infrastructure, transport and communication systems had been a recurring theme in both political and popular forecasts about cyber security and CIP in America. This attack scenario has dominated Congressional discussions on cyber security for decades and been the subject of numerous hearings and policy documents. For years, many debates about cyber-terror or cyberwar were stymied by the lack of a tangible public act – an 'electronic Pearl Harbour' as it had come to be known. There were various theories about why, given the enormous vulnerability of the United States on the Internet, had there not been a more substantial attack. Events in Estonia shifted the paradigm from the stuff of fiction and Hollywood to a very real issue for IR and state power. It was now clear that states were vulnerable to cyber-attacks impossible to attribute to the perpetrator. Belligerent states could cripple the infrastructure of a rival state and maintain 'plausible deniability' while they did it. This upsets conventions of state-to-state aggression which are based on understanding the identity of the parties involved.

This incident reinforced the paradigm for 'disruption' of information and communications technology (ICT) as a form of state vulnerability in the US political consciousness. This paradigm continued to develop over the ensuing years as 'wars of disruption' rather than 'destruction' came to be understood in academic and policy circles as characterizing future conflict, thereby adding weight to concerns about cyber security. At this point, the Internet was seen less as a conduit for the economic growth and more as an integral platform for the effective delivery of civil, military, political, social and economic functions in the United States. Disruption signalled another key shift in approach to the relationship between US power and Internet technology from a *source* of power as Al Gore had expressed it to a vulnerability and, therefore, potentially a *challenge* to power.

Critical changes to telecommunications law

One of the less discussed aspects of the relationship between state power and Internet technology is the impact of an expanded group of stakeholders on government policy. Few (if any) technologies prompt as wide and divergent a set of claims from individuals, commerce, interest groups, the international community and the public sector as Internet technology does. For states like the United States where the Internet is integrated into so many aspects of public and private life, managing expectations and balancing stakeholder requirements have complicated the relationship between state power and technology. Certainly, other examples such as nuclear technology provoke a set of debates and questions about how that technology should be used and developed in the context of state power. However, the implications of those policy choices affect most people in an oblique manner rather than having a direct, discernable impact upon everyday interactions.

One example of the impact of a broad range of stakeholders with an interest in technology policy is illustrated by the necessity of amending communications law to adapt to new ICTs. Debates around this type of legislative overhaul throw a light on the perceptions of politicians about how such technology fits into a larger view of the national interest. They also draw in debates about which values, norms and interests should be privileged in policies which shape and influence the technology and how these factors relate to state power. In the United States, these debates have largely revolved around the issue of network neutrality and this generates the third empirical issue examined in this book.

While much of the US political attention and energy was siphoned off to the pressing problems in Iraq and Afghanistan during the first decade of the 2000s, telecommunications law was under review in the United States. Stakeholders with an interest in the Internet had expanded both in numbers and in influence as so many functions of the state came to rely upon the 'information infrastructure'. Private companies, the military, individuals, civil and human rights groups, the education sector and, of course, the government all had an interest in and an opinion on how the Internet should develop and be managed. Understanding and attempting to reconcile these sometimes competing interests while maintaining a view of what was best for the national interest occupied many Congressional hearings. Adapting legislation designed to deal predominantly with fixed line telephones to the emerging rigours of advanced telecommunications proved complex and difficult.

There were two important developments which moved communications law into the spotlight in America. The first was a shift in online revenue streams which fundamentally impacted on previous economic models for Internet-related commerce. Previously, large private sector telecommunications firms had paid for the necessary infrastructure such as exchanges and the laying of cables. They then leased these back to the public, private and government sector for a fee and these services formed the economic foundation of the information technology sector. However, during the 'dotcom' boom, content and service providers like Google, Yahoo and eBay emerged as business enterprises which used that infrastructure to generate massive returns for very low relative investment. These companies had very low overheads compared to the owners of telecommunications infrastructure and yet they were able to generate massive returns. The telecommunications firms who owned the infrastructure soon began to argue that they had a right to a share of these profits – a contention which has been fiercely rejected by not only the dotcoms but by a large sector of the Internet community who believe in the principle of 'network neutrality', the principle that information travels across the network unexamined and without interference.

The second development which prompted debate over communications law was the advent of 'streaming media' necessary for playing live, multi-user video games, viewing video files and using voice over internet protocol (VoIP) to make phone calls over the Internet including services like Skype. Data travelling across the Internet is broken down into small 'packets', moved across the network through the fastest possible route and then reassembled upon arrival at the destination address. With simple data like text files, delays have less impact because although transmission may be slowed during peak traffic periods, documents eventually arrive fully assembled. However, with streaming media, delays in packet delivery result in the video or voice call being disrupted – sometimes even unintelligible. These services not only use considerably more bandwidth than ordinary data transmission but are reliant on an *uninterrupted* flow of data. In order to provide this, network operators sometimes have to 'manage' the data flows, privileging streaming media packets over ordinary data packets so as to ensure some quality of service to their customers. However, this practice leaves open the potential for misuse and this has been at the core of the debates about network neutrality – taken up in detail in Chapter 6.

A key player in these debates and in the renovation of communications law has been the Federal Communications Commission (FCC) – an independent government agency responsible for regulating the telecommunications sector in the United States.[9] In 2002, in an early attempt to address some of the complex issues which arose from the privatization and commercialization of the Internet in the mid-1990s, the FCC made what would later be regarded as a landmark decision for the future of the Internet. It relegated Internet communications from Title II of the 1934 Communications Act which governs common carriage telephone communications to the less stringent Title I regulations which govern interstate information services.[10] This meant that common-carrier regulations that impose rigorous access and anti-discrimination requirements to telecommunications like telephones would not apply to information services like Internet access. As a consequence, this ruling is regarded by many as the policy genesis of the 'network neutrality' debate which is explored in depth in Chapter 6. The 2002 FCC ruling effectively deregulated Internet broadband service supply, thus opening the door for private operators to discriminate against data. In the 2006 Senate hearing into network neutrality, Senator Byron Dorgan identified the FCC ruling as the fundamental cause of the political debate. 'If [the FCC] had made the decision this was a telecommunications service, the common-carrier rules would apply and ... the issue of neutrality and content and so on would not be before us' (Dorgan, 2006a, p. 35).

The FCC ruling was highly controversial – even at the time it was taken – with one of the five commissioners issuing a dissenting statement as part of the ruling document. Michael J. Copps argued strongly against the ruling on the grounds that the decision placed broadband services outside of 'any viable and predictable regulatory framework' (Copps, 2002, pp. 73–5). He refers explicitly to the failure of the ruling to stipulate open access requirements which would force owners of the infrastructure to make it available to competing ISPs. Without these open access requirements, the small number of telco and cable providers in the United States would be able to minimize competition and dominate the market – often in monopoly or duopoly situations which remains the case today.

Michael K. Powell, the FCC chairman at the time of the ruling, also included a statement. In it, he argued that the FCC was bound by law to interpret the existing statute – rather than use its discretion to determine the appropriate definition according to its preferred regulatory approach

(Powell, 2002, p. 70). He also made the point that the FCC should by no means be considered 'neutered' in this respect. 'Congress invested the Commission with ample authority under Title 1 ... to guard against public interest harms and anti-competitive results' (Powell, 2002, p. 70).

In 2006, a major bill aimed at a comprehensive overhaul of the Communications Act of 1934 was introduced to the Senate. The *Communications, Consumer's Choice and Broadband Deployment Act of 2006* was not passed into law but it generated serious debate about how the Internet was to be ordered and structured in the future. The act was the subject of two Senate hearings before the Committee on Commerce, Science and Transportation – the second of which (held on 25 May 2006) was dedicated solely to the net neutrality issue. The Congressional record reveals that when the bill was later debated in the Senate on 28 June 2006, net neutrality again dominated the speeches almost to the exclusion of any other communications issues addressed by the bill. In February 2015 in what was regarded by net neutrality proponents as an important victory, the FCC reclassified broadband access as a telecommunications service to which the Title II regulations apply.

Network neutrality had become a highly contested political issue over the recent decade and is now understood to have the potential for comprehensive and long-lasting effects on America's Internet experience and infrastructure. Perceptions held by American politicians about how these issues should best be managed in order to enhance US power are driven and divided by competing conceptions of 'freedom' on the Internet, the role of innovation in promoting and sustaining state power and the legitimacy of governmental intervention in the way the Internet is used and managed. These are examined comprehensively in Chapter 6.

The Obama administration

In 2009, Barack Obama was inaugurated as the 44th president of the United States. His campaign had positioned him as much more in touch with modern communications technology than his predecessor. He refused to give up his Blackberry maintaining that he could not function personally or professionally without an Internet connection. He had also run a very successful social networking fund-raiser during his campaign which raised not only money but also his profile as a politician who understood the Internet and would be able to provide some leadership on the complex problems the state faced – including cyber security.

Over the preceding few years, a series of intense cyber-attacks had emanated from China. In 2003, an incident referred to by the Pentagon as 'Titan Rain' came to light. Over a matter of months, attacks which appeared to originate from southern China accessed and extracted a huge amount of valuable and sometimes classified information from Defense computers (Norton-Taylor, 2007; Mazanec, 2009). In addition, a number of states including Germany, India, the United Kingdom and South Korea publicly denounced China for either aiding or abetting cyber-attacks upon their state functions (Tung, 2007; Connolly, 2009; Maples, 2009, p. 60; Leppard, 2010). The role of the Internet in US strategic competition with China featured in a 2008 report for the incoming 44th president which stated that 'America's failure to protect cyberspace is one of the most urgent national security problems facing the new administration' (Lewis, 2008, p. 11).

Within months of taking office, Obama called for a 90-day review of cyber security issues. In May 2009, the outcome of that study was published as the *Cyberspace Policy Review*. It argued that 'the continued exploitation of information networks and the compromise of sensitive data, especially by nations, leave the United States vulnerable to the loss of economic competitiveness and the loss of the military's technological advantages' (Hathaway, 2009a, p. 1). In contrast to the Bush administration which had strategically focused on the Internet primarily as a source of domestic vulnerability due to the reliance upon it of critical infrastructure, the Obama administration made an explicit link between cyber security, the economy and American hard power.

In the *2010 National Security Strategy*, President Obama declared cyberspace a 'strategic national asset' – essentially acknowledging unequivocally that although the Internet had been an engine of economic growth and innovation, US power could also be undermined by the Internet. President Obama argued in the *2010 National Security Strategy* that America must 'enhance our resilience — the ability to adapt to changing conditions and prepare for, withstand, and rapidly recover from disruption' brought about by a cyber-attack (Obama, 2010, p. 18). Even more explicitly, he argued that '[O]ur prosperity serves as a wellspring for our power. It pays for our military, underwrites our diplomacy and development efforts, and serves as a leading source of our influence in the world' (Obama, 2010, p. 9). Finally, cyber security is linked to global leadership in the tradition of the Sputnik response: 'the United States – the nation that invented the Internet, that launched an information revolution, that transformed the world – will do what we did in the 20th century and lead once more in the 21st' (Obama, 2009b).

In addition to President Obama's vision for the relationship between US power and the Internet, Secretary of State Hillary Clinton also introduced some innovative new policy. The '21st Century Statecraft' was Clinton's interpretation of the manner in which US power should be exercised abroad and understood at home. This doctrine articulated a new view of US power which was closely integrated with Internet technology. Clinton's speeches and policy documents were framed in social constructivist terms which expressed both the authority and responsibility of the US government to shape Internet technology in such a way as to promote this new view of power.

The emphasis of 21st Century Statecraft was on 'people to people' diplomacy in recognition of the view that diplomatic outcomes are no longer defined solely by what elites prefer but also by what the general population strives for. A key element of this approach was the understanding that the wider population can be motivated or stimulated to force change at an elite level and this is linked to the projection of US power. Clinton argued that 'to advance American interests and values and to lead other nations in solving shared problems in the 21st century, we must rely on our diplomats and civilian experts as the first face of American power' (Clinton, 2010c). This was referred to by the State Department as 'civilian power' and it formed the bedrock of 21st Century Statecraft.

21st Century Statecraft was promoted as a response to the information age. In a speech at the Newseum in January 2010, Clinton argued that the spread of information networks is 'forming a new nervous system for our planet' (Clinton, 2010a). 21st Century Statecraft, she argued, is the US response to this 'nervous system' in which traditional foreign policy tools can be complemented 'with newly innovated and adapted instruments of statecraft that fully leverage the networks, technologies, and demographics of our interconnected world' (Clinton, n.d.).

A fundamental element of 21st Century Statecraft is 'Internet freedom' which is the protection of human rights online – specifically freedom of information and freedom of expression. Discussing this during the Newseum speech, Clinton acknowledged 'the great irony' of the information age which President Obama had articulated. After extolling the many advantages which Internet freedom offers to the projection of US power, Clinton also remarks that 'these technologies are not an unmitigated blessing' (Clinton, 2010a). She goes on to observe that the same technologies which promote human rights also allow Al-Qaeda to operate globally.

In November 2010, Internet freedom faced a major challenge that highlighted its highly normative and value-based footings. The

WikiLeaks website began to release some of the hundreds of thousands of classified diplomatic cables which had been stolen from an unsecured computer in a military camp in Iraq. Clinton's response to this was unequivocal. She argued that the leak was not only an attack on America's foreign policy interests but also 'an attack on the international community – the alliances and partnerships, the conversations and negotiations that safeguard global security and advance economic prosperity' (Clinton, 2010b). When challenged over how she could reconcile this with the US stance on Internet freedom, Clinton argued that freedom of information did not include stolen information. Essentially, Internet freedom is a view which maintains that freedom to information is only appropriate for those with similarly aligned normative ideas about how it should be used. With 21st Century Statecraft, the Obama–Clinton administration appears to be ushering in a new era of US determination to shape the global Internet environment in such a way as to best protect and promote US power (Carr, 2013, pp. 621–37).

One of the defining issues of the Obama administration in this context will surely be the leaks by former NSA contractor, Edward Snowden. In 2013, Snowden revealed details of the US intelligence community's collection, storage and use of personal data. This is taken up in Chapter 4 and provides an excellent lens for the examination of politicians' expectations of the ways in which Internet technology can both enhance and undermine US power in IR.

4
Cyber Security

The information age 'power paradox' discussed in the Introduction to this book is particularly stark in the context of debates about cyber security. Those states which have most successfully adopted and exploited the opportunities afforded by the Internet are also most vulnerable to the range of threats which accompany it.[1] President Obama acknowledged this in 2009 when he referred to 'the great irony of our Information Age – the very technologies that empower us to create and to build also empower those who would disrupt and destroy. And this paradox – seen and unseen – is something that we experience every day' (Obama, 2009b). President Clinton had made clear the relationship between emerging cyber threats and US power 11 years earlier in his *Presidential Decision Directive-63* where he argued that '[t]he United States possesses both the world's strongest military and its largest national economy. Those two aspects of our power are mutually reinforcing and dependent. They are also increasingly reliant upon certain critical infrastructures and upon cyber-based information systems' (Clinton, 1998b, p. 1).

One of President Obama's first acts in office was to call for a national cyber security review (NCSR) in order to assess how the United States had arrived at a point of such vulnerability and what could be done to address this problem. He described cyber security as 'one of the most serious economic and national security challenges we face as a nation' (Obama, 2009b). President Obama concluded from the findings of the review that it was 'clear that we're not as prepared as we should be, as a government or as a country' (Obama, 2009b). The following year, in his first National Security Strategy (NSS), the president nominated the digital infrastructure 'a strategic national asset' and argued that protecting it was now a national security priority (Obama, 2010, p. 27).

How can a state with so many resources and capabilities, which has been so attuned to the threat of cyber insecurity for so long and which has a long history of deriving power from technology, remain so exposed to these threats? How is it that the United States has been unable to overcome the 'paradox of power' in the information age? Through an analysis of the way politicians' conceptions of power influence and shape technology, this chapter on cyber security produces some surprising findings which go some way to answering these questions.

Security and power are not, of course, the same thing. Indeed, their relationship is a key debate in international relations (IR) literature, particularly amongst realist scholars. Some realists (Hans Morgenthau and John Mearsheimer) regard states as power maximizing (Morgenthau, 1978; Mearsheimer, 2001). States seek power, they argue, because it is the most reliable means to ensure survival. Other realists like Kenneth Waltz (1979) invert this assumption and argue that states are actually security maximizing. In this view, power is simply a means to an end because it is useful for ensuring security. The distinction raises questions about whether power should be regarded as absolute or relative. Do states seek power absolutely or do they seek to acquire just enough relative to other states in order to ensure their own security?

In the following analysis, the concerns expressed by politicians lean towards the latter view. Cyber security is opening up a new field of global conflict – one on which the United States does not retain the same relative power that it has had in terms of conventional military capacity. Some small actors including terrorist groups and less developed states, which were previously regarded as possessing little power, potentially become relatively powerful in cyberspace. Absolute power in this context seems to have less meaning than it did in the more straightforward context of industrial technology. The United States is already regarded as in possession of an unprecedented proportion of power, yet it appears that it is not sufficient to ensure security in this realm. Either small actors are disproportionately powerful in cyberspace or a security-maximizing view has more currency here than a power-maximizing view. In fact, this chapter reveals that politicians do pursue a security-maximizing approach to state survival in cyberspace but, perhaps surprisingly, they do so through the pursuit of social power rather than material power.

One of the basic arguments running through this book is that the technology itself does not determine outcomes. While it is true that important Internet protocols were developed with little consideration for security, this is only a partial explanation for the persistence of cyber insecurity. The social construction of technology reminds us that although technology does impact on society, society in turn shapes and influences the development of technology. So why have US politicians not been more effective in formulating solutions to a problem they have regarded as so pressing?

US politicians have been aware of cyber security as a national vulnerability almost since the Internet's inception, though it took on added significance following the commercialization of the Internet in the mid-1990s. Cyber security has been the subject of numerous congressional hearings, reports, legislative action, presidential directives and debates, many of which were detailed in Chapter 3. As early as 1995, the General Accounting Office reported to Congress that ensuring security on the 'information superhighway' (as the Internet was then referred to) would pose a major challenge in the future (Willemssen, 1995, pp. 18–23). The following year, the same office issued a report on the rising threat of attacks pointing to the rapidly increasing number of people with access to the Internet as a source of elevated exposure for the Department of Defense systems. It also found that this exposure posed a 'serious threat to national security' as it allowed strategic competitors with less conventional material power to gain advantage at a low cost (Brock, 1996, p. 4). The report predicted that 'this will become an increasingly attractive way for terrorists or adversaries to wage attacks' (Brock, 1996, p. 4).

Twenty years later, these projections remain salient if not even more pressing. President Bush pointed out in 2003 that 'the healthy functioning of cyberspace is essential to our economy and our national security' (Bush, 2003a, p. 1). The Internet has opened a door for a new wave of criminal behaviour, anonymous state belligerence, terrorist attacks and significant economic expense. Control of critical infrastructure, the banking system and stock exchange, trade and commerce, communications, access to essential information, all of these functions and many more are now conducted using systems connected to the Internet and consequently exposed to risk of attack. The advantages of efficiency and enhanced productivity which Internet connectivity affords have to be weighed against the increased security risks. Melissa Hathaway, the Obama administration's former cyber security advisor, observed that 'during the last decade and a half the United States has been seduced by phenomenal business and economic growth enabled by the effectiveness and efficiency of high performance global networked environments' (Hathaway, 2009b, p. 13). President Obama has acknowledged that 'we've failed to invest in the security of our digital infrastructure' (Obama, 2009b) and cyber security was referred to as the 'soft underbelly' of America by Representative Daniel Lungren, while he was chairman of the Subcommittee on Emergency Preparedness, Science and Technology (Lungren, 2005, p. 50).

This chapter reveals that politicians engage with two different conceptions of power in the context of cyber security debates. When articulating how cyber insecurity poses a problem for US power, they employ a material view of power which references the impact of the Internet on the economy, the likely outcome of global conflict and geopolitics. In a sense, this reflects conventional approaches to security and power – an old recipe with the added ingredient of Internet technology.

The solution to these problems has been almost exclusively regarded as grounded in the 'public/private partnership'. This is a normative arrangement (as opposed to an institutionalized or formalized agreement) whereby politicians expect the private sector to lead the way in cyber security technology and practice in order to protect this important aspect of state power. This resonates with an instrumental view of technology which looks for the solution to technological problems in technology itself and relies on market forces to produce them. An analysis of this arrangement reveals that despite the importance of cyber security for US material power, politicians believe that the government lacks both the capability and the authority to more proactively shape technology in this regard.

This chapter also reveals that politicians regard cyber security in terms of the way it relates to social factors of power. Here they emphasize the importance of promoting norms and values such as privacy, freedom of speech and access to information – both domestically and internationally. Politicians argue in these debates that adherence to these 'universal' values has been a fundamental source of US power in the past and will continue to be in the future. In contrast to the material conception of power which is combined with an instrumentalist approach to technology, this social conception of power is accompanied by a social constructivist approach to technology. This approach lends agency and authority to politicians allowing them to assume responsibility for the direction of the technology. In this view, politicians regard themselves (and the society they represent) as empowered and enabled to shape and influence cyber security in such a way that it reflects the ideas, norms and values which they regard as most important to US power.

It is this second conception of power that has most significantly shaped cyber security technology in the United States. Indeed, the policies which emerge from this conception effectively undermine the earlier material conception of power and Internet technology. While there have been attempts by politicians to reconcile the two approaches, they are fundamentally at odds, a tension that has been acknowledged by former Secretary of State Hillary Clinton who suggested that, at best, the United States must aim for a balance between material and social factors.[2]

There are a number of arguments which emerge from these findings. The first has implications for how we approach the 'paradox of power' in the information age. This chapter finds that although politicians demonstrate an acute awareness of the threats which cyber insecurity poses to US material power, they have been unwilling to undermine those social factors of power which they believe have been fundamental to the state's success. This analysis finds that politicians consider both material and social factors of power in the context of cyber insecurity and that they privilege those which they regard as most likely to sustain US power in the future – and these are social. Cyber insecurity is, to some degree, then the consequence of conscious choice – or, at least, a reasoned calculation.

The second argument is that the approach to technology with which politicians engage has implications for the degree to which conceptions of power influence decisions about technology. In the context of framing the *problem* of cyber insecurity – in which politicians adopt a material view of power and an instrumental approach to technology – instrumentalism has two concurrent effects on the way these politicians regard their role and agency. It both absolves them of responsibility and diminishes their authority. If technology develops naturally along the 'best' path, then we must adapt to it, rather than seek to change or reinterpret it. This approach to technology is reflected in the stasis of cyber security debates which have been unable to envisage a more proactive path to ameliorate the threats of cyber insecurity to US material power.

In contrast, when politicians decide on cyber security policy, they do so through a social power framework and a social constructivist approach to technology. They openly discuss the technology as reflecting and projecting American values. Here they perceive it as their responsibility to ensure that Internet technology continues to develop in such a way as to protect and project those values. This approach to technology imbues politicians with authority as they regard it as both possible and necessary that the technology develops in such a way as to continue to reinforce the norms and values which they believe best promote US power.

This second argument is particularly important as it will re-emerge in each of the case studies and contributes to the conclusion of the book. In each case, the way in which politicians approach technology has implications for the degree to which their conceptions of power shape and influence the technology – more specifically, it has implications for how they perceive their *authority* to make decisions that shape technology. This was an unexpected finding for this study and it is not possible to draw a clear conclusion from this research about the exact nature of the causal relationship between approaches to technology, conceptions of power and authority. That is, it is not clear whether politicians adopt a particular approach to technology *based* on their perception of their authority to act or whether their approach to technology *causes* them to perceive their authority in a certain way. In other words, do politicians feel disempowered to take certain policy decisions and so adopt a determinist or instrumental approach to technology? Or does their social constructivist approach to technology lead to a sense of authority? A separate study would be required to determine the exact nature of the causal relationship here but this study finds that there exists a relationship between these factors.

The chapter begins with a technical brief – as does every case study in this book. This section is designed to introduce some of the key technological factors which influence the issues under examination for those with little technological knowledge – others will skip these sections. In this case study, the technical brief explains why networked computers are insecure and how the Internet complicates conventional security measures. In addition, this section will provide a brief explanation of how America came to be so reliant upon an uninterrupted flow of traffic over the Internet. This entails a brief discussion of the business practices and government policies promoting the privatization of public infrastructure which have increased national vulnerability to cyber threats. Finally, this section will provide some background on what exactly a 'cyber-attack' might entail.

The chapter moves on to an analysis of how US politicians perceive cyber security as linked to power in the context of IR. This section draws upon both IR theories of power and concepts from the philosophy of technology in order to engage with how politicians regard the 'problem' of cyber insecurity. It reveals that politicians debate these issues predominantly within a material power discourse which focuses on power as capabilities. They regard three key factors as the loci of cyber security vulnerabilities. First, they consider the impact on the economy – not only the potential for economic loss (which is substantial) but the broader implications of this for financing conventional military hard power. Second, politicians regard cyber security as linked to US power through the potential for the Internet to be deployed as a 'weapon' by a wide range of actors from terrorists to strategic competitors like China. Finally, politicians express concerns about how cyber security can undermine other factors of material power like geopolitics and how all of the above factors are perceived to impact on national security.

This is followed by an analysis of the ways in which politicians have sought to address material problems of cyber insecurity. As noted above, the most significant policy solution has been the 'public/private partnership' which has been referred to as the 'cornerstone' of US cyber security policy by successive US presidents. Its endurance as a policy approach and its relevance make the public/private partnership an excellent mechanism through which to access the conceptions of power which shape the technology.

The final section of this chapter looks at the social conception of power which politicians express through cyber security debates. In this view, politicians seek to adhere to values and norms which they believe have formed the foundation of American success in the past and will again in the future. In his first *NSS*, President Obama argued that 'if we compromise our values in pursuit of security, we will undermine both; if we fortify them, we will sustain a key source of our strength and leadership in the world – one that sets us apart from our enemies and our potential competitors' (Obama, 2010, p. 10). This conception of power links cyber security to foreign policy on human rights. Increasingly, access to the Internet is being defined by international institutions, as well as many governments, as a 'basic human right' and this has implications for how politicians view anonymity and censorship – two elements of cyber security. The social conception of power also engages with some of these same issues but in a domestic context. Here, politicians debate the role of civil rights in cyber security policy with reference to values of privacy, individual rights and freedom of information. This view of US power as emerging from norms and values provides a framework for the social power conception.

The conclusion of this chapter summarizes the findings referenced previously about how competing conceptions of power have influenced the development of the Internet in the context of cyber security. It also draws out the implications of these findings for understanding the relationship between power and new technology in the information age. It is evident in this case study that there exists a schism between how politicians regard cyber security as related to US power (in material terms) and how they seek to influence it (through a social power framework). Ultimately, it is the determination of politicians to adhere to ideas, norms and values which most profoundly impacts on cyber security technology.

Cyber security: Technology and concepts

Cyber security is a broad and indiscriminate term. It is used inter-changeably to refer to both the security *of* the Internet infrastructure and security from attacks *over* the Internet, and a lack of clarity about this is frequently a source of confusion in debates about cyber security. From a 'technology as artefact' approach (discussed in more detail in Chapter 2), cyber security might refer to the protection or vulnerability of the root server machines which are critical to the domain name system (see Chapter 5). It might refer to the cabling and wires through which individual computers connect to the Internet or the submarine cables which connect one continent to another. US politicians do regard this physical infrastructure as a factor in cyber security. Over the course of the 2000s, as American reliance on the smooth functioning of the Internet increased, political concepts of 'critical infrastructure protection' (CIP), which used to refer to factors like the electricity grid, expanded to incorporate *information.* Thus, 'critical information infrastructure protection' (CIIP) steadily gained traction as a policy issue and a cyber security concern.

An alternative definition of technology is one which incorporates how individuals or social groups interact with and use the physical artefact. What we do with the artefact is, in this definition, a constitutive element of technology. In this approach, not only is cyber security the protection of 'critical information infrastructure', but it also encompasses the *practice* of launching attacks over the Internet. These attacks might be carried out on critical information infrastructure; they might be targeted at completely unrelated critical infrastructure which happens to be connected to the Internet; or they might be attacks on systems which run over the Internet like banking and communications. This definition of cyber security encompasses not only the physical artefact and the virtual artefacts like software and web protocols, but also human engagement with all of these as well as the practices which result.

US politicians adopt a holistic approach to cyber security in the context of US power. During congressional debates about cyber security, the issues range from the physical security of US and global Internet infrastructure to the wide spectrum of practices which politicians regard as a threat to US power. These include criminal behaviour which undermines US economic power or the state's power to enforce the law. They also include terrorist threats and threats from other states either directly *on* the Internet or *over* the Internet. As this study is concerned with how conceptions of US power influence the development of Internet technology, it is these perceptions held by US politicians that are essential to the interpretation of the material and, for this reason, a broad definition of cyber security is necessarily employed here.

Technical brief

Prior to the development of the Internet, cyber security was an issue but on an infinitely smaller scale. Stand-alone computer systems were always vulnerable to damage and intrusion – malicious or otherwise – but prior to networking, one had to be physically in front of a computer in order to interact with it. As detailed in Chapter 3, the technology to connect one computer to another developed in the 1960s and, over the ensuing decades, became rapidly integrated into the commercial sector. With computers networked together, it was no longer necessary to carry a storage device like a floppy disk from one machine to another in order to share (or steal) data – files could simply be transferred across the network. These computer networks were typically confined to an organization or institution. Although security breaches were more problematic as a consequence of remote access, these were closed networks with access restricted to authorized personnel only and activity monitored by a system administrator who worked for that organization. Therefore, while security breaches occurred more easily over these networks than they had on stand-alone machines, there was a limited pool of people who had access and, consequently, the attribution of theft or damage was much easier than it is now.

The introduction of the Internet amplified network security problems exponentially. One of the key principles of the Internet is that it is built upon an open architecture. This means that the software protocols upon which it was constructed were intentionally designed so that anyone could contribute and 'innovate without permission'. Unlike more conventional software platforms, nobody 'owns' the Internet code or can prevent individuals or groups from pursuing innovative solutions to perceived needs or problems. This openness is at once a strength and a point of vulnerability for the Internet. The same architecture which allowed Larry Page and Sergey Brin to develop and give away the Google search engine, transforming the way we access information, also permits the theft of data, the sabotage of systems and the exchange of illegal goods and services – and all with a high degree of anonymity. Security was a low priority during the early development years and it has been technologically difficult to reverse engineer more secure features into Internet and web protocols.

Connecting systems to the Internet which were previously isolated or maintained on closed networks has meant that unauthorized access is infinitely easier. Once a security vulnerability is identified in the coding of a software program or operating system (e.g. like Microsoft Windows), it can be exploited remotely on hundreds, thousands or even millions of machines.

A range of malicious software or 'malware' has evolved over the life of the Internet. Viruses may be the most widely understood. These are essentially small software programs written intentionally to penetrate a system and cause it to malfunction in some way. They are often written to be self-replicating and travel quickly through mechanisms like email attachments and address books. A Trojan Horse is a particular type of malware which appears benign and is embedded in a system providing cover for a future attack. It can be a way of re-entering a system or it can contain malware which will be activated at a later date. Robot networks or 'botnets' are comprised of computers upon which code has been installed to allow them to be co-opted into illicit activity that requires a large number of coordinated machines. A botnet was used in the attacks on the Estonian infrastructure in 2007 which involved millions of computers around the world that simultaneously requested information from those critical sites. Often the owners of machines that are part of a botnet have no knowledge that they are contributing to this criminal activity.

Cyber insecurity as a problem for US power

These technical security vulnerabilities are compounded by the problems of attribution and this will be more fully developed as the chapter progresses. It has always been (and remains) very difficult to track movements over the Internet. The sheer volume of traffic means that keeping data logs is simply not feasible unless they are very narrowly defined. Also, information travels across the Internet in unpredictable ways – constantly searching out the fastest route. When an attack takes place over the Internet, the perpetrator (with any sophistication) will hop from location to location and because these hops are very quickly covered up, the origin of the attack becomes very difficult to determine. A report to Congress explained that difficulties of attribution mean that 'a terrorist group could possibly be set up by others to appear as the guilty cyber attacker in order to draw attention away from the actual attacker who may be located elsewhere' (Wilson, 2003, p. 15). Thus, with limited capability to identify who is responsible for illegal behaviour, state-controlled mechanisms such as deterrence, retaliation and punishment prove less effective. The problem of attribution produces a number of 'knock-on' implications for cyber security policy and practice which also feed into the political calculations discussed in this chapter. One of these is the legal implications of responding to attacks.

Conventions of a legal system rely upon punishment acting as a deterrent to undesirable behaviour and this framework is seriously undermined by the inability of law enforcement to identify perpetrators. Responding to aggression with reciprocal force over the Internet is therefore problematic for law enforcement pursuing cyber criminals – both those committing conventional crimes but using the Internet to do so and also those who commit Internet-related crime. It also has implications for global conflict and IR. First, as explained above, tracing data movements over the Internet is extremely time sensitive. It requires a rapid response and the immediate cooperation of authorities in the host country or countries – not always possible across borders without an aligned legal framework. A congressional report concluded that the US Department of Defense believes that it lacks 'sufficient policy and legal analysis for guiding appropriate responses to intrusions or attacks on DOD networks' (Wilson, 2006, p. 5). Under international law, the determination of what constitutes the use of force in the context of a cyber-attack remains unclear – one of the key problems highlighted by the attacks on Estonia in 2007 (Grove et al., 2000, pp. 89–103). In this case, although NATO conceded that Estonia was suffering a cyber-attack, the NATO charter lacked sufficient clarity to permit collective action (Applebaum, 2007; BBC, 2007; Sydney Morning Herald, 2007; Traynor, 2007).

In addition to these difficulties associated with attribution, the fact that so much civilian infrastructure relies upon the Internet generates concerns about the potential for reciprocal military action to have unintended civilian consequences. For example, if a state launched a cyber-attack which interrupted Internet access in another state, they may successfully repel an ongoing attack but they may also inadvertently interfere with civilian systems such as transport or energy which could potentially lead to a loss of life. The congressional report referenced above goes as far as to speculate that reciprocating against an attack may lead to 'possible accusations of war crimes if offensive military cyber-weapons severely disrupt critical civilian computer systems, or the systems of other non-combatant nations' (Wilson, 2006, p. 1).

These legal impediments to addressing cyber security vulnerabilities – in both a civilian and military context – amplify the challenges to US power by limiting the range of responses. These mechanisms of law enforcement, punishment and deterrence are constrained for states which adhere to this juridical framework nationally and internationally.

What is a cyber-attack?

In September 2010, it was widely reported that a worm known as 'Stuxnet' had damaged the centrifuges in an Iranian nuclear facility (Beaumont, 2010; Seltzer, 2010). There was speculation that the level of sophistication indicated nation-state involvement in the development and deployment of Stuxnet. If so, this would be an example of the type of cyber-attack about which US politicians have been concerned for the past 15 years. As discussed in Chapter 3, an attack on critical systems connected to the Internet or vulnerable to malware spread through the Internet is a dominant theme in debates about US power and cyber security. Why and how this emerged as a cyber-attack scenario can be explained through the widespread privatization of critical infrastructure and the concurrent adoption of supervisory control and data acquisition systems (SCADA systems).

An attack on critical infrastructure remains one of the dominant themes of debates about cyber insecurity in the United States. As explained in Chapter 3, from the late 1990s, the security problems outlined above were compounded by the connection of SCADA systems to the Internet. One no longer needed physical access to the facility in order to tamper with the computerized control systems. As long as network security remained a problem, intruders would theoretically be able to carry out attacks on computer systems from remote corners of the globe. In a congressional hearing into SCADA vulnerabilities, Representative Bill Pascrell stated that 'we *know* that vulnerabilities within these systems are abundant, and we *know* that the threat of a terrorist attack against these systems is real' (Pascrell, 2005, p. 3). Over the course of the past five years, this type of attack has emerged not only as a terrorist threat but also in the context of state-to-state conflict as was demonstrated in Estonia in 2007 and Georgia in 2008. This type of attack which targets critical infrastructure is referred to colloquially as a 'Die Hard 4' attack or a 'Firesale' attack – after the Hollywood film which is based on such a threat scenario (Carlin, 1997).

Although this scenario still garners significant attention in political debates about US cyber security, a new threat concept has recently been gaining momentum – the notion that America is *already* under attack and has been for some time. This scenario is based on a conception of the economy as a target. The assertion that cyberwar may not follow the 'Die Hard 4' script but rather may entail a war of attrition through economic espionage has been asserted by James Lewis of the Center for Strategic and International Studies (CSIS) (Lewis, 2010, pp. 12–17). Lewis has pointed out that America reportedly loses $1 trillion per year in systematic intellectual property and data theft (Akerman, 2009). Accurately identifying those behind these thefts is extremely problematic but allegations of steady infiltrations from American strategic competitors Russia and China have fuelled concerns about cyber-attacks which do not fit the preconceived pattern of overt disruption and destruction of services, property and, ultimately, lives (Messmer, 2008; Paget, 2010; Rogin, 2010; Choate, 2011; Grow and Hosenball, 2011). While it is not clear that this is indeed a state-based attack, it raises concerns that there is more strategy behind this relentless financial drain than the theft itself. This emerging concern will be taken up in more detail later in the chapter where it feeds into broader concerns about the impact of cyber security on US economic power.

The evolution of cyber security as a 'problem' for power

As foreshadowed in the introduction to this chapter, politicians regard cyber insecurity predominantly as a problem for US power in the context of three factors of material power: the likely outcome of global conflict, the impact on US economic power and the endurance of geopolitics as a factor of US power.

Periodically, the executive branch of the US government prepares an NSS for Congress which identifies key security concerns and outlines how the administration intends to address them. Cyber security had been a component of these documents since 1998; however, in 2009, President Obama ordered the first *National Cyber Security Review* (NCSR) – an indication of how seriously these concerns had come to be regarded. An analysis of successive NSS documents provides an overview of how ideas about national security, US power and new technology evolved; it also provides a background to the analysis of how specific threats translated to a problem for US power.

The *NSS* documents of the Clinton administration reflected an adjustment in the perception of post-Cold War threats to the United

States. They also began to refer to computer technology as relevant to US power but, through most of the 1990s, this was restricted to state investments in innovation and the relationship between new technology and the economy (Clinton, 1998a, p. 19). By 1998, following the commercialization of the Internet, an explicit link emerges in the NSS which lists 'transnational threats' immediately below 'regional or state-centered threats'. In describing these, the NSS specifically points to cyber-attacks:

> Threats to the national information infrastructure, ranging from cyber-crime to a strategic information attack on the United States via the global information network, present a dangerous new threat to our national security. We must also guard against threats to our other critical national infrastructures – such as electrical power and transportation – which increasingly could take the form of a cyber-attack in addition to physical attack or sabotage, and could originate from terrorist or criminal groups as well as hostile states.
>
> (Clinton, 1998a, p. 6)

This statement demonstrates the comprehensive approach to cyber security defined earlier in this chapter. It is an early acknowledgement that cyber security encompasses both attacks *on* the Internet infrastructure as well as attacks *using* the Internet to damage other infrastructure.

The 1998 NSS also lists foreign intelligence collection using the 'national information infrastructure' (as the Internet was then referred to) as a threat 'more diverse, complex and difficult to counter than ever before' (Clinton, 1998a, p. 6). Central Intelligence Agency (CIA) chief George Tenet told the Armed Services Committee in 2000 that cyber security was 'one of the most complex issues I've put on the table'. He went on to make the point that information warfare, in the assessment of the CIA, had the potential to be a 'major force multiplier' (Tenet, 2000, p. 8). Tenet outlined four key reasons why this was the case. First, it enables a single entity to have a significant and serious impact – a point of difference from weaponized technologies of the past. Second, it is a weapon that 'comes ashore' and can affect the homeland. Third, information warfare gives a force projection capability to those who have never had it before, and it can be used as an asymmetric response. Finally, Tenet projected that information warfare would be a basic capability of modern militaries and intelligence services around the world in the near future (Tenet, 2000, p. 8).

This militarized view of the Internet which interprets security threats or vulnerabilities as having implications for power featured in the 2002 NSS. Although specific references to cyber security are notably absent in both of the George W. Bush administration NSS documents, the 2002 NSS foreshadows the potential for 'modern technology' to compete with conventional US military power.

> Enemies in the past needed great armies and great industrial capabilities to endanger America. Now, shadowy networks of individuals can bring great chaos and suffering to our shores for less than it costs to purchase a single tank. Terrorists are organized to penetrate open societies and to turn the power of modern technologies against us.
>
> (Bush, 2002, p. 3)

These themes of asymmetry and the use of modern technology to 'attack' the United States which emerged from the 9/11 attacks (as detailed in Chapter 3) began to permeate debates about cyber security as well. The 2006 NSS was almost bereft of any mention of cyber security except to acknowledge it as a 'disruptive challenge' from state and non-state actors who may employ technologies (including the Internet) in new ways to counter 'military advantages the United States currently enjoys' (Bush, 2006, p. 44).

In contrast, the Obama administration's first NSS in 2010 elevated cyber security to a 'strategic national asset' and declared that protecting it was now a 'national security priority' (Obama, 2010, p. 27). President Obama also reinforced the long-standing view that technology enhances power by arguing that 'we must see American innovation as a foundation of American power' (Obama, 2010, pp. i–iii).

This continued approach to Internet technology more generally and cyber security specifically as linked to material power provides a background to the following analysis of some of the factors which politicians who are closely engaged with these issues debate most: the role of cyber security in future global conflicts, its impact on the US economy and the way in which it redefines geopolitics.

Cyber security and global conflict

Asymmetric power

The asymmetric nature of global order has shaped politicians' view of cyber security as it relates to US power. Cyber security (or more accurately, those tools such as worms and malware introduced in the technical brief which threaten cyber security) is regarded as a material factor – a weapon which may be deployed by less resourced opponents and used to move global conflict from the playing field on which the United States is able to dominate on to one on which it is 'asymmetrically vulnerable'.

A link between post-Cold War American military preponderance, asymmetric actors and cyber vulnerabilities was one of the early conceptions of how cyber security might relate to US power. This stemmed in part from the understanding that with the demise of the USSR, the United States had more material power than any other state or group of states by such a margin that it would be unlikely to face a challenge on the military field. With this threat mitigated, there was speculation in the United States that adversaries may seek other means of competition. President Clinton spoke to this in the 1998 *Presidential Decision Directive* when he argued that 'because of our military strength, future enemies, whether nations, groups or individuals, may seek to harm us in non-traditional ways including attacks within the United States' (Clinton, 1998b). A 2003 congressional report found that 'many Pentagon officials reportedly believe that future adversaries may be unwilling to array conventional forces against U.S. troops, and instead may resort to "asymmetric warfare", where a less powerful opponent uses other strategies to offset and negate U.S. technological superiority' (Wilson, 2003, p. 1).

This view was not limited to cyber security concerns; it was an observation about US power more generally. However, the low cost, potentially high impact and anonymity of cyber-attacks made them appear particularly well suited to adversaries engaging in asymmetric conflict with the United States. CIA chief George Tenet told the Armed Services Committee that America's power was so preponderant that its enemies would be looking to alternative fields of combat where they might gain a strategic advantage and that cyber security was one such domain (Tenet, 2000, p. 8). This opinion was echoed by FBI senior official Michael Vatis in testimony before a 2000 Senate hearing into Internet security. He testified that states which were unable to match the American military with conventional or 'kinetic' weapons may regard Internet attacks as a way to 'hit what they perceive as America's Achilles heel – our growing dependence on information technology in Government and commercial operations' (Vatis, 2000, p. 26).

A related consequence for American power is voiced by Defense Director of Intelligence Michael Maples at a 2009 hearing before the Senate Armed Services Committee. Maples points out that not only does cyber security offer an asymmetric advantage to states unable to compete with conventional and preponderant American military power, but cyber-attacks are of special concern because they undermine 'the pronounced military advantages that the United States has traditionally derived from information networks' (Maples, 2009, p. 38). In the 2010 *NSS*, President Obama argued explicitly that 'the threats to our people, our homeland, and our interests have shifted dramatically in the last 20 years ... In addition to facing enemies on traditional battlefields, the United States must now be prepared for asymmetric threats, such as those that target our reliance on space and cyberspace' (Obama, 2010, p. 17).

This link between material power and cyber insecurity is not limited to the conditions of asymmetry in global conflict. As speculation has grown about the emergence of China as a strategic competitor, politicians have broadened their perception of the threat to consider how cyber security might feature in more conventional state-to-state conflict.

China

The discourse on China's rise dates back to the mid-1990s and stems from speculation that China's considerable economic growth might be channelled into conventional military strength (Kristof, 1993; Overholt, 1993). The perception amongst politicians that the United States may face a new challenge to maintaining the established global order (or regional order in East Asia) provides a backdrop, as asymmetry also did, for how they perceive the threat to US power from cyber security vulnerabilities. In this context, concerns arise about the potential for China to develop information warfare strategy, doctrine and capability. The publication in 1999 of a Chinese document entitled *Unrestricted Warfare* (English translation) fuelled speculation that China was developing new and innovative ways to elevate its position as a strategic competitor (Qiao and Xiangsui, 1999).

Since that time, China has been implicated in many cyber-attacks on the United States. In 2003, an incident referred to by the Pentagon as 'Titan Rain' came to light in which a substantial amount of valuable and sometimes classified information was extracted from Department of Defense online systems (Lewis, 2005; Thornburgh, 2005). These attacks were traced to computers in the south of China although the Chinese authorities denied any knowledge of the operation. In June 2007, the Office of the Secretary of Defense was forced to take its information systems offline in order to defend against a serious attack which was also attributed to computers within China (Sevastopulo, 2007). In April 2009, reports surfaced that the Pentagon's $300 billion Joint Strike Fighter project had been penetrated and 'several terabytes of data related to design and electronics systems' had been downloaded (Gorman et al., 2009). Although attribution was not possible, the *Wall Street Journal* quoted former US officials as claiming that the attacks appeared to have originated in China (Gorman et al., 2009). A 2009 report to Congress by the US–China Economic and Security Review Commission stated explicitly that a 'large body of both circumstantial and forensic evidence strongly indicates Chinese state involvement' in a range of serious Internet attacks against the United States (Bartholemew, 2009, p. 167).

In February 2013, security firm Mandiant released a report that they claimed provided evidence linking a multi-year, enterprise-scale computer espionage campaign to the People's Liberation Army (PLA) of China (Mandiant, 2013). Although much of the material linking what was clearly a significant attack to the PLA appears to be unsubstantiated and circumstantial, the report was a significant boost to US attempts to counter China in cyberspace.[3] President Obama took the unprecedented step of indicting five PLA officials over the allegations made in the Mandiant report. In his statement, Attorney General Eric Holder said that '[T]his Administration will not tolerate actions by any nation that seeks to illegally sabotage American companies' (Department of Justice, 2014).

While China's rise and the intensity of attacks originating from within its borders have resulted in special attention from politicians, it is not the only state understood to be building cyber capabilities – that is, developing the tools for penetrating and damaging systems as well as preparing doctrine and strategies for implementing them in a conflict situation. Cyber security is increasingly perceived as a likely component of future conflicts. The Senate Committee on Armed Services heard testimony from the CIA in 2000 that there was evidence that 'several key states are aggressively working to develop their IW [information warfare] capabilities and to incorporate these new tools into their war-fighting doctrine' (Tenet, 2000, p. 8). This was reiterated later that same year by a top FBI official at a hearing into Internet security. 'The prospect of "information warfare" by foreign militaries against our critical infrastructures is perhaps the greatest potential cyber threat to our national security. We know that several foreign nations are developing information warfare doctrine, programs, and capabilities for use against the United States or other nations' (Vatis, 2000, p. 26). By 2009, the intelligence community was more explicit about the source of the threat. Director of National Intelligence, Dennis Blair, reveals that 'We assess that a number of nations, including Russia and China, have the technical capabilities to target and disrupt elements of the U.S.

information infrastructure and for intelligence collection' (Blair, 2009, p. 37). Following the Stuxnet attack, concerns were expressed that Iran may reverse engineer the attack code and relaunch it against similarly vulnerable US critical infrastructure (Clarke, 2012, p. 5).

Congress has been repeatedly briefed by top intelligence and military officials of the threat America faces from a nation-state deployment of cyberweapons. At a hearing in 2000, CIA Director George Tenet reported that America's security would increasingly depend on the unimpeded and secure flow of information. 'Any foreign adversary that develops the ability to interrupt that flow or shut it down will have the potential to weaken us dramatically or even render us helpless' (Tenet, 2000, p. 8). This is perceived as a problem for US power not only because of the damage which may be carried out through a cyber-attack, but also because the difficulties of attribution mean that an attack could be used to entrap other actors in conflict. Thus Michael Vatis argued that the possibility exists that 'nation-states not directly involved in American retaliatory action could launch cyber attacks against U.S. systems under the guise of another country that is the focus of the war on terrorism. This is of particular concern as it is possible to disguise the origins of information attacks with relative ease' (Vatis, 2001, p. 13). Interestingly, this also came up in discussions about Iran's intentions in cyberspace. In testimony before the Committee on Homeland Security, a witness from the Homeland Security Policy Institute argued that 'given Iran's history to employ proxies for terrorist purposes, there is little, if any, reason to think that Iran would hesitate to engage proxies to conduct cyber attacks' (Cilluffo, 2012, p. 11). Ultimately, the view expressed by President Obama that 'our technological advantage is a key to America's military dominance' serves to highlight the concerns of politicians when they consider the challenges that cyber security poses to US military power (Obama, 2009b).

The cost of cyber insecurity

In Chapter 3, it was made clear that almost from its inception the Internet has been regarded by politicians as having enormous potential for the growth of US economic power. Politicians consistently refer to the Internet as the 'backbone of the U.S. economy' (Davis, 2000, p. 6; Akaka, 2005, p. 5). In an analysis of how politicians regard cyber security as a problem for US power, economic factors feature significantly. Indeed, in a 2009 speech entitled *Securing Our Nation's Cyber Infrastructure*, President Obama stated definitively that 'America's economic prosperity in the 21st century will depend on cybersecurity' (Obama, 2009b).

There are a number of ways in which politicians perceive cyber security to be linked to the economy and to have the capacity to undermine US economic power. One of the most frequently cited is that the US economy is now so heavily dependent on the Internet that a consumer-driven loss of confidence could have substantial impact on trade. E-commerce (trade which is carried out over the Internet) in the United States was at $132 billion in retail sales for 2008 (Obama, 2009b). The estimate of US retail e-commerce sales for the first quarter of 2015 alone was $80.3 billion (Department of Commerce, 2015). Consequently, there is a strong belief that anything which jeopardizes the security of online transactions is dangerous – not only for the potential revenue loss of the particular transaction, but because of the broader implications of consumer trust and market confidence which are essential to continued growth rates (McLoughlin, 2002). If consumers do not believe that it is safe to conduct financial transactions over the Internet, e-commerce could retract with a consequential negative impact on the US economy and power (Cashell et al., 2004).

One of the early alerts to the potential for Internet insecurity to negatively impact on consumer confidence came in February 2000 in the form of a distributed denial of service (DDoS) attack on several booming commercial sites including eBay and Amazon. DDoS attacks involve bombarding a site with data – usually in the form of requests – which overwhelms the site and effectively causes it to shut down. Although the attacks resulted in little material harm, both targets were nascent consumer retail sites which were leading the trend for increasing online transactions. A month after the attacks, the Senate Committee on Commerce, Science, and Transportation held a hearing on Internet security to attempt to ascertain the extent of the problem. Senator Conrad Burns made the point that 'real damage was done, especially to Internet users' confidence' (Burns, 2000, p. 1). Indeed, the fear generated was sufficient to cause a significant sell-off in technology stocks. Senator Burns regarded the attacks as particularly alarming, 'as they were specifically designed to disrupt electronic commerce' (Burns, 2000, p. 1). These sentiments were echoed by William Reinsch, a senior official from the Department of Commerce. 'If we are to reap the benefits of the information age, we need to take action to maintain public confidence in a secure business environment that ensures both our national security and the growth of our economy' (Reinsch, 2000, p. 16).

In addition to undermining consumer confidence in online transactions, politicians also regard cyber security as potentially undermining US economic power through the billions of dollars of wealth which have been extracted from the United States in the form of commercial and military information obtained illicitly. In this more recently developed view, damage to the economy is not a *by-product* of cyber-attacks but rather the economy is the *target* of attacks. Industry estimates have put the global theft of public and private intellectual property and data at as high as US $1 trillion (Akerman, 2009; Mills, 2009). A 2012 report issued by the Department of Commerce revealed that intellectual property-intensive industries directly supported almost 30 per cent of US jobs (Department of Commerce, 2012). At a Senate hearing into US cyber security vulnerabilities, Eugene Spafford, Executive Director, Purdue University Center for Education and Research in Information Assurance and Security (CERIAS), testified that 'the Nation is under attack, and it is a hostile attack, it is a continuing attack. It has been going on for years, and we have largely been ignoring it' (Spafford, 2009, p. 28). He goes on to testify that the commercial losses alone, by best estimates, are in the tens of billions of dollars per year. 'To put that in context, imagine a Hurricane Katrina-style event occurring every year and being ignored' (Spafford, 2009, p. 28).

Politicians regard these costs as having implications for economic power both through the potential of cyber-attacks to undermine consumer confidence and thereby threaten trade and through the direct extraction of wealth through data theft. However, they also relate this to another aspect of material power – the state's capacity to fund military capability. President Clinton pointed out in the 1998 *Presidential Decision Directive* that 'our economy is increasingly reliant upon interdependent and cyber-supported infrastructures and non-traditional attacks on our infrastructure and information systems may be capable of significantly harming both our military power and our economy' (Clinton, 1998b). President Obama also recently argued that 'our prosperity serves as a wellspring for our power. It pays for our military, underwrites our diplomacy and development efforts, and serves as a leading source of our influence in the world' (Obama, 2010, p. 9). Therefore, cyber security is regarded as a problem not only because it undermines economic power but because this has implications for military power as well.

In the context of the economy, cyber insecurity raises concerns about US power in IR in three important ways. First, security breaches threaten to undermine consumer confidence in online trading – an important element of the US economy. Second, the direct theft of intellectual property in both commercial and state sectors is proving expensive. Commercially, it diminishes profits and reduces the economic base. The theft of military and science developments means that money invested in these projects by the state is appropriated by others at little cost which impacts on US competiveness. Finally, these negative effects on the US economy impact on the state's capacity to invest in conventional military power, thus producing a second-order threat to material power.

Shaping geopolitics

One final way in which politicians link cyber security to US power is through its impact on conceptions of geopolitics. This issue is taken up by broader debates about the effects of globalization but elicits some specific concerns about power in the context of cyber security. While some scholars like Stanley Brunn (2000, pp. 144–9) have suggested that the 'new geopolitics' of the Internet supersedes the old as time and space take on different dimensions, others like Ronald Deibert (2009, 323–36), Jack Goldsmith and Tim Wu (2006) have argued that the Internet adheres more closely than we might think to established power structures determined by state borders and geography. Significant for this study, however, is the perception of US politicians that the concept of state sovereignty within determined physical borders may indeed be undergoing some renovation. Concerns about reconceptualizing the geopolitics of the Internet are one of the key ways in which US politicians link US power to cyber security as they perceive the geopolitics of the Internet to be distinct from the physical geopolitics which has for so long played a role in strategic decision making and power calculations in IR.

When politicians express concern about the Federal government's capacity to protect the nation against a cyber-attack, the issue of the geopolitics of the Internet frequently arises. At a hearing in 2000, Senator Robert Bennett produced a 'map' of the Internet pointing out to his colleagues that there were no oceans on it.[4] He made the point that 'when you start talking about either national security threats or commerce in a world in which there are no oceans and no continents, you realize that we are not talking about a new tool to use in commerce or a new weapon to use in war. We are talking about a whole new place. We are talking about a whole new universe that is different from any that we have structured our Government to defend or our economy to market in the past' (Bennett, 2000, pp. 33–4). Indeed, the concept of a 'Digital Pearl Harbour' enters the policy lexicon around this time, linking virtual threats to the trauma of the World War II attacks on American soil (Berinato, 2003).[5]

A deep sense of unease about this new geopolitical configuration was exacerbated by the homeland attacks on 11 September 2001. As discussed in Chapter 3, apart from the physical devastation of the attacks, there was also a reaction to the attack taking place on American soil. The realization that oceans and friendly states no longer provided an adequate buffer from hostile attack prompted a re-evaluation of the US geopolitical situation. This was articulated in the 2003 *National Strategy to Secure Cyberspace* where President Bush observed that in the last century, 'geographic isolation helped protect the United States from a direct physical invasion. In cyberspace national boundaries have little meaning' (Bush, 2003a, p. 7).

These perceptions of the transformation of a material factor of US power raise questions about the permanence of power – a concept discussed at length by Hans Morgenthau in *Politics among Nations*. Morgenthau cautions against assuming the permanence of any factor of power which he argues is a 'typical error of evaluation' in power computations (Morgenthau, 1978, pp. 160–3). For Morgenthau, this assumption of permanency ignores the dynamic nature of most elements of power. He argues that 'everyday changes, however small and imperceptible at first... add an ounce of strength to this side and take a grain of might away from the other' (Morgenthau, 1978, p. 158). This sense of impermanence is most frequently articulated when politicians discuss geopolitics in the context of cyber security – not just as a material factor of power which is diminished or undermined, but one which has undergone qualitative change.

In summary then, when politicians discuss the problem of cyber insecurity in the context of US power, they focus on the ways in which it threatens to undermine US power to prevail in global conflict, US economic power and the continuation of geopolitics as a factor that enhances US power. These are conventional security concerns which have been reinterpreted in the context of the Internet technology.

Interestingly, they have consistently adopted an *unconventional* approach to addressing these problems. Over successive administrations from President Clinton to President Obama, politicians have sought to mitigate the threats which cyber insecurity poses to US material power and national security through the promotion of the 'public/private partnership'. As the following section shows, this is an instrumental approach to technology associated with a deeply embedded sense that the government lacks the authority to pursue national cyber security and that somehow (hopefully) the private sector possesses the motivation to do it for them.

The public/private partnership: Cornerstone of US cyber security strategy

In 2003, the Bush administration's *National Strategy to Secure Cyberspace* referred to the 'public/private partnership' as 'the cornerstone of America's cyberspace security strategy' (Bush, 2003a, p. iii). President Clinton had used similar terminology in his 1998 *Presidential Decision Directive* aimed at reducing the US vulnerability to cyber security. The public/private partnership also formed the central plank of the 2000 *National Plan for Information Systems Protection* (Clinton, 2000), the 2003 *Homeland Security Presidential Directive 7* (Bush, 2003b), the 2005 *Interim National Infrastructure Protection Plan* (Ridge, 2005) and the 2009 *National Infrastructure Protection Plan* (Chertoff, 2009). In the face of suggestions that the market-driven approach to national cyber security had failed, President Obama's 2009 *Cyberspace Policy Review* found that the public/private partnership must 'evolve' but it remained central to the administration's strategy (Obama, 2009a, p. iv).

A central finding of this analysis is that politicians regard themselves and the government more broadly as without agency in this respect. That is, they recognize and worry about the extent of the problems of cyber insecurity but nevertheless believe that they are without the capacity or the authority to resolve these problems. It is important to note here that this is distinct from a circumstance in which the government may opt to leave a problem to be resolved by market forces. The analysis finds that politicians involved in these debates explicitly state that they (and the government more broadly) have neither the authority nor the capability to deal with cyber insecurity. Through the public/private partnership, they shift the responsibility for these problems onto the private sector which, perhaps unsurprisingly, remains unwilling to be drawn into funding or being liable for national security or law enforcement services.

This is a unique approach to national security issues which threaten to undermine state power and it is one that seems out of step with previously noted junctures of technology and US power. Certainly, the Sputnik crisis initiated a strong and authoritative government response as did the early years of Internet technology. As discussed in Chapter 3, while the Clinton–Gore administration intended that the Internet should be privately owned and operated, those politicians were clear about the role the government must play in order to shape Internet technology accordingly. Given the proactive policies that emerged to guide Internet technology in order to promote US economic power, it appears counter-intuitive that with regard to the pressing security concerns outlined above, the government would retreat to such a passive policy position leaving national cyber security largely reliant on the private sector.

What exactly is this 'cornerstone' of US cyber security, how is it expected to work and what impediments does it encounter? The public/private partnership concept emerges from the fact that 85 per cent of US critical infrastructure (commonly perceived of as a cyber target) is in private hands (*Agency Response to Cyberspace Policy Review*, 2009, p. 3). As a consequence of this relationship between the private sector and the public interest, politicians are of the opinion that they must engage the private sector through some sort of working framework in order to formulate an effective cyber security strategy. The framework which they have normatively promoted since the early years of the Internet's commercialization has been a 'partnership'.

Despite its centrality in successive cyber security policies, exactly what this 'partnership' entails has always been unclear. The language implies some sense of shared responsibility for critical infrastructure and national security without explicitly stating 'for what' or 'to whom'. The partnership is generally referred to in policy documents using normative, value-based language rather than clear statements outlining legal authority, responsibility and rights. President Clinton's *Presidential Decision Directive 63* states that addressing problems with cyber security will require a closely coordinated effort of both the government and the private sector which must be 'genuine, mutual and cooperative' (Clinton, 2000, p. iii). In the *National Strategy to Secure Cyberspace*, President Bush takes a similarly ambiguous and normative approach. The *NSSC* states that 'every American who can contribute to securing part of cyberspace is encouraged to do so' and to this end, the federal government 'invites the creation of and participation in, public-private partnerships' (Bush, 2003a, p. xiii).

Although politicians subscribe to the notion that there exists (or should exist) a deeply entrenched norm of cooperation between the government and private sector, this has not proven to be the case. The expectation that the private sector will, of its own accord and driven by market forces, provide effective solutions to cyber insecurity (and therefore challenges to US power) assumes that the private and public sectors share the same goals. In fact, both parties in this 'partnership' have interpreted their own role in promoting cyber security – as well as that of their partner – through the lens of differing agendas.

Government view

The dominant view among politicians engaged with these issues has been that the government has a very limited role to play in assuring the state's cyber security and that innovation and advances in the technology and practice of cyber security should arise from the private sector. This stems from two assumptions which are sometimes conflated: the first is that the government has limited *capability* to deal with cyber insecurity and the second is that it has limited *authority* and should not 'interfere' in the private sector. States may often find they lack the capability to project or protect power, and politicians have to deal with this. However, the notion that the government lacks the authority – or, indeed, the responsibility – for national cyber security is difficult to reconcile with the realist view of power which was evident in debates about the problems this poses for US power. In either a power-maximizing or security-maximizing view, the very survival of the state depends on security, and 'outsourcing' national security in this way is a unique approach.

It is useful to note here that while many functions of national security can be carried out by the private sector, for example, the private security firms that operated in the Iraq and Afghanistan wars, this is very different from the public/private partnership in the context of cyber security. Privately contracted soldiers simply replace salaried soldiers in a state-run conflict. The private sector is not expected to *conduct* the war; they simply provide personnel. There is a disjuncture in the way politicians usually regard their role in managing and projecting power and how they respond to this particular challenge. There is also a disjuncture in how they articulate power when discussing the problem and how they seem to remove it from the solution.

The Bush administration's *National Strategy to Secure Cyberspace* argued that in the United States, 'traditions of federalism and limited government require that organizations outside the federal government take the lead' in cyber security (Bush, 2003a, p. xiii). This interpretation of the government's limited authority is combined here with an assumption of its limited capability. 'The federal government could not – and, indeed, should not – secure the computer networks of privately owned banks, energy companies, transportation firms, and other parts of the private sector' (Bush, 2003a, p. 11). This resonates with earlier statements by President Clinton, who also argued in *Defending America's Cyberspace* that Congress neither 'could nor should dictate solutions to the private sector' (Clinton, 2000, p. iii).

While politicians believe that they do not have the authority to drive the development of cyber security technology, they also repeatedly express the opinion that 'in general, the private sector is best equipped and structured to respond to an evolving cyber threat' (Bush, 2003a, p. ix). At a 2000 congressional hearing, Attorney General Eric Holder argued that decision makers in the United States 'believe strongly that the private sector should take the lead in protecting private computer networks' (Holder, 2000, p. 12). This belief that the government has neither the authority nor the capability to deal with cyber security persists even when acknowledging the importance of cyber security to US power. In the same document in which President Clinton declared that the government neither could nor should interfere in the cyber security of privately owned critical infrastructure, he argued that 'America's strength [by which one might read "power"] rests on its privately owned and operated critical infrastructures' (Clinton, 2000, p. iii). At a 2000 hearing into cyber security, a senior official from the FBI testified that 'the prospect of "information warfare" by foreign militaries against our critical infrastructures is perhaps the greatest potential cyber threat to our national security'. He went on to describe 'America's Achilles heel' as 'our growing dependence on information technology in Government and commercial operations' (Vatis, 2000, p. 26). Despite these warnings, he later argued that cyber security is 'clearly the role of the private sector. The Government has neither the responsibility nor the expertise to act as the private sector's system administration' (Vatis, 2000, p. 24).

In this view, cyber security is critical to US power and yet the government has neither the authority nor the capability to deal with it. This is problematic for realist understandings of security and power. Whether the state is indeed security maximizing or power maximizing, in the context of this issue which is perceived as critical for both security and power, the state appears to have no agency. Instead, it relies upon the private sector to generate advances in technology and practice in order to deliver national security and protect state power.

Private sector view

As stated earlier, this approach to the public/private partnership is based on an assumption that both parties share a common goal of national security and state power. However, not only has the private sector expressed no willingness to *fund* national security, but industry representatives have made it clear that they do not wish to assume *responsibility* for it either. During a 2005 hearing into cyber security issues, Alan Paller of the SANS Institute, a major private sector computer security firm, highlighted these two main impediments to shifting responsibility for security back onto the private sector. First, he argued, the expense of ensuring cyber security to a national security level would be significant and, second, the litigious nature of American society means that industry would be very resistant to accepting liability for the security of their products or systems (Paller, 2005, p. 62).

The question of private sector security investment was further articulated by Sam Varnado of the Sandia National Laboratory who pointed out to a congressional hearing that industry believed that they need only increase security enough to protect against the low-level threat such as 'background noise, individual hackers, and possibly hacktivists' (Varnado, 2005, p. 95). He argued that 'it is industry's contention that government should protect against the larger threats – organized crime, terrorists, and nation-state threats – either through law-enforcement or national defense' (Varnado, 2005, p. 95).

Representative Jim Turner had speculated on this during a hearing in 2000. He commented that based on the testimony he had heard, the private sector would eventually argue that there was a point beyond which they would not spend the necessary money to meet national security needs (Turner, 2000, p. 163). Richard Clarke, former special advisor for cyber security during the Bush administration, has more recently reinforced this point, arguing that while the private sector will undertake security measures on a cost–benefit basis, it is not willing to fund or administer national security (Clarke, 2009, pp. 31–6). This space between public and private expectations was exploited by Sony Pictures in the 2014 hacking incident. Although the company had experienced severe attacks over the past few years and had a poor reputation for security, the narrative that the North Korean state was responsible for the attacks allowed Sony Pictures to shift the focus to the federal government provision of security and away from their own practices.

There exists a fundamental disjuncture between what politicians expect and hope the private sector will contribute to the public/private partnership and what the private sector regards as their responsibility. Deputy Attorney General Eric Holder's logic that the private sector should take responsibility and the state should step in only as law enforcement relies on a distinction between 'crime' and 'national security' and 'war' (Holder, 2000, p. 7). This distinction is one of the highly problematic aspects of cyber security for IR. Perceptions about the nature of an act of violence conventionally depend on the identity and intentions of the actor and, in this context, problems of attribution make that very difficult. Even in the instances when attacks are able to be tracked back to source machines, determining whether the individuals involved were working independently of any state apparatus is difficult or impossible, and plausible deniability still remains an option available to states in most cases. This means that a distinction between acts of crime, terrorism and war is very difficult and this is an important but generally overlooked factor in the difficulties that US politicians face in realizing some kind of cyber security 'partnership' between the public and private sectors.

Assessing the effectiveness of the public/private partnership

Despite the persistence of the public/private partnership as politicians' preferred solution to the problems for US power brought about by cyber insecurity, there is little to suggest that it has been regarded as a successful strategy. The perception that cyber insecurity has not been adequately addressed has been a consistent theme running through hearings and research reports since the late 1990s. Joel Willemssen, a congressional researcher, testified at a 2001 hearing that 'our most recent analysis... of reports published since July 1999, showed that federal computer systems continued to be riddled with weaknesses that put critical operations and assets at risk' (Willemssen, 2001, p. 4).[6] In 2003, the House Committee on Government Reform held a hearing entitled *Cyber Security: The Challenges Facing Our Nation in Critical Infrastructure Protection* in which the issues of conventional critical infrastructure were assessed simultaneously with cyber critical infrastructure. In the assessment of the performance of federal agencies, Representative Clay makes the point that despite the fact that Congress had 'steadily turned up the heat' on cyber security issues, recent reports indicated that the situation was consistently worse than expected (Clay, 2003, p. 7).

In a 2008 hearing into the global security assessment, concern was expressed by Representative Rick Larson that even though an official from the Office of National Intelligence testified to the hearing that the risk from cyber security was assessed as high, the budget appropriations did not reflect that (Fingar, 2008, p. 4; Larson, 2008, p. 10). By 2009, Senator Rockerfeller assessed the past decade of policymaking as poor. 'Mike McConnell, under President Bush, and Admiral Blair, under President Obama, both said that the number-one security threat to the United States of America was cybersecurity, or cyberterror, however you want to phrase it. I regard it as a profoundly and deeply troubling problem to which we are not paying much attention' (Rockerfeller, 2009, p. 1).

This has implications for the 'paradox of power' discussed in the introduction. Richard Clarke has argued that America's ability to 'defend its vital systems from cyber attack ranks among the world's worst' (Clarke, 2009, p. 34). He goes on to point out the relative advantages of some states including China which has 'implemented plans allowing them to shut the limited number of portals that connect their cyberspace to the outside world'. Other nations like North Korea, he argues, have such limited cyber dependence that there is almost nothing to defend whereas 'America's connectivity to the rest of the world is unlimited and controlled by no plan or agency' (Clarke, 2009, p. 34). President Obama's former cyber security advisor Melissa Hathaway agreed with Clarke. She wrote in a 2009 discussion paper that 'our reliance on the conveniences of remote access and the ability of our networked control systems to reduce costs and manpower needs have led to weaknesses that are being exploited by our opponents on multiple boards' (Hathaway, 2009b, p. 13). She has also stated that the failure over the past 15–20 years of cyber security policy to mitigate the threat means that 'the United States and our allies have become asymmetrically vulnerable because we have more to lose than our adversaries. Our vulnerabilities have increased year after year' (Hathaway, 2009b, p. 13). Not only does cyber security policy appear to be ineffective in the United States, but other states do not face the same threat which further increases their relative advantage.

After 15 years of promoting the public/private partnership while cyber insecurity continued to worsen, there have been some recent signs that political approaches to problems with cyber security in the United States are shifting – at least to the point of acknowledging some of these disjunctures. One recent development has been the Obama administration's explicit statement that the public/private partnership has not been an effective means for addressing cyber security issues (hence its need to 'evolve'). This sentiment was first foreshadowed in a CSIS commission report 'Securing Cyberspace for the 44th Presidency', which substantially influenced the Obama administration's *Cyberspace Policy Review*. In a 2009 Senate hearing, CSIS director James Lewis testifies that 'the United States has used a market-led approach to cybersecurity for more than a decade. It has failed us' (Lewis, 2009, p. 9). The CSIS commission report concluded that market forces (the contribution of the private sector to the public/private partnership) alone would not provide adequate national security. It also makes the observation that the US government has been timid on the question of regulation and routinely deferred to business interests over the issue of national security in this policy area (Lewis, 2009, p. 9).

In a major departure from previous thinking, the government's *Cyberspace Policy Review* also clearly articulates a sense of authority for the US federal government in dealing with cyber security. 'It is the fundamental responsibility of our government to address strategic vulnerabilities in cyberspace' (Hathaway, 2009a, p. iii). This is underlined by the key issue of apportioning responsibility and liability. 'The common defense of privately-owned critical infrastructures from armed attack or from physical intrusion or sabotage by foreign military forces or international terrorists is a core responsibility of the Federal government' (Hathaway, 2009a, p. 28). Although the review acknowledges that there remains some ambiguity over the extent to which the government is responsible for cyber as well as physical attacks, it also clearly states that the 'Federal government cannot entirely delegate or abrogate its role in securing the Nation from a cyber incident or accident' (Hathaway, 2009a, p. iv). Significantly, the review signals an awareness that in order for America to continue to use the Internet to enhance its power, it will have to recalibrate the balance between the 'public/private partnership' and accept greater responsibility for shaping the relationship between the Internet and state power. 'Our continued leadership and prosperity in the global economy may well hinge on our national commitment to act as leaders in bringing information assurance to the global information environment we have helped to create' (Akaka, 2000, p. 6).

This shift to a more proactive approach to cyber insecurity resonates with a social constructivist approach to technology and may well signal some important changes in US cyber security policy. If so, they will postdate this book but it could be a critical focal point for future analysis, as we see the problems that cyber insecurity poses for IR escalate rather than subside.

While the public/private partnership is essentially an expression of politicians' perceived lack of authority or lack of responsibility to protect and project material power, this is not the case when they engage with a more social conception of power. Here, they articulate a very clear sense of both authority and responsibility to promote the norms and values which they believe underpin US power and it is this conception of power which has most influenced the path of cyber security technology.

The role of norms and values in cyber security policy

We uphold our most cherished values not only because doing so is right, but because it strengthens our country and keeps us safe. Time and again, our values have been our best national security asset – in war and peace, in times of ease, and in eras of upheaval. Fidelity to our values is the reason why the United States of America grew from a small string of colonies under the writ of an empire to the strongest nation in the world.

(Obama, 2010, p. 35)

Hans Morgenthau wrote that 'national character' relates to national power as a shaping force which enables or disqualifies certain foreign policy choices (Morgenthau, 1978, pp. 138–40). He uses the example of American (and British) aversion to compulsory national service and large standing armies coupled with anti-militarism which Morgenthau argues can be understood as a 'handicap' in measures of national power. 'Frequently the military strength actually at their disposal will not be commensurate with the political commitments that their concern for the national interest imposes upon them' (Morgenthau, 1978, pp. 138–40). He further notes that 'the observer of the international scene who attempts to assess the relative strength of different nations must take national character into account, however difficult it may be to assess correctly so elusive and intangible a factor' (Morgenthau, 1978, p. 139). This concept proves helpful in understanding how a social conception of power influences the way in which US politicians approach solutions to cyber security threats.

In the following pages, a sense of how politicians understand the US 'national character' emerges. President Obama's argument that 'fidelity to values' has been the foundation of power is a sentiment echoed by politicians in debates about cyber security policies. He also said, in the same document, that 'our struggle to stay true to our values and Constitution has always been a lodestar, both to the American people and to those who share our aspiration for human dignity' (Obama, 2010, p. 10). Certainly in the debates of this section, these ideas dominate particularly when politicians are confronted with the kind of complexity and conflict which addressing cyber security vulnerabilities entail. When in doubt as to how they should act, politicians frequently articulate the view that they should adhere to the norms and values which they believe have led to US power in the past.

The following pages provide an analysis of how these ideas play out in two major debates. The first is the promotion of human rights in foreign policy which has substantially influenced the direction of cyber security technology. This deals with the key conflict of attribution – that while human rights concerns promote the protection of anonymity on the Internet in order to protect vulnerable people, anonymity also facilitates illegal and antisocial behaviour which potentially undermines US material power. The second example takes up some of the same concepts in a domestic setting.

The Internet as a human right: foreign policy and cyber security

A 2010 poll conducted for BBC World Service interviewed almost 28,000 adults across 26 countries and found that four out of five regard Internet access as a basic human right (BBC, 2010). This concept of linking Internet access to human rights has been evolving steadily over the past 15 years and has its roots in the UN Declaration of Human Rights. Article 19 states that everyone has the right to 'seek, receive and impart information and ideas through any media and regardless of frontiers'. In states where human rights violations take place, this can equate to the ability of political dissidents to mask their online identity in order to avoid persecution or prosecution for voicing opinions which run counter to those in power.

The difficulty of attribution over the Internet is not only a *problem* for cyber insecurity, but also a *safeguard* for global civil society. The same qualities of the Internet which afford anonymity to antisocial actors engaging in theft, espionage or disruptive behaviour discussed earlier also provide cover for political activists in non-democratic states who wish to voice their ideas and collaborate with other like-minded citizens. It can also mean that someone may post illegal material and never be traced or that state or corporate espionage can be undertaken in the guise of an individual untraceable on the Internet. The same technology which protected Iranian dissidents using Twitter also protects Al-Qaeda operatives who use the Internet for planning and communication. Anonymity on the Internet allows people to protect their privacy from criminals and also from the scrutiny of their own or foreign authorities.

In the context of human rights, better attribution has potentially dire consequences for those who choose to speak out against their governments or to seek access to information restricted by their government. The US approach has been to promote the rights of individuals to express their opinions online and to access information which their governments may seek to block. Throughout the 1990s, President Clinton's foreign policy was built around the core ideas of democratic enlargement through trade, the promotion of human rights and globalizing and liberating markets (Christopher, 1993; Clinton, 1993; Lake, 1993). A view of the world as open and connected through trade was promoted by the administration reflecting a fresh approach to the post-Cold War international climate and articulating these ideas as not only 'America's core values' but values with universal appeal (Lake, 1993). In the early years of the Internet, prior to its widespread take-up around the world, the Clinton–Gore administration focused predominantly on the domestic promise of a fully developed and implemented information infrastructure (Gore, 1993, 1994). By 1999, the concept of promoting human rights abroad and the relevance of the Internet in that pursuit united in the *NSS*, which listed information and communications technology as key to mitigating human rights abuses and promoting the free flow of information (Clinton, 1999, p. 26).

Although neither the promotion of human rights nor Internet technology occupied quite the same place of importance in the Bush administration's foreign policy, the concept that access to the Internet was a human right continued to develop. The 2006 *NSS* did pick up on the previous Clinton era view that the promotion of human rights abroad was in the interests of the United States. 'Championing freedom advances our interests because the survival of liberty at home increasingly depends on the success of liberty abroad' (Bush, 2006, p. 3). Throughout the Bush years, a number of bills were introduced (though not passed), designed to combat state-sponsored censorship and monitoring of Internet use. The *Global Internet Freedom Bill* expressed the view that the United States should 'denounce governments that restrict, censor, ban, and block access to information on the Internet' and 'deploy technologies aimed at defeating state-directed Internet censorship and the persecution of those who use the Internet'.[7] The US government's efforts to defeat the blocking of Internet access included funding to provide counter-censorship software to Chinese Internet users and, later under the Obama administration, the issuance of similar software to target states including Iran, Sudan and Cuba. This, it was argued, would enable citizens of these states to 'exercise their most basic rights' by using the Internet to communicate with each other and with the outside world (Lum, 2006; Kellerhals, 2010).

As mentioned in Chapter 3, under the Obama administration, Secretary of State Hillary Clinton developed the '21st Century Statecraft' doctrine which was essentially an effort to broaden diplomacy from a sole focus on government to government to the potential for 'government-to-people, people-to-government, and maybe even people-to-people' (Sifry, 2009). It relied on the belief that US interests are best pursued not solely through material power but also through the promotion of US values, with Clinton regarding social networking technology as a key mechanism for the spread of these ideas. In early 2010, senior State Department official Michael Posner argued that 'it's very hard to change countries from outside. Countries change from within... So this [Internet freedom] is really a vital piece of what we're trying to do when we talk about linking human rights, democracy, and development' (Posner, 2010).

Anne-Marie Slaughter, who would go on to produce the first *Quadrennial Diplomacy and Development Review* for Hillary Clinton, points out that this is a contention in debates about the wisdom of privileging of values over interests which remains unresolved in the literature. Slaughter calls this an 'overworked dichotomy' and argues that interests and values are often too simplistically defined – a view which resonates with the findings of this book (Slaughter, 2011).

This approach is built upon an understanding of the universal nature of specific values including freedom of speech and freedom to access information. Posner further argued for 'one standard of freedom, one standard of free expression that applies across the board to every government, to every country. Everybody ought to be entitled to the same access to information' (Posner, 2010). The State Department website clearly stated that the 'United States believes that "certain core principles," such as the freedom of expression as outlined in the Universal Declaration of Human Rights, apply to everyone around the world' (Kaufman, 2010).

The 21st Century Statecraft doctrine linked the Internet to human rights in two ways. First, it perpetuated the approach developed over the previous decade that access to the Internet should be regarded as a human right. In this context, Clinton repeatedly linked the Internet to the *Universal Declaration of Human Rights* and indeed this is a key component of her concept of 'Internet Freedom' (Clinton, 2010a). Clinton then expanded this to define the Internet as a new 'site' of human rights abuses derived from what she dubbed the 'freedom to connect' – like the freedom of assembly, only in cyberspace (Clinton, 2010a). 'I talked about how we must find ways to make human rights a reality. Today, we find an urgent need to protect these freedoms on the digital frontiers of the 21st century' (Clinton, 2010a). Hillary Clinton's Senior Advisor for Innovation, Alec Ross, explained that 'we're elevating Internet freedom from a piece of foreign policy arcana to something that's more central to our statecraft' because, in this administration's view, Internet freedom 'really lives at the convergence of security issues, human rights issues, and economic issues' (Ross, 2010).

The difficulties of attribution in this context then act as a safeguard to protect vulnerable identities and promote human rights of access to information and the capacity to voice an opinion. This poses a dilemma for politicians engaged with cyber security policy. While better attribution appears to be an essential element of addressing the material power vulnerabilities discussed earlier in this chapter, the ability to hide one's identity is critical to the preservation of human rights on and over the Internet. The promotion of norms against government restrictions on the Internet coupled with the distribution of technology to circumvent these practices when they do occur relies on a positive view of anonymity on the Internet as it relates to US power.

Privacy vs. security: The role of civil liberties

In contrast to the 2006 *NSS* which stated that the promotion of US values abroad would support the continuation of US values at home ('Championing freedom advances our interests because the survival of liberty at home increasingly depends on the success of liberty abroad', Bush, 2006, p. 3), the 2010 *NSS* takes the reverse view. American values in this document must be upheld at home because the very act of doing so translates to a source of US national power abroad. 'Fidelity to our values is the reason why the United States of America grew from a small string of colonies under the writ of an empire to the strongest nation in the world...America must demonstrate through words and deeds the resilience of our values and Constitution' (Obama, 2010, p. 35).

This approach to US power provides a framework for understanding how the issues of cyber security outlined in the previous section on human rights also apply to civil liberties in the United States. Privacy and security have been conceptually linked from the very early years of the Internet. A 1994 report from the National Research Council presciently argued that it was 'imperative to develop at the outset a security architecture that will lay the foundation for protections of privacy, security, and intellectual property rights' (Kleinrock et al., 1994, p. 5). As an understanding of the implications of attribution evolved, it became clear that 'privacy' was not necessarily compatible with 'security and intellectual property rights'. A 1995 Government Accountability Office report identified several services which it argued would be essential for network security in the future. They included: 'identification and authentication – the ability to verify a user's identity and a message's authenticity' and 'non-repudiation – the ability to prevent senders from denying they have sent messages and receivers from denying they have received messages' (Willemssen, 1995, p. 20). Based on the section which explained the material power considerations of cyber security, it is clear how these policies, if implemented, might have reshaped cyber security technology. However, they could not be reconciled with the values and norms associated with civil liberties such as privacy, freedom of information and rights of the individual, and an alternative approach was adopted.

In 2000, the US government produced the first national plan for the protection of the information infrastructure – *Defending America's Cyberspace*. In it, President Clinton asserts his commitment to civil liberties, reassuring the American people that enhanced cyber security 'cannot and will not come at the expense of our civil liberties. We must never undermine the very freedoms we are seeking to protect' (Clinton, 2000, p. iii). The implementation of this into policy is demonstrated in Program 10 of the plan which states that 'incorporated in every other program and is making what we do in the protection of critical cyber systems conform to Constitutional and other legal rights' (Clinton, 2000, p. v). This duality of security and privacy is acknowledged throughout the plan, but ultimately it argues that 'while safeguarding our critical infrastructures is vital, protecting our civil liberties is paramount' (Clinton, 2000, p. xxxvi).

This interrelationship between security and privacy continues to evolve in the context of hearings into cyber security. Thirteen years before the Prism program debates unleashed by Edward Snowden's leaked files, Michael Vatis testified at an Internet security hearing that FBI information-gathering activities were conducted in strict adherence to constitutional and statutory requirements regarding personal privacy. His testimony is typical of the strongly worded belief in these institutions and norms. 'These rules are founded first and foremost on the protection of privacy inherent in our constitutional system. Respect for privacy is thus a fundamental guidepost in all of our activities' (Vatis, 2000, p. 32).

In the 2003 *National Strategy to Secure Cyberspace*, President Bush attempts to reunite security and privacy on the same side of the policy arena by arguing that 'the abuse of cyberspace infringes on our privacy and our liberty. It is incumbent on the federal government to avoid such abuse and infringement. Cybersecurity and personal privacy need not be opposing goals' (Bush, 2003a, p. 14). However, despite a certain public tolerance for national security prerogatives following September 11, the privacy imperative was not easily erased from Internet security debates. In a 2003 congressional hearing, Representative Clay evoked an ideational approach to US power when he argued that 'If we sacrifice the fundamental principles of our society in the name of security, we have won neither security nor freedom' (Clay, 2003, p. 8). In this view, values rather than capabilities lead to power.

More recently, in a speech announcing the appointment of a Cybersecurity Coordinator to the National Security staff, President Obama explained that 'to ensure that policies keep faith with our fundamental values, this office will also include an official with a portfolio specifically dedicated to safeguarding the privacy and civil liberties of the American people' (Obama, 2009b). The following year, the 2010 *NSS* stated that 'our digital infrastructure, therefore, is a strategic national asset, and protecting it – while safeguarding privacy and civil liberties – is a national security priority' (Obama, 2010, p. 27).

This overview of the role of civil liberties in political debates about cyber security solutions demonstrates that although there were policy proposals in the mid-1990s which argued for the identification and authentication of Internet users, this approach failed to take hold in US politics. Although the intelligence community clearly had other priorities, the Prism program can be understood better as a failure of adequate oversight than as a political approach to technology. Even though the proposals discussed here directly address the problems that cyber security is perceived to pose for US power, politicians continuously privileged values and norms in the belief that these underpin US power more significantly in this context than do material capabilities.

While she was criticized for being inconsistent, Hillary Clinton exhibited an honesty and understanding of the interrelationship between a problem grounded in material power and solutions derived from an ideational power framework. Rather than ignore or play down these apparent contradictions as had happened in the past, Clinton acknowledged them. She argued that 'liberty and security, transparency and confidentiality, freedom of expression and tolerance – these all make up the foundation of a free, open, and secure society as well as a free, open, and secure Internet where universal human rights are respected, and which provides a space for greater progress and prosperity over the long run' (Clinton, 2011). Ultimately, Clinton observed that the United States will have to struggle to balance ideational and material power concerns and that, in a sense, this will be a key feature of US power in the information age (Clinton, 2011).

Conclusion

This chapter has examined the way in which conceptions of US power have shaped and influenced cyber security. The research revealed that, rather than a single conception of power, there have been two competing conceptions of power that drive debates about cyber security technology in the United States. A material view of power dominates discussions about how cyber insecurity threatens to undermine US power. The impact on outcomes of conflict, the economy and geopolitics were found to be the three most significant concerns. The policy response to these problems has been the public/private partnership in which politicians have expected the private sector to deliver solutions to cyber insecurity. This conception of power has been coupled with an instrumental approach to technology which undermines the agency and authority of social actors – in this case, politicians. Politicians have consistently expressed the view that the government has neither the authority nor the capability to address what they regard as significant threats to US national security and power.

Rather than privilege these material power concerns when formulating policies guiding cyber security technology, politicians have instead sought to promote a set of norms and values which they also associate with US power. They have regarded the protection of anonymity in the context of human rights and the protection of privacy in the context of civil liberties as essential to the sustenance of US power. Significantly, this conception of power is associated with a social constructivist approach to technology which imbues a sense of authority and responsibility. Politicians regard their actions to steer cyber security technology in this direction as legitimate and necessary and it is this conception of power which has been most influential in shaping cyber security technology.

The case study leads to a number of findings and implications for understanding the relationship between power in IR and new technology. One of the key findings of this case study has been that a conception of power based on values and norms can override material concerns even in the face of very serious risks. Politicians have regarded policies which undermine deeply embedded norms and values as a greater threat to US power than those which undermine material capabilities. Speeches and policy statements which elevate the role of values and norms can sometimes be regarded as rhetoric – particularly in the context of security concerns. However, in the case of cyber security, politicians' determination to adhere to a social view of power when engaging with solutions to a problem they frame in material terms is all the more significant in the face of the perception that the United States remains dangerously exposed to cyber security threats.

This illustrates the role of *choice* exercised by states when dealing with these issues. And this leads to one of the key arguments that motivated this book – that is, the Internet does not have universally applicable effects on state power. Certainly the effects of the Internet can be *observed* on material and social factors of power. However, without understanding the *choices* which politicians make – first, about which factors they regard as most significant and, second, about how they shape technology in order to promote those factors – it is not possible to reach meaningful conclusions about the relationship between this new technology and state power in IR.

The second key finding of this case study is that the philosophical approach to technology with which politicians engage has implications for how they perceive their authority and agency to shape and influence technology. When they articulate the ways in which cyber insecurity challenges US power and when they discuss the public/private partnership as a solution to those challenges, politicians engage with an approach to technology which is predominantly instrumental. This approach regards problems which arise from technology as best addressed by more technology. It also expects those solutions to emerge from market forces which continue to drive innovation in the 'best' direction without intervention from government. This correlates with the views expressed by politicians that they have neither the authority nor the capability to shape or influence this aspect of technology. In contrast, when discussing the social power factors of cyber security, politicians readily claim authority and indeed responsibility for influencing the development of this technology in such a way as to best promote those aspects of US power. They believe that they can and should shape technology according to their conception of power and, in fact, they do so by insisting on the preservation of anonymity and privacy over the benefits that more accurate attribution offers.

5
Internet Governance

Internet governance was initially perceived as a narrowly defined technical function of little interest other than to those tasked with managing it. However, it soon came to be recognized as an important form of power exercised globally. Through the mechanisms of Internet governance, decisions are made about how the Internet is used, how it grows and how it is controlled. Processes are institutionalized that determine who participates in governance, which voices are privileged and how decision makers are held accountable. These processes and decisions affect economies, impact on national identity formation and undermine sovereignty in a number of important ways. Indeed, they have deeply political implications.

By the mid-1990s, Internet governance had emerged as a problem. An exponential increase in those connecting to the Internet put existing governance mechanisms under considerable strain and it was proving difficult to register new domain names and Internet protocol (IP) addresses quickly or to resolve disputes about conflicted names in a timely manner. Politicians were concerned that this 'bottleneck' was preventing the Internet from fulfilling its commercial potential by inhibiting growth and expansion. This, it was believed, would have negative implications for US economic power – the focus of so much expectation in the 1990s.

In 1998, the US Department of Commerce responded by establishing a private, not-for-profit corporation to administer Internet governance. The Internet Corporation for Assigned Names and Numbers (ICANN) was awarded full control of Internet governance not only in the US but globally. In doing so, the US government was able to set the agenda, define the parameters of debate and establish their own objectives and interests as the primary function of ICANN. In short, they established hegemonic control over Internet governance which profoundly shaped the way the Internet works today. Indeed, hegemony – defined here as not only a preponderance of power but the ability to set the agenda and shape the preferences of others – is one of the key concepts to emerge from the analysis in this chapter (Jervis, 1993, p. 53; Layne, 2006, p. 46). ICANN's agenda and its oversight by the US Department of Commerce ensured that Internet governance evolved in such a way as to shape the Internet into an environment designed to promote commerce and enhance US power.

The coordination of such a huge computer network was without precedent and while there has been no debate about the necessity of a stable mechanism for carrying out this function, exactly *how* this should happen and *who* should control key governance functions has become a globally significant issue which is increasingly contentious for economic, commercial and political reasons. These debates will be located within the broader literature on global governance in order to not only connect the case study to some of the perennial questions about governance, authority and power but also highlight some of the ways in which ICANN differs from other global governance bodies. ICANN's distinctive structure as private sector body which formulates important policies for a global system generates a range of impediments to effective governance including important accountability measures. These, it will be shown, have implications for legitimacy – both of ICANN itself and of US oversight of Internet governance. Those implications for legitimacy in turn have implications for US power.

Legitimacy is an important concept in this case study – particularly as it relates to hegemony. Hegemony raises concerns because others realize that the hegemon's power could threaten their own interests (Walt, 2005a, p. 107). As the political nature of Internet governance came to be more widely understood, questions arose about whose interests were being promoted through the established mechanisms for Internet governance and whether the US should continue to exercise control over key decisions about the technology. Both ICANN and the US government experienced independent but related challenges to their legitimacy. ICANN faced these challenges as a consequence of its own internal governance processes which were regarded to be lacking in transparency and accountability – issues which Milton Mueller argues emerged partly due to its unorthodox structure (2009). The US government faced challenges to its legitimacy as the hegemonic power due to the realization by other state actors that it exercised unilateral control over a system upon which most of the world now heavily relied. However, at the same time, it had become apparent to US politicians that control of ICANN was an important source of power. They had been able to shape Internet governance in such a way as to promote their agenda of economic growth which was specifically intended to enhance US power. In order to prevent other norms or interests derailing that trajectory, retaining control of ICANN – or at least, preventing any other state or institution from gaining control – was regarded as important to the pursuit of US power. As a consequence, while facing increasing pressure to distribute governance of the Internet, politicians became less inclined to release control and more concerned about how sharing control might undermine US material power. In addition to the Internet serving as a 'source' of economic growth, and consequently US power, the continued control over Internet governance came to be regarded as an *expression* of US power over a global resource.

Through the tension produced by this struggle for power and legitimacy, the US government embarked upon a series of negotiated concessions with the international community in order to relinquish enough control over Internet governance to maintain international support – which they regarded as essential to the continued promotion of a commercial agenda – without undermining their explicitly stated material power objectives. Their perception that they must balance the demands of both material and social factors – that continued control over Internet governance relies on some degree of legitimacy – echoes broader debates in international relations (IR) about the relationship between power and legitimacy (Nye, 2002; Walt, 2005b; Reus-Smit, 2004; Joffe, 2006). Ultimately, the evolution of Internet governance is a story of the interaction of hegemonic power and legitimacy and these two themes drive the narrative of this chapter.

There are three important findings to highlight in this case study. First, in the years immediately preceding the establishment of ICANN, changes in the international order combined with advances in information and communications technology (ICT) to create a political shift in approaches to US power – particularly within the Clinton–Gore administration. Ideas which emerged from this linked the Internet to US economic power in such a way as to impact significantly on the structures subsequently put into place to govern an increasingly global Internet. These ideas have had a lasting impact and continue to shape Internet governance today. The second finding is that when Internet governance came to be recognized as a bottleneck, US politicians combined this material view of power with a social constructivist approach to technology. These two elements together formed a framework which not only clearly articulated the way in which the technology *should* develop but lent authority and agency to the politicians making these decisions – and this is perhaps the most powerful combination in political approaches to technology. The third important finding is that when this arrangement encountered legitimacy challenges, US politicians responded through a social conception of power – that is, they sought to enhance their legitimacy credentials.

The chapter begins with an introduction to Internet governance from both a technical and a conceptual perspective. The technical section explains key terms and concepts which will recur throughout the chapter and are integral to understanding Internet governance. This is intentionally brief so as to avoid rewriting the technological history which has been covered so abundantly in other studies but substantial enough to promote a better understanding of the depth and breadth of the challenges of Internet governance. The conceptual section of this introduction to Internet governance locates the issue in broader debates about global governance and power. Here, it becomes clear that ICANN is a unique case due to its hybrid structure which is distinct from state governments, inter-governmental or non-governmental organizations (NGOs) and conventional private sector bodies which typically occupy debates about global governance. This unique structure emerges as an important factor later in the chapter during the discussion on legitimacy challenges to ICANN which are significantly enhanced by a lack of accountability – a key element of governance.

Following this introduction to Internet governance, the chapter looks at the evolution of the set of ideas which have framed this issue in US political debates. There was a synergistic confluence of events – both technical and political – which combined over the course of the 1980s and late 1990s to shape politicians' approach to Internet governance. In addition to outlining these factors, this section draws out the relevance of politicians establishing the commercial sector as the 'relevant social group' in Internet governance considerations. The relevant social group is a methodological tool borrowed from the social construction of technology (SCoT) which allows for the identification of the actor or actors whose requirements and expectations are privileged in decisions about how technology should develop. It is understood that this has a substantial impact on how technology evolves as it guides decision making.

The next major section of this chapter analyses how politicians (unselfconsciously) combined this conception of power with a social constructivist approach to technology in their efforts to influence and shape the establishment of ICANN. By the late 1990s, there was a growing perception amongst US politicians that the existing, somewhat informal Internet governance structure was inadequate to facilitate the commercial opportunities that they envisaged for it. This was regarded by them as critical given the important role they believed that new technology, generally, and the Internet, specifically, could play in restoring US power to a globally dominant position.

The chapter moves on to explain the role of legitimacy in Internet governance. Plagued by accusations of illegitimacy brought about by a perceived lack of transparency and accountability, procedural ambiguity and an expanding mandate, ICANN continues to operate under the purview of the US Department of Commerce through the National Telecommunications and Information Administration (NTIA) – though at the time of writing, the Internet Assigned Numbers Authority (IANA) contract was scheduled for transition to the global multi-stakeholder community at the end of September 2015. US politicians have expressed growing concern that poor governance practices which undermine ICANN's legitimacy could threaten the status quo which has been established to preference US objectives. Indeed, politicians link legitimacy to the US ability to 'fend off interference from the UN and from governments' (DelBianco, 2006, p. 33). Their response is to take steps to shore up legitimacy – both for ICANN and US oversight and they do so through a series of contractual concessions which will be covered in this section.

This chapter concludes by drawing out some implications of these findings for our understanding of the relationship between power and new technology. These fall into two categories: the first is the relevance of broader tensions between power and legitimacy in the context of Internet governance and the second is the importance of understanding the relationship between conceptions of power and approaches to technology.

Internet governance: Technology and concepts

In order to understand the issues at play in this chapter, it is necessary to have a basic understanding of the 'domain name system' (the DNS) which is the main focus of ICANN's governance. The following paragraphs offer a very basic introduction to this technology which will help to contextualize the rest of the chapter. This will be followed by locating the issue within concepts of governance both to link it to broader debates and to define the ways in which ICANN is unique.

Technical brief

To manage a computer network and to ensure that packets of information are routed to the destination they are intended for, each destination must be allocated a unique identifier or 'address'. In the context of the Internet, these identifiers are referred to as Internet protocol addresses – or IP addresses. As IP numbers are long and not easily recalled, they are coupled with 'domain names'. This allows the user to simply type in www.icann.org rather than '192.0.34.163' – the actual IP address. In addition to managing the allocation of IP addresses so as to avoid conflicting numbers, these domain names and IP addresses must be constantly recorded and updated in a central database and made readily available to global traffic on the Internet to facilitate the rapid and accurate transfer of information. These details are retained in a kind of register or 'phone book' file stored on 13 computers known as 'root servers', located all over the world. The system as a whole is referred to as the domain name system (DNS).

Ensuring that these names and addresses are issued and controlled in an orderly manner is a significant aspect of Internet governance. Administering and resolving the names and numbers on an ongoing basis (referred to as 'universal resolvability') becomes a key element of the security and stability of the Internet. Universal resolvability means that every computer connected to the Internet has access to the same information about which address relates to which number. Without this, directing packets of information to the correct destination is impossible. Indeed, the DNS is absolutely critical to the operability of the vast number of services which have come to rely on the Internet.

For many years while the network was restricted to the academic and military communities, the DNS was managed by a single individual – Jon Postel, a computer scientist from the University of Southern California. After the commercialization of the Internet in 1992, the US government contracted the management of the DNS out to a private firm – Network Solutions. However, with the extraordinary expansion of the Internet, the task of managing the DNS rapidly escalated both in scope and in relative importance, outgrowing the somewhat informal governance mechanisms that were in place. Furthermore, as the Internet community broadened to include businesses, individuals, NGOs – all across international boundaries – these governance functions came to be understood as not simply technical, but highly political as well, due to their implications for sovereignty, state economies and cultural distinctions. These developments (discussed in more detail later in this chapter) led to the establishment in 1998 of the ICANN – a private, not-for-profit organization which was awarded full responsibility and control over the DNS by the US government.

Conceptual approach to governance and the Internet

In addition to these technical details, there are some important conceptual factors here. As governance is the mechanism through which authority and power is exercised in this case study – and over which legitimacy is challenged – it is useful to locate these debates about Internet governance in the context of broader literature about global governance. Too often, Internet governance is discussed as entirely unique without due reference to existing lines of scholarship that can provide useful frameworks for analysis and consideration. And too often, global governance literature looks at a whole range of interesting problems and challenges – except this one.

Michael Barnett and Raymond Duvall have nominated global governance 'one of the defining characteristics of the current international moment' and certainly, it has implications for a wide range of transnational concerns including the environment, economies, communications and trade (Barnett and Duvall, 2005, p. 1). Thomas Weiss regards debates about global governance as emerging from a growing realization amongst IR scholars in the 1970s and 1980s that both a realist state-based approach and liberal-institutionalist theories focused on interdependence were failing to adequately incorporate the 'vast increase, in both numbers and influence, of non-state actors and the implications of technology in an age of globalization' (Weiss, 2000, p. 796). In addition to this quantitative increase in actors on the world stage, scholars like Klaus Dingwerth and Philipp Pattberg argue that there has been a quantitative shift as well. They suggest that a 'plethora of forms of social organization and political decision-making exist that are neither directed toward the state nor emanate from it' (Dingwerth and Pattberg, 2006, p. 191).

The Internet prompted speculation about how global governance might translate to cyberspace. As early as 1998, Robert Keohane and Joseph Nye observed that 'rules will be necessary to govern cyberspace, not only protecting lawful users from criminals but ensuring intellectual property rights' (Keohane and Nye, 1998, p. 82). The normative assumption that intellectual property rights (as a commercial concern) should be central to Internet governance has been deeply embedded in US debates around this issue from the beginning and rarely challenged in academic or policy debates.

Keohane and Nye further argued that 'classic issues of politics – who governs and on what terms – are as relevant to cyberspace as to the real world' (Keohane and Nye, 1998, pp. 82–3). This was a view encapsulated in the 'Tunis Agenda for Action', one of the final outcomes of the United Nations (UN)-sponsored World Summit on the Information Society in 2005 (Tunis Agenda, 2005). This document defines Internet governance as 'the development and application by governments, the private sector and civil society, in their respective roles, of shared principles, norms, rules, decision-making procedures, and programmes that shape the evolution and use of the Internet' (Tunis Agenda, 2005). This definition resonates with basic regime theory but it also implies an affinity with the social constructivist approach to technology in that it acknowledges the role of social groups in shaping technology. It links global governance back to perennial questions for the study of power in both the virtual and physical environment.

Barnett and Duvall link governance to power not only through questions like 'who governs?', but significantly for this case, 'how are institutions designed to check the potential abuse of power?' (Barnett and Duvall, 2005, p. 2). In their view, 'the rules, structures, and institutions that guide, regulate, and control social life' are fundamental elements of power (Barnett and Duvall, 2005, p. 2). In the case of ICANN, these questions lead to some provocative answers. In fact, one of the defining debates about ICANN is that as an institution, it has been designed *without* measures to check the potential abuse of power and this will be explored in more depth in the section on ICANN and US power.

Literature on global governance provides a framework for what might be expected of ICANN and its functions. It also helps to illustrate how ICANN does not meet those expectations. ICANN, it will be explained, is a unique organization due in part to its unusual structure and also due to its mixed mandate of governing a globally significant resource upon which many state functions rely while, at the same time, operating a commercial enterprise.

From guns to butter: A new conception of US power

A SCoT approach urges the close examination of changing priorities for any technology, for it is at these junctures of change when long-held assumptions are sometimes challenged and reassessed that the ways in which social groups shape technology can become most apparent (MacKenzie, 1996, p. 6). Relating changing priorities to technological developments also allows for the analysis of where those priorities emanate from, whose priorities are being addressed and how those priorities shape technology. Chapter 3 discussed how changes in conceptions of US power from primarily military to President Clinton's emphasis on the importance of economic growth led to a shift in priorities for Internet technology. In President George H. Bush's approach to power, the Internet had little if any relevance; however, in the Clinton–Gore view, it became an important element of future economic growth and, consequently, US power.

The Clinton–Gore conception of US power as dependent on economic growth (and also projected through economic engagement) repurposed the Internet from a military/science project (as it was perceived during the Cold War and by President Bush). This led to a shift in priorities about how the technology should be managed and in which direction it should be encouraged to develop. First, in order to maximize its commercial potential, it was desirable that the Internet move from an elite tool to be broadly available. This was evident in the discourse of the *National Information Infrastructure* and the bills which arose from it. As discussed in Chapter 3, there was a marked transition from the first *High Performance Computing Act of 1991* which focused on the National Research and Education Network (NREN) – a network primarily targeted at researchers – to the *National Information Infrastructure Act of 1993* (HR 1757) which placed greater emphasis on the general population as users of the network. The Internet was regarded by the Clinton–Gore administration as an essential element of the national infrastructure like roads and electricity and it was discussed using that terminology – as the 'information superhighway' (Gore, 1989b).

A second outcome of the shift in priorities of the Clinton–Gore administration was the privatization and commercialization of the Internet. Although it is rarely discussed in these terms, the privatization and commercialization of the Internet was in large part a political development – not a technological or even commercially driven one. As also detailed in Chapter 3, policy documents clearly state that the intention of the US government was to privatize and commercialize the network in order to maximize its potential for contributing to US economic growth and thus improve the state's international standing.

A third outcome of this period was that these factors all combined to contribute to an exponential increase in the registration of domain names and numbers, putting existing mechanisms for Internet governance under considerable strain. By the mid-1990s, and in the context of the Clinton–Gore ambitions for Internet technology,

Internet governance had come to be perceived as a problem. Existing mechanisms were perceived as preventing the Internet from fulfilling its commercial potential by proving inadequate to deal with the extraordinary growth and expansion of the 1990s.

As the Cold War wound down, eventually concluding with the fall of the Soviet Union, there was an attendant shift in dominant ideas about both US power and Internet technology. Politically, ideas about American power and new technology, which had been steadily gaining traction within some quarters of US politics, found firm ground with the election of the Clinton–Gore administration. Ultimately, foreign policy, economic policy and technology policy would converge in the early 1990s to emphasize the importance of global social, political and economic networks to American power. In President Clinton's words, 'From beyond nations, economic and technological forces all over the globe are compelling the world towards integration. These forces are fuelling a welcome explosion of entrepreneurship and political liberalization' (Clinton, 1993). At the same time, Internet technology which was rapidly evolving and changing was reprioritized by US politicians from a military/science project to having potential to contribute to the US economy. The network was privatized and opened to commercial traffic, the World Wide Web was invented and there was rapid movement of both commercial enterprise and private access to the Internet.

Internet governance as a problem for power

Establishing who should govern the Internet and how might have been a question left to the technical community had it not been for the expectations of the Clinton–Gore administration that the Internet would play a role in rejuvenating US power. At heart, the 'problem' of Internet governance for US politicians was its capacity to undermine commercial confidence in the network. The dot-com boom of the 1990s had already substantially reinforced those ideas about the relationship between new technology, the economy and US power. During this period, small single person or small partnership companies (Google, eBay) that provided an innovative web service generated unprecedented levels of wealth with very low overheads.

There is an assumption in much of the literature and most of policy documents that the Internet has a 'natural' or normative relationship with commerce. However, in studies like this one which seek to understand how actors shape technology, it is important to remain aware that technology does not have a predetermined path. Rather, it reflects the expectations, norms and values which actors with the power to do so lay upon it. Given that the Clinton–Gore administration now regarded the Internet as integrally linked to US economic power, resolving the problem of managing the DNS was perceived as an issue with some political gravity. An early policy paper justifying US government intervention in Internet governance argued that 'many businesses and consumers are still wary of conducting extensive business over the Internet because of the lack of a predictable legal environment governing transactions' (Clinton and Gore, 1997). The DNS needed to be stable and secure so as to provide a reliable operating environment for private enterprise. The Internet, and particularly Internet governance, is oriented primarily towards commerce because that was the vision which the Clinton–Gore administration had for the technology, and the policies which they developed were devised to shape the technology into that purpose.

When decisions are made about technology, they are made with reference to the needs, expectations or desires of a particular actor or group of actors. Decisions about how technology should evolve or be incorporated into society do not have universal appeal. They generally privilege some while disadvantaging others. Identifying this nuance in how decisions about technology are made provides insight into how those in power exercise that power and interpret the most desirable outcomes for technology. The following pages explain how Internet governance came to be perceived of as a 'problem' by US politicians and how they identified the commercial sector as the 'relevant social group' for whom they were devising solutions to that problem. That is, they perceived that privileging the interests of the commercial sector was the best way to promote their agenda of enhancing US power.

In the latter half of the 1990s, political decisions about the Internet (including privatization and commercialization) combined with technological developments such as the invention of the World Wide Web and the Mosaic browser led to an explosion in registrations of IP names and numbers as the user base for the Internet grew from predominantly research and military users to include government departments, businesses of all sizes and individuals. In 1989, there were 159,000 hosts registered. By the end of 1994, there were 5 million and by 1998 when ICANN was established, there were 30 million (Zakon, n.d.).

Quite apart from the exponential increase in users due to the popularity of the web, there was also an underlying technical function which placed a strain on the DNS by increasing the demand for domain names.

Tim Berners Lee and his colleagues designed the web to use a 'uniform resource locator' (URL) to identify resources on the web, including documents, images, downloadable files and services. As its starting point, the URL uses the domain name which encouraged the registration of new domain names in order to shorten URLs (Mueller, 2002, p. 108). Rather than have one's biography page located at the address 'http://ips.cap.anu.edu.au/ir/studies/phd/carr.php', it is preferable in many cases (particularly in a commercial context) to simply register the domain name 'www.madelinecarr.com'. The URL quickly became part of the image of a product or person online and as this preference for more direct addresses became the norm, domain names and numbers were in much greater demand.

An early Internet pioneer and computer scientist at the University of Southern California, Jon Postel had recorded and released IP addresses under the auspices of the IANA (Berners Lee, 2000, p. 127). Initially, these were contained in a paper notebook, but as the task grew Postel migrated the data to a text file. In the early years, while there was a relatively small number of people and organizations who required IP addresses, this system worked well but even prior to the post-commercialization explosion in requests for IP addresses in the mid-1990s, it became clear that the Internet had outgrown these governance arrangements and that the task had outgrown the capacity of a single individual.

In 1992, the US government (through the National Science Foundation) contracted a private firm, Network Solutions, to manage the .com, .org and .net domains. This was not a long-term solution to Internet governance as Network Solution's privileged position and ability to generate substantial revenue through domain name registrations led to dissatisfaction amongst their competitors while their inability to deal quickly and effectively with the onslaught of new copyright disputes led to dissatisfaction amongst their clients (Leiner et al., 1997; Abbate, 2000; Mueller, 2002).

By the late 1990s, it had become clear that Internet governance was failing to meet the needs of the commercial sector. By doing so, it was also inhibiting the economic growth and consequent increase in US power which politicians believed would follow. In framing the problem of Internet governance in this way, it followed that when they debated possible solutions, politicians privileged the needs and expectations of the commercial sector. In SCoT terms, they had determined that the commercial sector was the 'relevant social group'. In the case of Internet governance, the relevant social group might alternatively have been identified as global or domestic civil society, the Department of Defense that funded so much of the research or state governments. Had any of these been identified as the relevant social group, Internet governance may have evolved very differently.

ICANN and hegemony as the solution

In the post-Cold War period, broader conceptions of US power in the context of unipolarity had refocused attention on questions about the nature of hegemonic power, some of which were replicated in the microcosm of Internet governance. IR scholar Robert Jarvis writes that in addition to the 'usual and crude measures of power', a preponderance of power can result in a state's capacity to 'establish, or at least strongly influence, "the rules of the game"... the intellectual frameworks employed by many states, and the standards by which behaviour is judged to be legitimate' (Jervis, 1993, p. 53). Essentially a Gramscian approach to hegemonic power, this was significant in the establishment of the policies, practices and institutions that were developed to manage the governance of the Internet.

In a 1998 journal article, Keohane and Nye argue against a technologically determinist view which regards information technology as a levelling influence, empowering small states and disempowering large, powerful states. They point out this technology can also reinforce existing power structures because 'first movers are often the creators of the standards and architecture of information systems' (Keohane and Nye, 1998, p. 88). They were referring specifically to the use of the English language in domain names but the same principle applies to the way in which the United States took unilateral control of Internet governance and embedded it in an institutional framework which was designed to address their objectives and interests. In doing so, the United States exercised a form of hegemonic power which allowed it to steer Internet governance in such a way as to specifically address the US-defined agenda of economic growth. By assuming authority to manage Internet governance, these politicians were able to establish the 'rules of the game', the agenda and the terms of reference and these would have a lasting effect on the technology.

An analysis of relevant policy papers which preceded the establishment of ICANN demonstrates how politicians conceived of the solution to the problem which inadequate Internet governance posed for the future of US economic power in a cohesive and targeted way from early on. They had clear objectives and they purposely set about establishing and institutionalizing a mechanism for Internet governance which would best address those objectives.

Three significant policy papers were released by the US government between July 1997 and June 1998. These were the *Framework for Global Electronic Commerce* (July 1997), The Green Paper on Internet Governance (February 1998) and *The White Paper on Management of Internet names and Addresses* (June 1998). Together, these policy papers articulated the approach of the Clinton administration to the future of new technology and the policy vision for its potential contribution to US power. In addition, they formally charted a path from the existing Internet governance mechanisms to a future which was based on the establishment of ICANN.

Framework for Global Electronic Commerce

The Framework for Global Electronic Commerce (GEC) was issued by the Clinton administration in July 1997. Largely authored by Ira Magaziner, Clinton's 'technology czar', the GEC articulated the administration's 'vision for the emergence of the Global Information Infrastructure (GII) as a vibrant global marketplace' with a particular focus on the Internet which the paper refers to as a revolutionary force in the commercial sector (Clinton and Gore, 1997). The GEC proposed five principles for Internet governance:

- The private sector should lead development of mechanisms to facilitate the successful operation of the Internet.
- Governments should avoid undue restrictions and regulation.
- Governmental involvement should be limited to supporting and enforcing a predictable, minimalist, consistent and simple legal environment for commerce.
- Governments should recognize the unique qualities of the Internet and not assume that existing regulatory schemes are appropriate for new technology.
- Electronic commerce over the Internet should be facilitated on a global basis.

The GEC was specifically addressing electronic commerce, so it is not surprising that the principles express belief in the value of the private sector and market forces, minimal government regulation and the power of global trade. However, taken in context with the policy documents which followed, it is an early indication of the privileging of the commercial sector which would form the basis of Internet governance. The GEC explicitly states that 'widespread competition and increased consumer choice should be the defining features of the new digital marketplace' and it specifies that problems with Internet governance had led 'businesses and consumers to be cautious' (Clinton and Gore, 1997).

While this policy document suggested that any government influence should be light handed and flexible so as not to 'impede' the natural growth of the Internet and the US economy, it also stressed that the Internet was in need of some 'shaping' by the government. 'Governments can have a profound effect on the growth of commerce on the Internet. By their actions, they can facilitate electronic trade or inhibit it' (Clinton and Gore, 1997). These policy proposals laid the groundwork for the following 'Green Paper' on Internet governance.

The Green Paper

In the United States, a 'Green Paper' represents an opportunity for the government to gauge and compile the opinions of stakeholders on an issue prior to settling on policy. Although it was widely acknowledged that Internet governance had to evolve in order to address the increased demand for names and numbers, there was significant contention amongst the technical and business sectors about how this should happen. This discord was referred to in the Green Paper. 'Recognizing that no solution will win universal support, the U.S. government seeks as much consensus as possible before acting' (Improvement of Technical Management of Internet Names and Addresses: Proposed Rule, 1998, p. 8827). In 1998, the NTIA, an agency of the Department of Commerce, published a Green Paper under the title 'Improvement of Technical Management of Internet Names and Addresses: Proposed Rule' (Improvement of Technical Management of Internet Names and Addresses: Proposed Rule, 1998, pp. 8826–33). It articulated the strong beliefs within the Clinton–Gore administration about the commercial potential of new technology, the benefits of global trade, the need for legitimacy and the benefits of private sector solutions. In the Green Paper, these all point towards the establishment of a private entity which appears independent but comes within the purview of US control. The problems and solutions expressed in this policy document are very much in line with the principles expressed in the GEC – that the private sector should take the lead in Internet governance with government playing an important but limited role, that the scope needed to be recognized as global and that the focus was to be commerce.

Articulated in the Green Paper were government's reasons for implementing changes to the structures of existing Internet governance. They included

- the 'widespread dissatisfaction about the absence of competition in domain name registration',
- the growing numbers of Internet users who reside outside the US and 'want a larger voice in Internet coordination',
- the understanding that as domain names and numbers acquired commercial value, they could not be managed by an entity which was 'not formally accountable to the Internet community', and
- 'As the Internet becomes commercial, it becomes inappropriate for U.S. research agencies to participate in and fund these functions' (Improvement of Technical Management of Internet Names and Addresses: Proposed Rule, 1998, p. 8827).

These same themes recur in the four principles articulated for the proposed governance system: stability, competition, private bottom-up coordination and representation. These, the Green Paper states, were derived from stakeholder consultation and were designed to accommodate an uncertain future (Improvement of Technical Management of Internet Names and Addresses: Proposed Rule, 1998, p. 8827).

Stability

'The introduction of a new system should not disrupt current operations, or create competing root systems' (Improvement of Technical Management of Internet Names and Addresses: Proposed Rule, 1998, p. 8827).

Competition

The Internet succeeds in great measure because it is a decentralized system that encourages innovation and maximises individual freedom. Where possible, market mechanisms that support competition and consumer choice should drive the technical management of the Internet because they will promote innovation, preserve diversity, and enhance user choice and satisfaction.

(Improvement of Technical Management of Internet Names and Addresses: Proposed Rule, 1998, p. 8827)

Private, bottom-up coordination

'A private coordinating process is likely to be more flexible than government and to move rapidly enough to meet the changing needs of the Internet and of Internet users' (Improvement of Technical Management of Internet Names and Addresses: Proposed Rule, 1998, p. 8827).

Representation

> Technical management of the Internet should reflect the diversity of its users and their needs. Mechanisms should be established to ensure international input in decision making. In keeping with these principles, we divide the name and number functions into two groups, those that can be moved to a competitive system and those that should be coordinated. We then suggest the creation of a representative, not-for-profit corporation to manage the coordinated functions according to widely accepted objective criteria.
>
> (Improvement of Technical Management of Internet Names and Addresses: Proposed Rule, 1998, p. 8827)

Of these, stability and competition were the two principles most fully realized through the establishment of ICANN. They are also the two most aligned with the Clinton–Gore vision for the Internet as a mechanism for enhancing US economic power. The flexibility of private coordination was realized but ICANN responded not to the 'changing needs of the Internet and Internet users' – they were far too diverse to be considered as a cohesive unit. Rather, ICANN responded to the agenda within which it had been created, a fact which will become apparent as the chapter progresses through an analysis of some of the problems ICANN later encountered. In addition, representation was never pursued through the establishment of ICANN. On the contrary, it has been a point of considerable contention and this will also be discussed at more length later in the chapter.

The White Paper

The Green Paper generated over 650 (submitted) responses. In May 1998, the subsequent White Paper was released by the NTIA responding to feedback and detailing the policy which would frame the establishment of ICANN (Department of Commerce, 1998). The four principles articulated in the Green Paper (stability, competition, private bottom-up coordination and representation) were sustained with 'stability' providing the justification for a continued role for the US government.

Although the White Paper did modify some elements of the Green Paper in response to the feedback received from the public, it did not deviate from the government's view on what the new governing body should be, how it should operate and, most importantly, which goals and norms it should promote and institutionalize. Indeed, the written justifications for not amending the White Paper further made it clear that only modifications which did not deviate from the intended policy were considered (Department of Commerce, 1998).

In September 1998 following these policy proposals and consultation with stakeholders, ICANN was established as a private, not-for-profit incorporated body subject to the jurisdiction of the state of California and placed under the purview of the Department of Commerce. The agreement took the form of a zero dollar contract for ICANN to administer the IANA contract – essentially the work that Jon Postel had carried out. Placing Internet governance under the purview of the Department of Commerce effectively set the parameters for future debates by moving commercial interests to the fore ahead of competing agendas such as security, human rights or national sovereignty. By institutionalizing the existing informal governance arrangements (which had been carried out predominantly by people based in the United States), the government ensured a level of future control over the development of the Internet. Despite the fact that the Internet was already a global network with no clear locus of 'ownership', the US government would retain the capability to further shape Internet governance through this relationship.

These policy processes, culminating in the formation of ICANN as a global Internet governance body, demonstrate how the conception of power outlined in the previous section has shaped technology. A material conception of power which linked Internet governance to US economic growth was combined with a social constructivist approach to technology in order to very effectively define the parameters of debate and guide the outcome to address the goals articulated by these politicians. A single-minded emphasis on commercial prerogatives like competition and private sector solutions over those of technological determinants (like alternative protocols), political norms (for example, addressing breaches of sovereignty) or security concerns (cyber crime and terrorism) has profoundly shaped not only ICANN but global Internet governance.

Essentially, the fact that ICANN has been administered by the Department of Commerce has had a determining impact on setting ICANN's agenda as this subset of US politicians has been the group assessing its conduct and to a large extent, affecting the vote on its future. Although the Department of Commerce policy was initially to be hands off and move ICANN to a fully independent arrangement as soon as possible, this has been countered by a very evident reluctance to relinquish control of an instrument so important to the US economy (Victory, 2002, p. 5).

ICANN and US power: Legitimacy versus hegemony

The previous pages have demonstrated how US politicians have exercised power effectively to shape global Internet governance so that it reflects their interests and values. However, almost immediately following the establishment of ICANN both the organization itself and the US government began to encounter legitimacy challenges to their respective roles in global Internet governance. These are often conflated in literature on Internet governance and although they are related, in terms of the implications for power, they are actually distinct issues.

The legitimacy challenge to the US government stems from the growing awareness that Internet governance has not only a technical function but economic, political and cultural implications. Some states, groups and individuals argue that a global system of such significance should be governed through a multilateral and truly representative body – not one dominated by the US Department of Commerce. This proposal directly threatens US power by proposing to divest the United States of its hegemonic control of Internet governance. Without this, actors with interests not necessarily aligned to those of the United States could be in a position to alter the course of Internet governance so that it no longer privileged the needs and expectations of the commercial sector – thereby working in harmony with politicians' conceptions of power. This more direct threat to US power will be discussed in greater detail later in this chapter.

On the other hand, ICANN's legitimacy challenges are a consequence of multiple factors – primarily to do with its structure and internal governance processes but also due to the general awareness that Internet governance entails important policymaking which goes beyond the purely technical functions initially envisaged. A brief overview of these provides the background to debates about international concerns over the legitimacy of ICANN as a global governance body and how these concerns relate to US power.

How ICANN works – or does not

The previous sections have detailed how a particular conception of US power which linked the Internet to economic growth culminated in the establishment of ICANN. Its unique structure as a private sector policymaking institution also reflects the late 20th-century American belief in private sector ownership of public infrastructure and an anti-regulatory norm which was prevalent in the Internet community. John Palfrey has observed that ICANN is an amalgamation of three distinct institutional models (Palfrey, 2004, pp. 410–73). First, it was established as a private corporation which is run from the top down by a board of directors. At the same time, it is understood to be an open space for the development of bottom-up consensus about policy. Finally, ICANN is regarded as akin to a governmental regulatory body, which should offer representation to affected stakeholder groups in a legislative process for the development of public policies. Palfrey regards ICANN's structure as 'a compromise in the worst sense of the word' (Palfrey, 2004, pp. 425–6). He suggests that the attempt to blend the best parts of these three models has resulted in 'a structure that does not carry the legitimacy or authority or effectiveness of any of its component parts' (Palfrey, 2004, p. 425).

Situated between these divergent approaches, ICANN has been plagued with problems almost from its inception as it has struggled to reconcile the role of a global governance body with the demands of the commercialized aspects of DNS management. The US-led privatization of generic top-level domains (gTLDs) has meant that each top-level domain represents a commercial opportunity as domain names and numbers are then on-sold to individuals or businesses which need them.[1] These sets of domain names are allocated by ICANN to registrars – private firms which manage and sell them. In its first year, in response to a shortage of names and numbers, ICANN administered a kind of 'bidding' system for the selection and allocation of seven new gTLDs. Registrars were invited to submit proposals but there were widespread complaints from unsuccessful applicants about the lack of transparency in the selection criteria, the non-refundable application fees (US$ 50,000) and the lack of a satisfactory appeals process. However, these arrangements continued to be negotiated bilaterally between ICANN and each commercial entity with the contents of the contracts remaining private.

Dissatisfaction with the process of this first allocation of new gTLDs led to a congressional hearing in early 2001 before the House Subcommittee on Telecommunications and the Internet.[2] Entitled *Is ICANN's New Generation for Internet Domain Name Selection Process Thwarting Competition*, the hearing addressed the gTLD allocation specifically as well as the emerging concerns about ICANN governance more broadly.

Politicians at the hearing articulated concerns that ICANN was 'anti-competitive and lacking in fairness, transparency, and accountability' (Dingell, 2006, p. 3). These problems, it was revealed, were in part a consequence of the fact that the ICANN board is appointed rather than elected, the board meetings are closed and the minutes are not published.

Internet governance scholar Milton Mueller has written extensively on these issues and he has detailed the insular way in which ICANN board members are appointed (Mueller, 2009). A Nominating Committee (NomCom) appoints all but a few board members and Mueller notes that the NomCom vets candidates in secret and selects board members on the basis of these private deliberations. In a circular arrangement, some of the Nominating Committee members themselves are appointed by the ICANN board. Despite a number of advisory groups (the 'At Large Advisory Committee', the 'Government Advisory Committee', the 'Supporting Organizations'), the ICANN board is not obliged to adopt any of the recommendations or policy proposals which are put forward by these groups. During the 2001 hearing, Representative Edward Markey expressed serious concern at the lack of transparency in ICANN governance when he suggested that 'events at the Vatican are shrouded in less mystery than how ICANN chooses top-level domains' (Markey, 2001, p. 5).

Problems of accountability

A corollary to a lack of transparency is the difficulty in establishing accountability. Ruth Grant and Robert Keohane define accountability as the implication 'that some actors have the right to hold other actors to a set of standards, to judge whether they have fulfilled their responsibilities in light of these standards, and to impose sanctions if they determine that these responsibilities have not been met' (Grant and Keohane, 2005, p. 29). They further argue that 'if governance above the level of the nation-state is to be legitimate in a democratic era, mechanisms for appropriate accountability need to be institutionalized' (Grant and Keohane, 2005, p. 29). The unique structure of ICANN means that it does not conform to this conception of accountability which normally applies to a private corporation, a public institution or a global governance body.

Mueller has suggested that ICANN uses extensive public participation to generate legitimacy while avoiding accountability – a 'learned behaviour' which he regards as a response to 'the political and organizational tensions inherent in ICANN's DNA' (Mueller, 2009). ICANN holds four major open meetings each year in locations all over the world. These meetings are open to any member of the public who wishes to attend and they provide an opportunity to directly question the ICANN board members on issues of concern in an open forum. While ICANN is at liberty to incorporate any of the input which it receives through these or other channels – or reject all of it – this emphasis on public participation helps to generate a form of legitimacy without account- ability. Public participation in this context, Mueller argues, can 'displace accountability rather than improve it' (Mueller, 2009).

Concerns about accountability feature significantly in hearings into ICANN as expressed by Representative Markey. 'To whom are the ICANN board members accountable, to the Internet community, to the Depart- ment of Commerce? Is the Department of Commerce performing ade- quate oversight? Is it simply an eyewitness to history?' (Markey, 2001, p. 5). Unlike other private sector bodies, ICANN does not have share- holders or members to which it must answer. As pointed out above, its own board is appointed by individuals who themselves are appointed by the ICANN board. Significantly, there is also no competition in the mar- ketplace for ICANN. ICANN has a monopoly on Internet governance. These concerns about ICANN's lack of accountability are a key compo- nent of challenges to its legitimacy. Another important element is its unanticipated and unintended capacity for policymaking.

ICANN's policy agenda

When ICANN was established in 1998, it was on the understanding that it would undertake necessary technical oversight and management of the root – a function which seemed relatively apolitical at that time. However, as the use of the Internet spread both in scope and size, it became increasingly apparent that the distinction between technical decisions about the Internet and politics and policymaking is at best grey and at worst artificial. Mitchell Kapor, the founder of Lotus soft- ware, has stated unambiguously that 'architecture *is* politics' – in other words, the way technological systems like the Internet are constructed and managed (governance) is inherently political (Kapor, 2006). A SCoT approach would argue that it was ever thus, but more significant to this study is the growing realization amongst US politicians of this relation- ship. While (as this chapter argues) there were politically driven ideas about the relationship of US power to the Internet which motivated and guided the process of establishing ICANN, the understanding of broader political implications emerged only over time as the use of and dependence upon the Internet spread.

The political implications of managing the DNS became apparent over the early years of ICANN's existence and were unsettling not only for the private sector or the international community but for US politicians as well. Those politicians involved in ICANN's oversight were soon confronted by a new understanding of the organization as a non-governmental body, setting policy in what is regarded as a critical sphere of US power and governance of a global resource. Edward Markey observed during a 2006 hearing into ICANN governance that 'many have lamented that ICANN appears to set policy when it was simply set up to do rather narrow technical issues' (Markey, 2006, p. 8). The following quote by John Dingell is more explicit:

> Some suggest that ICANN has morphed from a nongovernmental, technical standards-setting organization to a full-fledged policymaking body. If that is true, there is cause for serious concern. ICANN was not given authority to assume that function, and it appears to be accountable to no one, except perhaps God Almighty, for its actions.
>
> (Dingell, 2001, p. 8)

These concerns arose from the realization that what had initially been regarded as a narrow technical function, which the US government directed towards commerce, also had deeply political implications. As well as the gTLDs, the globalization of the Internet led to the establishment of a further two-character country code top-level domain or ccTLD (.au, .uk, .jp). From a technical perspective, these are unremarkable and are uncontentious. However, from a political perspective the names and numbers give rise to concerns about sovereignty and autonomy. Originally drawn from the ISO 3166 list published by the International Organization of Standardization (ISO) which allocates two-character codes to all recognized states, the ccTLDs have to be amended periodically following civil war or newly independent states such as happened after the Bosnian conflict. ICANN, then, is essentially in the position to 'create' a state's own cyberspace by allocating it a ccTLD.

In addition to issues of diplomatic recognition, the exclusive use of the Latin alphabet in gTLDs and ccTLDs has also been the subject of debate amid increasingly widespread calls for the inclusion of alternate scripts such as Arabic and Mandarin.[3] These ccTLDs (and the gTLDs which come under them) are increasingly regarded as the domain of individual states and, as such, a reflection of national identity. Predictably, this has resulted in an expectation that when navigating the

Internet – at least to domestic or local sites – users should be able to do so in their own script and language. At the June 2009 ICANN meeting in Sydney, a Chinese delegate also pointed out that, for a gTLD, three characters is one too many to make sense in Mandarin and even if alternative scripts were adopted, China would have to be allowed to register gTLDs of two characters – a configuration not permitted under the current protocol.[4]

While some US politicians appear resigned to the merging of technical, commercial and political in ICANN, others like Senator Conrad Burns strongly resist it. 'Simply put, ICANN was never meant to be a super national regulatory body' (Burns, 2002, p. 4). Ultimately, regardless of one's position on whether or how ICANN should be spanning the technical/political divide, the same conclusion is reached, that it *does* – and this has global implications.

Despite the fact that the United States is the only state with any direct oversight of ICANN, even US politicians question how much control they have over Internet governance. When Representative Edward Markey asks rhetorically whether the Department of Commerce is providing adequate oversight of ICANN or is 'simply an eyewitness to history' (2001, p. 5), he articulates a concern issued by many of his colleagues. This sense of 'history in the making' is a feature of US political debates about ICANN. In the hearings, there was a general awareness that in the establishment of ICANN, something had been set in motion, possibly without due consideration of future implications. Representative Charles Pickering draws a direct parallel between the establishment of ICANN and the Constitution of the United States. 'Many I believe did not realize that, in essence, by setting up ICANN... [what we were] doing was fundamentally the Constitution of the Internet, just as our Founders set up the decision making process of a representative democracy' (Pickering, 2001, p. 92).

The expected outcome, when ICANN was established in 1998, was (perhaps optimistically) that it would both garner international legitimacy and continue to promote US interests. The previous pages have outlined how ICANN has been confronted by challenges to its legitimacy, both for poor internal governance (particularly a lack of accountability) and because it is now acknowledged that, in addition to technical functions, ICANN is actually in a position to make important policy decisions. It is these policymaking implications which are most unnerving for politicians as they threaten to compromise the established agenda which was put in place by the US hegemonic control over Internet governance.

In some ways, ICANN's legitimacy problems have served to strengthen the case for US oversight as (in the absence of alternate forms of accountability as discussed above) this remains the strongest form of accountability in a relatively unconstrained organization. Certainly, not only are US politicians reluctant to grant ICANN full independence but also many in the commercial sector have raised questions about where they would turn for mediation if the US Department of Commerce no longer exercised oversight. In an unexpected manner, ICANN's failure to achieve international legitimacy generates support for continued US hegemony in Internet governance oversight.

As part of the proposed IANA transition process announced by the NTIA in 2014, the Cross Community Working Group on Enhancing ICANN Accountability (CCWG-Accountability) was established specifically to propose mechanisms and practices that could address the accountability deficit in ICANN. As of May 2015, the CCWG-Accountability had released a draft proposal for public comment but had gone no further.

In addition to these problems of legitimacy which ICANN has encountered, the US government has also faced challenges to the legitimacy of its continued oversight of ICANN. This raises a separate set of issues about power which is not perceived to have any hidden or obvious benefits.

US oversight faces a crisis of legitimacy

One of the primary findings of this case study is that in continuing to exert some level of dominion over Internet governance, US politicians perceive that the United States has had to balance a need for political legitimacy with a desire to retain control. The following section will demonstrate how, as understandings of Internet governance evolved from a dominantly technical concern to become politicized, accusations of US hegemonic control have led to problems of political legitimacy and calls from the international community for greater representation. The ensuing debates have pitted very fundamental beliefs about national interest held by US politicians against the perceived costs and benefits of international cooperation. In these debates, explicit comments on US power have been articulated by committee members in congressional hearings. The hearing transcripts reflect an acknowledgement by committee members that in order to retain control of ICANN, a degree of legitimacy amongst the international community is either necessary or at least desirable. In 2006, Congressman John Dingell argued that 'Our constituents ... need to know that this Nation, because of the way we are managing these things, is not losing the support of the international community, a matter of concern to me' (Dingell, 2006, p. 4).

Given the previously described emphasis on the relationship between US economic power and the Internet, politicians argue that Internet governance must continue to operate under some form of US stewardship for two reasons. First, the failure of ICANN to implement a widely accepted and respected corporate governance structure has undermined its legitimacy and brought into question its readiness to act independently of US government oversight. Second, given that the US government does not regard ICANN as adequately established to be wholly independent of some form of governmental oversight, the alternatives are decidedly unappealing.

However, since 1998, there have been increasing calls from some in the international community for the United States to either make ICANN completely independent or to move Internet governance to a more conventional global body such as the International Telecommunication Union (ITU) of the UN (Meyer, 2009). While the United States has made incremental concessions in response to demands to loosen its grip (to be detailed in the following pages), there has been no support for the notion of moving Internet governance to the UN.

It was initially intended that ICANN would come under some control of the Department of Commerce only initially and once it was fully functioning it would become independent of government oversight. Although an exact time frame was not specified, this transition was anticipated as likely to take place within a few years (Improvement of Technical Management of Internet Names and Addresses: Proposed Rule, pp. 8826–33). More than 15 years later, ICANN continues to be subject to some level of US government control and perhaps, not surprisingly, this has become a source of contention.

In response to ongoing pressures to relinquish control of ICANN over the past decade and a half, the US government neither agreed to move Internet governance to an international body nor did they overtly assert any right to control it. Rather, they adopted an approach of 'historic authority' and took a series of steps to try to shore up their power in this sphere by enhancing their legitimacy. In 2005, the US NTIA issued a set of principles on the DNS. The first principle reads as follows:

Given the Internet's importance to the world's economy, it is essential that the underlying DNS of the Internet remain stable and secure. As such, the United States is committed to taking no action that would have the potential to adversely impact the effective and efficient operation of the DNS and will therefore maintain its historic role in authorizing changes or modifications to the authoritative root zone file.

(Department of Commerce, n.d.)

This principle of 'historic authority' reflected the approach taken to date and served as a framework for future amendments to the US–ICANN relationship.

Move to the UN – or not

Despite the politicization of Internet governance, any calls for the transfer of ICANN or its functions to an international body like the UN have been strongly resisted by US politicians. They repeatedly express that they regard the Internet as far too critical to the US economy and (increasingly) to its security to risk the network's destabilization or indeed the introduction of interests not aligned to their own. Representative Cliff Stearns summed up the status quo approach when he argued in a 2006 hearing that he was 'not interested in making changes that would in any way endanger what has proven to be one of the most powerful tools in history for empowering American commerce and the American consumers' (Shimkus, 2006, p. 9; Stearns, 2006, p. 6).

Proposals to involve the UN in Internet governance elicit quite adamant responses from US politicians involved in ICANN oversight possibly reflecting broader anti-UN sentiment which had gained traction in some US political circles – particularly after the failure of the Bush administration to obtain Security Council approval for the invasion of Iraq and President Bush's subsequent statement that 'we really don't need anybody's permission' to go to war (Bush, 2003c). This general disaffection for the UN was illustrated in another ICANN hearing in 2006. During that week, Venezuelan President Hugo Chavez had likened President George Bush to the devil in a speech in front of the UN General Assembly.[5] Representative John Shimkus referred to this in the ICANN hearing when he remarked that 'with what has gone on at the U.N. the last couple of days, the last thing we would want is any movement in an international community. Could you imagine the farce and the jokes that would create of the World Web and the Domain Names System?' (Shimkus, 2006, p. 9).

Representative Fred Upton summarized in a 2006 hearing: 'Although some have complained about the lack of transparency of ICANN, moving its function to the U.N. is no way to fix the problem. In fact, it will likely make it worse' (Upton, 2006, p. 2). Representative Cliff Stearns argues that 'Heavy-handed government involvement, particularly by supra-national institutions like the United Nations, I think, would spell disaster for a system that is thriving around the world' (Stearns, 2006, p. 5). He explicitly states that he 'will oppose any efforts for a number of reasons to put it under the U.N. jurisdiction' (Stearns, 2006, p. 5).

These debates came to a head in December 2012 during the World Conference on International Telecommunications (WCIT). The WCIT was convened by the UN International Telecommunications Union (ITU) with the intent of reviewing the International Telecommunications Regulations (ITRs), which serve as part of the binding global treaty designed to facilitate international interconnection and interoperability of information and communication services. The ITRs had not been updated since 1988 and the ITU proposed that the text needed 'to be updated to reflect the dramatically different information and communication technology (ICT) landscape of the 21st century'. This was widely promoted by the United States as a bid by the UN to 'takeover' the Internet and the negotiations failed to achieve the consensus needed to change the treaty. Significantly though, 89 countries voted for the changes with only 54 other countries lining up behind the US view.

While US politicians express no support for the transfer of Internet governance to an international body like the UN and while (until 2014) they generally resist relinquishing Department of Commerce oversight, the allegations of illegitimate control over the global DNS have resulted in a number of incremental concessions in an attempt to find a balance between international consensus and continued US power to control the Internet. These concessions have taken the form of periodically renegotiated contracts between the Department of Commerce and ICANN.

Concessions to discontent

Misgivings about ICANN independence based on issues of corporate governance (transparency, process, accountability) coupled with concerns about leaving a power vacuum have contributed to a lack of US political will to move Internet governance to a more independent or international structure. However, there are also complications internal to ICANN's mandate which arise from the US conception of Internet governance as a commercial function which gives pause to US politicians considering the prospect of fully relinquishing control over Internet governance.

The original Memorandum of Understanding (MOU) between ICANN and the Department of Commerce was amended six times between 1998 and 2003.[6] These amendments were intended to address the concerns of the growing community of people who expressed concerns about ICANN – either because they wanted ICANN to be more independent of the United States or (conversely) because they felt it required additional oversight due to its own internal flaws. In 2006, the MOU was replaced with a 'Joint Project Agreement' (JPA)[7] which was widely heralded as a step towards greater independence from the US government though the Internet Governance Project (IGP) – an independent group of analysts – called it a 'cosmetic response' to public feedback about ICANN's lack of transparency, representation and accountability (Mueller, 2006). The IGP's Milton Mueller wrote that the transition from the MOU to the JPA was in fact 'old wine in new bottles' since ICANN still received policy guidance from the Department of Commerce and still reported to it (Mueller, 2006). The JPA lasted for three years and, in 2009, it was replaced by yet another agreement – the Affirmation of Commitments (AOC) in September 2009 (Beckstrom, 2009).

As with the end of the MOU, the transition of the JPA to the AOC was widely reported as ICANN 'gaining its independence' – including by ICANN itself which referred to the transition as a 'dramatic step' towards full management of the DNS (ICANN, 2006). However, while the new agreement introduced a broader level of review and oversight, the US government had not relinquished control of Internet governance. ICANN internal reporting was consequently to be submitted to a review board (the selection of board members remains contentious) in addition to the Department of Commerce (Beckstrom, 2009).

The most recent chapter of this ongoing process was initiated in the wake of the Snowden revelations about the National Security Agency's collection and use of data. ICANN's director Fadi Chehade worked with the Brazilian President Dilma Rousseff to convene a global meeting (called NetMundial) to discuss the future of global Internet governance. Hosted in Sao Paulo, Brazil, in April 2014, the meeting became a focal point for these simmering tensions and debates about the US role in global Internet governance. One month before the meeting took place, the NTIA announced that they intended to transition the IANA contract to the 'multi-stakeholder' community, thereby ending the contract between ICANN and the Department of Commerce. The transition was anticipated to take place when the existing contract ran its term at the end of September 2015, but at time of writing, the outcome remains uncertain.

Conclusion

The Clinton–Gore administration articulated a particular view of the role they expected the Internet to play in enhancing US power. They regarded it as an engine for economic growth which would ensure continued dominance in the international system. Langdon Winner (a prominent philosophy of technology theorist) commented on this narrow focus in a journal article in 1993. He likened the Clinton administration's vision of the future of the 'National Information Infrastructure' to a 'national money pump' into which technology is poured at one end, mixed with some additional ingredients like education of the work force and incentives for business and out the other end comes economic growth (and through this, economic power). Winner argued that a more appropriate metaphor would be one of fabric – the fabric of society into which we weave additional threads of infrastructure. As these threads are introduced, the fabric is changed and this reweaving results in 'a reshaping of some of the roles, rules, relationships, and institutions that make up our ways of living together' (Winner, 1993, p. B1).

This metaphor of interwoven threads allows for an enhanced understanding of change which has been so important in this case study. Donald Mackenzie reminds us that the adoption of technology can also change it. Those who use it, improve, exploit, adapt and shape technology (MacKenzie, 1996, p. 5). In this process, priorities about how technology should develop, in what ways and to serve which purposes as well as the means by which success is measured, may change.

The first section of this chapter explained how a new conception of US power – one premised upon economic strength rather than simply military dominance – formed a framework for a new prioritization of Internet technology. In this new conception, the Internet was regarded by a key set of US politicians (initially the Atari Democrats and later the broader Clinton–Gore administration) as a potential source of economic growth which, if managed correctly, would contribute considerably to US power. These politicians articulated a clear set of guidelines including a strong emphasis on stability of the network and private sector competition for the distribution of domain names and numbers. These norms were carried through successive policy documents and expressed repeatedly in speeches detailing this approach. Ultimately, those norms resulted in the issue of Internet governance being placed under the purview of the Department of Commerce – a step which would define the parameters of future debate.

By the mid- to late 1990s, Internet governance was becoming understood as a 'problem' in that it was potentially preventing the Internet from performing in the way these politicians envisaged it should – that is, in support of US economic power. Politicians through this period regarded the growing inadequacies of existing Internet governance structures as an impediment to the commercial growth they so strongly believed would eventuate given the right conditions. A lack of commercial confidence in the process for dealing with copyright issues as well as a shortage of available names and numbers was believed to be stifling economic growth in related industries. For these politicians, setting up a new structure which could deal with growth and continue to shape the Internet in their vision without raising concerns about US hegemonic control of the network was the policy goal. This was institutionalized in the establishment of ICANN.

This chapter then deals with the ongoing operation of ICANN during which the issues which preoccupy politicians have to do with the nature of ICANN's operations and its capacity to undermine US legitimacy through unpopular governance – thus potentially leading to a further loss of control for the US government. US politicians believed that retaining control of the Internet through ICANN was desirable partly because of their growing understanding of its impact on the national interest but also because they believed that American norms and values formed the foundation of the Internet's success and that they are also the key to its future. Transparency, free markets, freedom of individuals, access to information and due process are repeatedly referred to as integral to these politicians' vision of the Internet. They enact policies which they believe will promote these elements and this becomes an example of the way that technology can be understood as an *expression* of norms and values.

Finally, this study of Internet governance and ICANN highlights persistent concerns about the balance between the need or desire for international legitimacy and the cost in terms of the national interest. America's continued challenge of exercising its power in a state of primacy or hegemony is directly reflected in the problem of ICANN. International cooperation in the management of ICANN is regarded by US politicians as a trade-off against the national interest and as the national interest is increasingly linked to the smooth functioning of the Internet, the effective exercise of American power to retain control of it becomes a more and more significant issue.

In an effort to understand how conceptions of US power have influenced the development of Internet technology, the issue of Internet governance clearly demonstrates that the Clinton–Gore administration's view of US power as linked to economic growth impacted on Internet technology in a number of direct ways. It established the commercial sector as the relevant social group by placing Internet governance under the purview of the Department of Commerce. It led to the establishment of a unique organization which was neither a public regulator nor a wholly independent private organization. While this organization faltered in meeting political expectations by eliciting allegations of illegitimacy, the US government had become convinced not only of the economic importance of the Internet but of its own control over the DNS as an additional source of power. Given this new conception of the relationship between US power and Internet governance, politicians no longer wished to relinquish control of ICANN and embarked upon a number of amendments to the agreement between ICANN and the Department of Commerce which sought to find a balance between calls for its independence and the US political desire for control – project that continues today through the negotiations to transition the IANA contract.

The implications of these factors for understanding the relationship between new technology and power in IR are threefold. The first implication is that a broad approach to the definition of power is most useful here. In this case study, there are two clear articulations of power which US politicians refer to: economic power and social power in the context of hegemony and legitimacy. The second implication is that it is necessary to examine closely what objectives states have for technology and how exactly they envisage it relating to their power. States make certain choices about technology which emerge from a set of expectations and priorities which can be formulated externally to that technology. Without understanding how states expect technology to relate to their power, technological development can appear to take on a life of its own forcing states to constantly adapt. The third implication is that technology like the Internet which is fundamentally about relationships between computers, routers and the people who operate them has a social element which emphasizes social aspects of power. Primacy may be just as desirable as it is in the context of military capability but legitimacy is an important force.

6
Network Neutrality

Network neutrality refers to the principle of an agnostic network, that is, one which does not discriminate against the content which travels across it or the applications or hardware which engage with and connect to it. The understanding that the network itself is 'dumb' and the packets of data which travel across it will not be interrogated during transmission is considered by many to be fundamental to the original architectural conception of the Internet and integral to privacy, equality of access and freedom of information.[1] In the early years of the commercialized Internet, there had been minimal interference in the order in which data packets were delivered but a number of compelling developments emerged to challenge this 'hands off' practice. These developments prompted political debates about how the Internet should function, how the power to control information should be distributed and the implications of these decisions for US power.

In common with the previous two case studies, network neutrality is regarded by politicians as having implications for both material and social factors of US power. Network neutrality is a politically divisive issue but politicians from both sides of this debate agree on some key points. They all regard network neutrality as having implications for how the Internet can best continue to enhance US economic power although they differ fundamentally on which policies are most likely to achieve this. Those politicians in favour of network neutrality argue that the huge economic benefits delivered through Internet growth in the past were largely a *consequence* of the principles of network neutrality. These principles, they argue, promote material power through innovation which stimulates economic growth and social power by establishing the United States as 'leaders' in Internet technology and by promoting 'freedom' which they regard as a norm that underpins

US power more broadly. This is a view which regards US power as emerging from a set of norms, values and principles much in the way discussed in the social power conception in Chapter 4.

Those politicians opposed to network neutrality believe that recent changes to Internet technology and to the way we use the technology place greater demands on the network that can only be effectively managed if certain principles of network neutrality are relaxed or dispensed with. These politicians fear that network neutrality will prove an *impediment* to future economic growth by limiting fiscal incentives for further private sector investment in the Internet infrastructure which is already regarded as steadily declining in international competitiveness.

Politicians on both sides of this debate regard network neutrality as a critical issue which, if mismanaged, threatens to undermine US material power through lost economic opportunity but also due to social power factors like leadership in much the same way the 'Sputnik crisis' did.

The findings of this case study are unique in a number of ways from the first two case studies. In the previous two case studies, politicians have engaged with multiple conceptualizations of power and the one which has been most influential on Internet technology has been the conceptualization associated with a social constructivist approach to technology. In the context of cyber security, this was a social conception of power which privileged norms and values of human rights and civil liberties. In the Internet governance case, a material conception of power was most influential, and again it was associated with a social constructivist approach to technology. The research for this case also revealed multiple conceptualizations of power although until quite recently, none of them could be regarded as significantly shaping or influencing this aspect of Internet technology. As discussed in Chapter 3, one key decision taken by the Federal Communications Commission (FCC) in 2002 fundamentally reshaped the network neutrality landscape. This was overturned in February 2015, but up until then politicians opposed to network neutrality needed only to maintain the status quo while those politicians in favour of network neutrality had been unable or unwilling to claim the necessary authority to shape the Internet in this way.

This is a point of continuity which runs through all the case studies. The empirical research has revealed that conceptions of power are influential in shaping technology only when associated with a social constructivist approach to technology. None of the conceptions of power in the network neutrality case were associated with a social constructivist approach to technology and in none of them did politicians demonstrate a clear sense of authority. Rather, they drew on external sources of authority.

In seeking to understand why this case study produced a unique finding (conceptions of power were not found to influence the technology), we may consider three distinctions between this case study and the previous two.

First, this case deals with issues outside the parameters of conventional debates about state power. Security and governance are both issues which are clearly linked to power in international relations (IR) literature and in political discourse. Politicians have a framework for understanding security threats to the state and how those threats interact with US power. In Chapter 4, these included economic power, the ability to prevail in global conflict and geopolitics. Governance of the Internet broke more new ground in that it dealt with an organization without precedent. The Internet Corporation for Assigned Names and Numbers (ICANN) was set up in a completely unique manner to existing (or subsequent) governance bodies. It was established to govern a global technical function which, as it turns out, has deeply political implications. Still, principles of governance are obviously familiar territory for politicians and have provided a framework for conceptualizing power in this case study. Certainly, interpreting these issues of security and governance in the context of Internet technology has been a significant challenge, but the debates begin from a familiar framework.

Network neutrality, in contrast, is a case that is driven by telecommunications regulation. It is not an issue that politicians have conventionally identified as relating to state power. As with the other cases, technology has generated problems for US power but in this case, those problems do not fit within an existing framework for discussing power. It would seem that the further we move from conventional power frameworks, the more difficult it becomes to clearly articulate and pursue a conception of power through decisions about technology.

Without a familiar power framework within which to interpret the implications of Internet technology for US power, anti-network neutrality politicians revert to a status quo position. That is, if they are unsure of the future, rather than try to shape it, they opt to 'stay out of the way' and let market forces take over to shape the technology. In an instrumental view, they believe that this ultimately results in the 'best' path for Internet technology as long as it is left alone to evolve 'naturally'.

Pro network neutrality politicians take a different view. In a determinist approach, they regard the Internet as possessing a set of norms and values which have led to the growth in US economic power and they believe that unless those norms and values are protected, the United States will experience a decline in power. This is essentially the same argument as their political opponents put forward. In this view, the Internet has a path which it is destined to follow. Pro-network neutrality and anti-network neutrality politicians differ only on whether their responsibility is to avoid getting in the way or to make sure that the technology does adhere to this path.

The second way in which this case study is distinct from the first two is that network neutrality has been a divisive debate in US politics. In both the cyber security case and the Internet governance case, the competing conceptions of power were broadly shared. Politicians regarded both conceptions as important but they privileged one over the other or tried to balance the two. With regard to network neutrality, there exist sharp political divisions which result in pro-network neutrality and anti-network neutrality camps. Part of the analysis of this case study entails working through the similarities and differences of these two groups with regard to their conceptions of US power and how it relates to network neutrality.

The third distinct feature of network neutrality as a case study is a relatively new issue. Both cyber security and Internet governance have been regarded as closely related to US power since the mid-1990s. They date back to the commercialization of the Internet and consequently, we have access to almost two decades of empirical material to study. In fact, although these debates have evolved over time, clear conceptions of power were articulated by politicians right from the beginning in the context of issues raised in the first two case studies. In contrast, the first congressional hearing into network neutrality was not held until 2006. The combination of the issues falling outside the parameters of an established framework for discussing power, the divisive nature of the debates and the short timeframe seem to contribute to what Marianne Franklin refers to as attempts to 'reconcile competing visions of internet futures with contested versions of the internet's brief past' (Franklin, 2010, p. 80). Perhaps not all that surprisingly, network neutrality has not been an easy issue either for politicians or scholars.

Despite the fact that the case study does not demonstrate the influence of conceptions of power on technology, it produces some useful findings about the relationship between power and Internet technology in this context. First, we can observe how politicians draw on alternative sources of authority in order to try and support their agenda. Instead of drawing on their own sense of authority to shape the Internet into what they believe will best promote US power, politicians on both sides of this debate defer to external sources of authority. Pro-network neutrality politicians draw on sources of legitimacy which emanate from the technology itself – either based on the views of Internet pioneers like Vinton Cerf and Tim Berners Lee or grounded in the architecture of the Internet which they argue was built upon principles of net neutrality and therefore prescribes certain norms and values such as equity, freedom of access and a non-hierarchical structure. This approach has elements of technological determinism in it as it regards technology both as 'path determined' and also as possessing some values of its own.

Those politicians opposed to network neutrality draw on 'market forces' as their source of authority. Through a liberal understanding of limited government, they claim that they have no mandate to interfere with the market forces until such time as it is proven to fail. Their view of technology leans towards instrumentalism which regards technology as value neutral and best driven by commercial imperatives for innovation.

The second finding is that innovation emerges here as an integral element of US power in much the same manner as it was perceived in the Sputnik crisis. That is, innovation is regarded not only as the means to develop advanced technology which will be translated into a power advantage (material power), but it is deeply understood as reflecting US prestige and leadership (social power).

The third important finding is that while politicians on both sides of the network neutrality debate regard protecting 'freedom' on the Internet as essential to promoting US power, they differ significantly in how they interpret 'freedom'. While 'Internet freedom' has been demonstrated to be a driving concept in the context of cyber security policy, network neutrality debates reveal conflict and contention in how politicians regard freedom as it relates to US power. As Senator Barbara Boxer astutely observed in a 2006 hearing, 'freedom is an issue here [but] it depends on how you look at what freedom is' (Boxer, 2006, p. 44). Pro-network neutrality politicians regard it as 'freedom of access', 'freedom of information' and 'freedom to innovate' and they believe that these freedoms best promote US power – economically and socially. Anti-network neutrality politicians believe that the most essential freedom is freedom from government interference – that it has been a source of US power in the past and must continue to be protected in the information age.

Background to network neutrality

Technical brief

There are a number of technical issues that are necessary to understand in order to engage with debates about network neutrality. The following explanation of 'bandwidth', 'streaming media', 'voice over Internet protocol (VoIP)' and 'network management' will be useful to the non-technical reader.

Bandwidth

In the context of the Internet, bandwidth refers to the amount of information which can be transmitted over a connection. This impacts on how quickly an Internet connection works. A useful analogy is water running through a hose. If the bandwidth is low (or the hose narrow), the information has to trickle through more slowly than if it were coming through a fast or 'broadband' connection. While waiting for information to download on the Internet was acceptable in the early years, there is an expectation now that we will be able to access information as quickly as if it were stored on our computer's hard disk. Broadband speed is one of the key markers of Internet functionality that is used to rate services and the demand for faster and faster connections has been a consistent market driver in Internet technology.[2]

Streaming media

One of the most significant recent technological developments which moved network neutrality into the spotlight was the advent of streaming media necessary for viewing video files and playing live, multi-user video games. Previously, one might download a video file to the hard disk of a computer and then play it from there. In this situation, the data is local and the computer need only reference its own hard disk in order to keep the video flowing. However, when the video file is actually being played across the Internet (as it is with YouTube), it is referred to as 'streaming media' and this introduces a special set of problems. As explained in the previous chapter, ordinary data travelling across the Internet is broken down into small 'packets', moved independently through the fastest possible route and then reassembled upon arrival at the destination address. With simple data like text files, delays have less impact because although transmission may be slowed during peak traffic periods, documents eventually arrive fully assembled. Streaming media relies upon an uninterrupted flow because it is being transmitted and viewed live in real time. With streaming media, delays in packet delivery can result in the video or audio being disrupted – sometimes to the point of becoming unintelligible. Streaming media has substantially increased demands on bandwidth. Increasingly, Internet users expect streaming media to operate smoothly over their Internet connection and this places demands on commercial network operators to ensure that it does.

Voice over Internet protocol

One application of streaming media which is of particular relevance to this study is that of VoIP.[3] This is the protocol which allows for telephone calls to be made over the Internet through applications like Skype. VoIP is streaming media because the conversation takes place live (as with any phone call) and if there is not an adequate bandwidth, the voice call breaks up and can become unintelligible. This particular application will feature significantly in this chapter because it potentially undermines the conventional business model of some telecommunications corporations which own Internet infrastructure in the United States. These firms argue that without the revenue generated by phone calls, their profits are not adequate to build out the necessary infrastructure. In the United States, where the government relies on the private sector to provide this, these problems have implications for state infrastructure.

Network management

Network management is an outcome of the previous three technical factors. Advances in streaming media including VoIP have placed greater demands on bandwidth. Consumer expectations of streaming media working properly (fluidly and without interruption) have led to an increase in network management practices in order to enhance the 'quality of service' (QoS). This involves prioritizing certain data packets over others so that packets associated with streaming media arrive promptly at their destination rather than in a jerky, disrupted fashion. With no network management, streaming media may work perfectly – particularly if other demands on the network are low at that time. However, during peak periods, streaming media may not perform well without some network management which ensures the packets arrive sequentially and consecutively. This practice of network management is one of the key areas of contention in network neutrality debates. Some object to any prioritization of data packets at all and regard packet discrimination is an antithesis to the open and agnostic nature of the Internet.[4] Others regard it as increasingly necessary arguing that there has always been the technical capacity for prioritizing packets and network management is increasingly necessary to accommodate the uptake of streaming media.

Changes to the 'business' of the Internet

In the early years of the commercial Internet, there were two broad revenue streams: one was associated with advertising existing businesses and the other was related to building and leasing the additional infrastructure which had become necessary. With regard to the infrastructure, telecommunications firms and cable operators initially offered Internet access over their existing infrastructure. As consumer demands grew both quantitatively and qualitatively for Internet connections, so did the telecommunications sector's plans for additional infrastructure including faster methods of delivery such as wireless and digital subscriber lines (DSL).[5] In this business model, the network operators (telecommunications firms and cable operators) invested in the necessary infrastructure and then leased it out to individuals, government and commercial operators. Each user paid for their own access and use in the same manner as they paid for other utilities like electricity or telephone calls. If they exceeded their stipulated data limit, they may be charged an additional 'download' fee but the commercial exchange was between the network operators and those wishing to connect to the Internet. Whether those customers were connecting to develop their own commercial website or whether they were connecting in order to access websites posted by others was immaterial. It was the access to the Internet which one paid for and there were no costs associated with the number of visitors to one's website.

The second broad revenue stream associated with the early commercial years of the Internet was the means of advertising existing businesses. At this time, online business activity was regarded merely as an adjunct or supplement to an existing commercial enterprise. Referred to as 'Web 1.0' or the 'brochure' phase, websites in this period were used as an alternative means of providing a point of contact, offering an explanation of products and/or services offered, and later, with the advent of e-commerce, an opportunity to remotely purchase those products and services. The Internet in this incarnation was equated to other advertising platforms like television, print media and radio.

In the mid- to late 1990s, it became evident that there was money to be made through the provision of stand-alone services offered over the Internet – wholly unrelated to existing, physical businesses. Broadly referred to as 'Web 2.0', this was a time during which search engines like

Google and Yahoo as well as the online auction service eBay demonstrated that websites could be more than just supplements for conventional businesses. They were capable of generating huge commercial returns in and of themselves. Subsequently, the commercial opportunities of the Internet which had previously been perceived of as limited to existing business on the one hand and new demands for infrastructure (cable, DSL, broadband) and associated services on the other – expanded to include a third group – service and content providers. Indeed, the 'dot-com' era was characterized by tiny start-up companies (often the product of one or two bright young minds) returning huge profits with comparatively little investment and minimal physical overheads.[6] It was these extraordinary profits which reinforced existing political views that the Internet was integrally linked to US power through its impact on the economy.

Chapter 5 demonstrated the repercussions of this business shift on the Internet protocol names and numbers which very abruptly acquired substantial commercial worth where none had previously existed. In the context of network neutrality, this shift had a similarly disruptive influence. In the wake of the dot-com boom, network operators became increasingly dissatisfied with supplying the means of transmission for content and service providers without sharing in the considerable profits the service providers were making. The commercial sphere of infrastructure provision and network operations was far less profitable in comparison. It became apparent that it would be fiscally advantageous for network operators if there were a financial relationship between infrastructure and content. Increasingly, these firms began to diversify their operations to include content provision.[7]

This in itself was not problematic but there were two concerns which arose from this development of the business model for network operators. First, they soon proposed a new financial arrangement which they regarded as more equitably distributing the huge profits generated by Web 2.0 Internet activity. Network operators wanted to be able to charge the owners of websites – specifically Internet service and content providers – a fee for each user who accessed their site or used their services. Under this model, the individual user would pay for their own access to the Internet as was already the case, but in addition companies like Google, MSN, Facebook and YouTube would also have to pay a fee for each individual who accessed their websites.

In 2005, CEO of AT&T Ed Whitacre gave an interview to *Business Week* in which he explicitly addressed this stating that 'what they [Internet businesses including Google, MSN and Vonage] would like to do is use my pipes free, but I ain't going to let them do that because we have spent this capital and we have to have a return on it' (O'Connell, 2005). In a somewhat more measured approach, Verizon CEO Ivan Seidenberg said in an interview the following year that 'We have to make sure that they [service providers] don't sit on our network and chew up bandwidth... We need to pay for the pipe' (Kapustka, 2006).

This proposal concerns those in favour of network neutrality because it sets up the 'two-lane highway' where those who can pay have access to the fast lane and others are relegated to the slow lane. Proponents of network neutrality believe that giving network operators such power (particularly in a semi-monopolistic business environment like the United States) could lead to anti-competitive behaviour whereby small, innovative companies which have previously used the net as a means of accessing the marketplace and driving development could be shut out due to excessive fees imposed upon their traffic. If, for example, Verizon were to charge Google an 'access fee', they would certainly pay it. However, they may not have been in a position to pay it when they first started and other new start-ups may be prevented from reaching a customer base by prohibitive fees. The next 'Google' may never reach the marketplace. This failure to nurture innovation which has been regarded as so important for economic power as well as leadership and prestige is very worrying for those politicians who take a pro network neutrality view.

The second reason why proponents of network neutrality are concerned by moves by network operators to integrate content provision is because they anticipate that this will lead to the network operators discriminating against competing content. In a market with plenty of choice for consumers, this would be of less concern, but in many sectors of the US market, Internet connectivity is dominated by a small number of firms. Those firms, if they were able to discriminate against content, would have the power to control what information is available on the Internet to their subscribers. One of the key ways in which network operators can and have done this is through network management. They have argued that in order to keep their network running well, they have had to demote some information in order to privilege other information.

This is obviously a concern for both consumers and the commercial sector trying to reach them over the Internet. However, it has additional political implications because of the way in which it challenges norms and values which politicians associate with US power – particularly freedom.

Network neutrality comes to Congress

As discussed in more detail in Chapter 3, a major revision to US telecommunications law took place in 1996 when Congress passed changes to the *1934 Communications Act*. This update to the legislation was intended to facilitate competition in local phone services in the wake of the historic break-up of the AT&T telephone monopoly (Crandall, 2005). Following this, the FCC took the important step of relegating Internet communications from Title II of the Communications Act which governs common carriage telephone communications to the less stringent Title I regulations which govern interstate information services.[8] This step essentially removed a layer of regulation from the telecommunications firms which own and operate networks in the United States and a series of conflicts arose from this action.

Madison River

In early 2005, VoIP provider Vonage Holdings accused network operator Madison River Communications of 'port-blocking' VoIP traffic (like Skype) through its Internet service provider (ISP). Essentially, Madison River was using its ability to control traffic over its infrastructure to prevent the transmission of data associated with VoIP calls made through Vonage's service. This was regarded as anti-competitive given that Madison River's core business at the time was the provision of fixed line voice services as a common carrier (conventional telephone lines) – a service in competition with, and considerably threatened by, new VoIP services which allow long-distance phone calls to be made free or at negligible cost. As Lawrence Lessig (2005) pointed out in his analysis of this case, VoIP 'not only explodes demand for broadband but effectively renders obsolete its major competitor, plain old telephone service'.

This was exactly the kind of behaviour which had been foreshadowed by those like Michael Copps who were opposed to the FCC Title I ruling in 2002. The FCC fined Madison River although there were some residual questions about its legal authority to do so (Goldstein, 2005).[9] Madison River paid the fine and the case was widely reported as a tentative win for net neutrality while, at the same time, serving to highlight the very real possibilities for network operators to be tempted to 'manage' Internet traffic in a way which privileged their own interests (Kapustka, 2005; Lawson, 2005; McCullagh, 2005).

Within months of the Madison River complaint being resolved, the FCC issued a policy statement which contained the following four principles of 'Internet freedom' in order to 'encourage broadband deployment and preserve and promote the open and interconnected nature of the public Internet':

- Consumers are entitled to access the lawful Internet content of their choice.
- Consumers are entitled to run applications and use services of their choice, subject to the needs of law enforcement.
- Consumers are entitled to connect their choice of legal devices that do not harm the network.
- Consumers are entitled to competition among network providers, application and service providers and content providers (FCC, 2005b).

The final paragraph of this policy statement asserted that the FCC would incorporate these principles into its future policies. However, this was footnoted with a line which read 'The principles we adopt are subject to reasonable network management' (FCC, 2005b). This caveat would prove instrumental in the second very public challenge to the FCC's authority.

Comcast

In 2007, complaints began to emerge about network operator Comcast Corp selectively blocking BitTorrent traffic – a peer-to-peer (P2P) file-sharing application. P2P applications like BitTorrent are used for exchanging large files – often video. As video files consume huge amounts of bandwidth relative to ordinary data files, heavy P2P traffic can impact negatively on the network's performance. While it is certainly used legitimately, BitTorrent is also a tool of choice for those seeking to download TV shows and movies illegally. This sometimes emerges in debates about this case and can impact on perceptions about the importance of the Comcast case, as illegal behaviour of BitTorrent users is conflated with the issue of selectively blocking traffic.

BitTorrent raises the issue of QoS discussed earlier in this chapter. QoS was increasingly becoming a consideration for network operators seeking to provide consistently fast service in the face of the huge growth of data flowing through the network. In order to achieve a standard of QoS, network operators argued that they needed the flexibility to undertake some 'management' of the data. However, just as Madison River was a telephone service provider found to be blocking competitive VoIP services, Comcast was a cable television provider blocking the download of video files. Consequently, allegations of anti-competitive behaviour arose again in this case.

After receiving a filed complaint, the FCC launched an investigation and found Comcast's practices exceeded what could reasonably be viewed as 'necessary network management' (FCC, 2008). Comcast was not fined, but the FCC ordered them to cease blocking and to publicly reveal their network management strategies. Comcast denied any wrongdoing – maintaining that their network management practices were both legal and necessary. More significantly though, they challenged the FCC's authority to enforce the four Internet principles without them being linked to a statute. The case went to the US Court of Appeals and in April 2010 the court found in favour of Comcast, ruling that the FCC lacked the authority to force ISPs to keep their networks open to all forms of content (Eggerton, 2009; Kang, 2010).

Although this appeared at the time to be a blow to net neutrality, it highlighted the vulnerability of the US Internet ecosystem that resulted from the FCC Title I relegation in 2002. After a sustained campaign by civil society groups like 'Save the Internet', the FCC overturned the decision and, in 2015, relegated Internet services back to Title II of the *Communications Act,* thereby reinstating their regulatory powers over the sector. By this stage, there was some congressional unanimity over the term 'net neutrality' (The Uncertain Future of the Internet, 2015). It had become politically unfashionable to argue against it after nearly 4 million Americans had filed comments on the FCC's public comment page (Obama, 2015). The division now was over the best way to ensure consumer rights and the future of US Internet infrastructure but apart from this discursive shift, the debates remained unchanged.

Network neutrality, US power and deferred authority

An examination of how politicians construct their authority to act completes the analysis of these two competing conceptions of how US power relates to network neutrality and how these two groups of politicians have sought to shape that technology. In the previous two case studies the research revealed politicians' perceptions about their authority to shape and influence Internet technology as closely associated with their philosophical approach to technology. In Chapter 4, it was found that while politicians expressed very serious concerns about how cyber insecurity impacts on US material power, this conception of power is associated with a determinist/instrumental approach to technology which does not promote a sense of responsibility or authority for these politicians to act. Rather, the social conception of power which emphasized the importance of norms and values was associated with a social constructivist approach to technology and it was the combination of these two views which has most influenced the development of cyber security technology. In the case of Internet governance, politicians expressed the belief that the government had a role to play in shaping this aspect of Internet technology so as to promote US economic power and this view was accompanied by a social constructivist approach to technology – again, resulting in a sense of authority which drove debates and ultimately influenced Internet governance very significantly.

In this case study, although politicians continue to express the belief that the Internet is essential to US power through both material (innovation-driven economic growth) and social factors (global leadership credentials), they do not express a sense of legitimacy to make decisions which might shape Internet technology. Instead, relevant policy approaches are mediated through alternative and external sources of legitimacy. Pro network neutrality politicians draw upon the technology itself as a source of authority. They refer to both the architecture of the Internet and the key engineers who devised it as their source of authority. This approach is informed by technological determinism which regards technology as imbued with a set of values – in the case of network neutrality these are understood to include freedom, equality and transparency. It is also an approach which has been found in the past two case studies to be associated with a diminished sense of authority and responsibility – a finding which is also upheld in this case study.

The anti-network neutrality politicians refer directly to market forces as their source of legitimacy. They make a normative argument that government should not take a role in shaping technology unless it is demonstrated that the market is unable to perform that function. This approach is a blend of liberal ideas of limited government and an instrumental approach to technology. Instrumentalism is an approach which regards technology as value neutral and driven by commercial innovation. It also emphasizes the capacity of technology to solve any problems it creates which anti-network neutrality politicians draw on as the solution to any potential problems which might emerge from the power to control information being located in network providers. An instrumental approach to technology is also associated with a diminished sense of authority and responsibility but anti-network neutrality politicians need only maintain the status quo – a position which does not demand the same active engagement which the pro network neutrality position does.

The following section outlines how politicians conceptualize network neutrality as an issue for US power and the ways in which they defer authority on both sides of this debate.

Material power: Innovation and the state of the net

When politicians engage with a material conception of power in the context of network neutrality, there are two key issues which dominate the debates. The first is the degrading state of US information infrastructure which lags behind many other countries and has failed to improve over the past decade. The poor state of the broadband performance is regarded as a problem for sustaining US economic competitiveness and economic growth – regarded as important factors in US economic power. There is an assumption in the United States that investment in this infrastructure must come from the private sector and the network owners use this expectation to apply pressure to politicians to oppose network neutrality. Poor broadband performance also has some important implications for social power which will be taken up in the next section.

The second issue which features in material power conceptions in the context of network neutrality is *innovation*. Innovation is closely associated with US material power in this case study both as a source of power and as a means through which to generate power. Innovation also intersects with a social conception of power which, again, will be taken up below. This, of course, links back to the post-Sputnik insecurity about the United States as a global innovator.

The state of the Internet in the United States

There are a range of measures used to determine the state of a country's Internet 'health' (Benkler, 2010).[10] Although there is some contention about the methodology and findings of studies which attempt this analysis, overall in terms of speed, penetration and price, US Internet services have been rated significantly below the top of the scale for some time now.

An independent report published in February 2010 that compared broadband in half of the Organisation for Economic Co-operation and Development (OECD) countries described the United States as 'a middle-of-the-pack performer on most first generation broadband measures, but a weak performer on prices for high and next-generation speeds'

(Benkler, 2010, p. 12). In 2015, using data collected by the UN International Telecommunications Union, the Internet Society placed the United States 21st in terms of broadband download speed, 18th globally in terms of Internet penetration and 12th for affordability (Internet Society, 2015).

Anxiety about the United States falling behind other states in broadband measures is a key feature of network neutrality debates. The revelation of poor rankings led to the conclusion in a Senate report that 'although the U.S. Department of Defense Advanced Research Projects Agency developed the Internet and provided the Nation with a platform for leading the world in Internet technology, the next generation of Internet applications may not be developed here without the right policies' (Committee on Commerce, Science, and Transportation, 2007, p. 2). It goes on to say that nations with more substantial broadband infrastructures 'may be home to the next wave of digital research and development because they could be better positioned to reap the economic benefits of the broadband era' (Committee on Commerce, Science, and Transportation, 2007, p. 2).

Internet infrastructure is not intrinsically linked to network neutrality but this becomes a problem for the United States because its infrastructure is privately owned and operated. For states that invest public funds in the infrastructure, network neutrality debates deal with separate issues. As explained in Chapter 3, the privatization of the Internet was politically considered necessary in the United States in order to allow for commercial activity. It was regarded as inappropriate for the private sector to profit from a taxpayer-funded network. At this time, the Internet was regarded by politicians as specifically a mechanism for economic growth. However, by the time network neutrality emerged as a problem for US power, the Internet had become a part of the critical infrastructure of the state. In some states, this transition has led to an expectation that the government will contribute funds towards improving the information infrastructure. The Internet is now regarded as integral to so many aspects of cultural, educational, commercial and political life of the state that expectations of the private sector funding necessary improvements to the infrastructure are waning and public money is used instead. However, in the United States this has not been the case and there remains an assumption that telecommunications infrastructure should be built, owned and operated by the private sector and this impacts on global competitiveness.

This contrasts with the previous two decades when US politicians were prepared to publicly fund the development of Internet technology but in the context of network neutrality this is never seriously discussed or debated. In several hearings, reference is made to states which have injected public funds into their Internet infrastructure and which now exceed the United States in Internet metric ratings. At a 2006 hearing into network neutrality, Vinton Cerf (one of the scientists credited with inventing the Internet) testified that 'promoting an open and accessible Internet is critical ... to our Nation's competitiveness – in places like Japan, Korea, Singapore, and the United Kingdom, higher-bandwidth and neutral broadband platforms are unleashing waves of innovation that threaten to leave the U.S. further and further behind' (Cerf, 2006, p. 9). This is most often met with the response that although that approach has been successful in other states, it is not appropriate for the United States. Senator John Ensign argues that although 'many other countries are taking a different approach than the United States; we're more of a free-market country. And I think that we should be that way' (Ensign, 2006, p. 4).

In this political context where politicians fear the United States is losing its competitive edge and thereby jeopardizing its power, expectations of the private sector providing critical infrastructure are high and the debate is focused on what sort of fiscal incentives are necessary or warranted in order to promote investment. The telecommunications sector argues vigorously against network neutrality, charging that if legislated it will deter further investment in an already substandard US infrastructure. Faced with such poor performance internationally, US politicians have been forced to give real weight to these arguments. In a 2006 hearing, Senator John Ensign acknowledges that 'you do deserve a return on your investment, is the bottom line, if you're going to build out these networks. Otherwise, if we can't give them a return on their investment, Wall Street is not going to loan them the money to do this' (Ensign, 2006, p. 5). As with the public/private partnership in Chapter 4, the government is reliant on the private sector to deliver a solution to this problem for US power.

Innovation and US power

> *We want to continue to see [the Internet] be a source of innovation and a strength for our economy.*
>
> (Wasserman Shultz, 2008, p. 85).

There is a convention in US politics of linking innovation – particularly technological innovation – to state power as well as to the state's position in the global order. Adam Segal writes that '[t]he United States' global primacy depends in large part on its ability to develop new technologies and industries faster than anyone else. For the last five decades, U.S. scientific innovation and technological entrepreneurship have ensured the country's economic prosperity and military power' (Segal, 2004). President Obama has argued that this history provides a compelling precedent for contemporary technology policy. 'The United States led the world's economies in the 20th century because we led the world in innovation. Today, the competition is keener; the challenge is tougher; and that is why innovation is more important than ever' (Obama, 2011b, p. 1).

While there is little digression from this assumption that innovation is linked to US power, there are contending views about how innovation is best promoted and these views relate to conceptions of power. Some politicians take the view that innovation needs to be guided and sometimes encouraged by government initiatives while others believe that regulation and governmental involvement tend to stifle innovation more than they enhance it. In the first view, innovation is regarded as a potential source of power similar to natural resources. It *can* result in increased state power, if directed to do so by appropriate government policies. In the latter view, innovation *is* power – particularly when wed to a market-led economy. As President Bush has expressed 'America's economy leads the world because our system of private enterprise rewards innovation' (Bush, 2004b). In this view, the government needs to 'stay out of the way' (DeMint, 2007).

These two approaches to innovation as it relates to US power more broadly are reflected in the debates on network neutrality. In his opening statement to a 2006 hearing on network neutrality, committee Chair Ted Stevens described net neutrality as 'one of the most difficult, but most important' issues before the committee (Stevens, 2006, p. 1). He goes on to state that changes to the nation's telecommunications laws will determine two things – first, whether the private sector can generate adequate revenue to justify the considerable investment needed in network infrastructure and second, whether the Internet remains 'a free marketplace of ideas with no gatekeeper' (Stevens, 2006, p. 1). Pro network neutrality politicians fear that without legislative reform to enshrine network neutrality principles in communications law, innovation on the Internet which has been so important to the US economy will be stifled by privileging large organizations which can pay for speed and access over the Internet while smaller organizations or individuals may find themselves on the 'gravel road' as Senator Byron Dorgan refers to the slow lane on the Internet (Dorgan, 2007). Anti-net neutrality politicians, on the other hand, fear that network neutrality will eliminate important economic incentives for large telecommunications firms to build out the state's ailing information infrastructure by preventing them from exploiting new revenue streams and garnering a portion of the profits of those companies which operate over the network.

Although network neutrality itself did not feature in congressional debates prior to the Bush administration, the approach of the Clinton–Gore administration more generally to government promotion of innovative technology was made clear in Chapter 5. Vice President Gore expressed a proactive approach many times stating that although the government's intention was that the Internet should become the domain of the private sector, government did have a role to play in establishing and promoting the technology (Gore, 1989b). This approach is consistent with that of President Obama who has also expressed an understanding of innovation as a resource – 'the key to meeting some of the greatest challenges facing our nation and the world' (Obama, 2011b, p. 4). He has anticipated innovation playing a pivotal role in protecting freedom, global competitiveness, a resilient economy and the attainment of essential national goals (Obama, 2011b, p. 4). Because of this, he has argued that 'a strategy is clearly needed to direct our government's funding and regulatory decisions in order to capture the innovation opportunity' (Obama, 2011b, p. 4).

President Obama declared during his presidential campaign that if elected he would support network neutrality. Once in office, the Obama administration released a major policy document outlining the administration's approach to innovation – including in the context of network neutrality. In the *Strategy for American Innovation,* the President argued that network neutrality was essential, in large part, because the US economy was increasingly dependent on the Internet. The President stressed the importance of telecommunications networks which were 'open to all lawful uses by all users' arguing that 'that's the way the Internet has always worked, and we want it to stay that way – not because we treasure our past, but because we care about our economic future' (Obama, 2011b, p. 14). President Obama draws explicitly on the Clinton–Gore technology initiatives of the early 1990s to illustrate his point arguing that innovation in the Internet technology sector was 'initially catalyzed and continuously supported by government investment' and as a consequence, has made key contributions to the US economy. 'Some experts estimate that the Internet adds as much as $2 trillion to annual GDP, over $6,500 per person' (Obama, 2011b, p. 5).[11]

Pro network neutrality politicians believe there is significant danger associated with allowing network operators to have too much power over the flow of information. This, they argue, will lead to anti-competitive behaviour which will stifle innovation. 'The small start-ups and the scores of others that began tiny and dreamed big were able to succeed because every user has had equal access to all the websites' argued Senator Ron Wyden in a 2006 hearing. 'So, I'm going to introduce legislation to try to keep it that way, and the legislation is essentially built on the idea that all information ought to be made available on the same terms, so that no "bit" is better than another one' (Wyden, 2006, p. 6). In 2005, Nancy Pelosi linked this issue to social power when she observed that the 'dynamic and virtuous cycle of innovation is what secured our status as world leader, and that status has remained unchallenged – until now' (Pelosi, 2005). The importance of this 'leadership' status is another key theme that drives network neutrality debates in the United States.

Social power: Leadership, prestige and freedom

As was found in both of the other case studies, a social conception of power plays a role in network neutrality debates. In this context, politicians focus on two aspects. The first is a strong belief in the relationship between US 'leadership' and power. Politicians express a deep anxiety about any other state leading the world in Internet technology; indeed, they express a strong sense that it is the US 'destiny' to lead. The debates here resonate strongly with the debates outlined in Chapter 3 which emerged after the Sputnik crisis.

The second social power factor which plays a role here is competing conceptions of 'freedom'. As was the case in the cyber security case study, politicians in this case study argue that promoting freedom is essential to the future of the Internet and to US power. They disagree quite seriously on what 'freedom' means in this context and this opens up a whole range of questions about what US politicians mean when they talk about the role of these norms and values with relation to US power.

Leadership and prestige

In addition to the assumption that the private sector should be solely responsible for US information infrastructure, there is also a somewhat conflicting assumption that the United States should 'lead' the rest of the world in Internet technology. In much the same way that the

Sputnik crisis shone a light on the failure of US science and technology research to dominate globally, the poor performance of US broadband is also regarded as undermining US leadership. While other states like South Korea, Denmark and Sweden achieve much more impressive results, politicians fear that US leadership in dictating how the Internet should develop cannot be assured.

This conception of power can be understood through Robert Gilpin's work on 'prestige' which he describes as 'the reputation for power' (1981, p. 31). A hegemonic capacity to control Internet technology has been found in both the previous case studies to be important to US politicians and they express concern that the US position of 'special responsibility', authority and leadership on Internet issues, which has been developed in the last two case studies, could be undermined by their failure to lead in terms of the implementation of technology. Technological leadership has material power implications but it is also regarded in a social power context in the United States as it has implications for US leadership and promotion of liberal values such as freedom of speech which are playing an increasing role in US foreign policy.

In general, there is consensus amongst US politicians that network neutrality is one of the issues which will determine whether the United States continues to play a leading role in global innovation or whether it falls behind. Senator Edward Kennedy has argued that

> We must continue to do all we can to stay on track with the pace of other industrialized countries in this new era of technology. If we are not careful, we will wake up one day soon to find that America has been left behind while other countries leap ahead with higher bandwidth and neutral broadband platforms.
>
> (Kennedy, 2006, p. 2)

Similar comments came from Senator Byron Dorgan who argued that 'how this issue is resolved could determine whether our Nation continues to be a world leader in the area of innovation and technology' (Dorgan, 2006b).

In these debates, there is a sense that not only does the United States have a 'special responsibility' to lead the world in Internet technology, it has a kind of 'manifest destiny'. In her opening statement before a hearing into the digital future of the United States, Representative Anna Eshoo laments the fact that 'no longer is the country that created the Internet and the most connected nation in a leadership position, and Americans shouldn't settle for 12th or 15th or 20th. That is not who and what we are' (Eshoo, 2007, p. 347). For President Bush, this 'destiny' emerges directly from the commercial sector. In his 2004 *Technology Agenda,* the President argued that '[a]s the birthplace of the Internet, and home to the world's most important information technology companies, the United States is well positioned to continue its leadership in technical innovations for years to come. This report highlights steps the President is taking to ensure that America realizes this promise' (Bush, 2004a, p. 1).

President Obama addresses these issues head on in the *Strategy for American Innovation* where he acknowledges that the 'United States once led the world in broadband deployment, but now that leadership is in question. Wireless networks in many countries abroad are faster and more advanced than our own' (Obama, 2011b, p. 2). He goes on to report that only 46 per cent of adults in rural households have broadband access, with the figures at only 67 per cent for non-rural adults. Despite these statistics, the President maintains that 'America should lead the world in broadband adoption and Internet access' (Obama, 2011b, p. 13). Indeed, this is articulated as a key goal for the *Strategy for American Innovation* (Obama, 2011b, p. 1). President Obama outlines his vision of America's future as one in which the nation leads the world 'in the technologies, innovation and discoveries that will shape the 21st century' (Obama, 2011b, p. 4).

Certainly, the United States has a lot of ground to make up in order to be anywhere near the top of the field in terms of Internet infrastructure. Presumably, any state would prefer to be as close to the top of the rankings as possible for many of the same reasons as these politicians have expressed. However, there is something uniquely American about this anxiety over maintaining a position of global leadership in Internet technology which is about more than commercial competitiveness. It has strong links to a sense of national identity and national character. Even more significantly, though, just as was the case during the Sputnik crisis, US politicians equate 'leadership' with power and global order.

Freedom

As was the case in the previous two case studies, in network neutrality debates politicians express the belief that adhering to certain values when deciding policy and formulating legislation has led directly to the enhancement of US power in the past and will continue to do so in the future. In this case, there is one value which dominates: freedom. Competing conceptions of 'freedom' and its relevance to US power have been at the core of network neutrality debates since the early 2000s. Freedom becomes a policy touchstone in net neutrality debates, a point of navigation for politicians confused about the best path forward although they are actually divided on what exactly 'freedom' in this context entails.

One of the more prevalent public debates about the Internet of the past 10 years in the United States has been the widespread opposition to censorship on the Internet. The target for these debates in the political sphere has most often been China (and more recently, Middle Eastern states) where government censorship and surveillance is perceived by US politicians (and others) as authoritarian and an antithesis to 'Internet values' of openness, free access to legal information, the unimpeded exchange of ideas and global connections between individuals.

In a sense, this foreign policy stance was in danger of being undermined by the absence of net neutrality safeguards in America. Delegating power for the control of information crossing over the Internet is an antithesis for this conception of Internet freedom, irrespective of whether that control is delegated to the state or to corporations. As discussed above, one of the dangers of not legislating for network neutrality is the capacity for telecommunications companies to block data which either directly competes with their own core business or fails to pay a levy. Legislating to ensure that US citizens can access any legal information and download data from any legal site they wish to without permission from their service provider is a core issue of network neutrality.

The potential for this kind of private sector censorship in the United States does not appear to set off the same alarm bells that censorship in other states like China or US government censorship does. However, while in a free market with plenty of competition, private sector censorship may not pose a problem, the US market is dominated by monopoly and duopoly service providers, and it therefore has serious implications (Wheeler, 2014).

Mueller links network neutrality to the outcomes of the UN World Summit on the Information Society (WSIS) held in Tunis in 2005. The agreement emerging from this meeting included a commitment to the development by states of globally applicable public policy principles (Mueller, 2007). Mueller points out that network neutrality principles not only encompass the rights of individuals to access any and all legal content, services and applications free from interference or moderation by service providers (or governments), they also serve to protect service providers from liability for the transmission of illegal or offensive material. He concludes that 'because Internet connectivity does not conform to national borders, net neutrality is really a *globally applicable principle* that can guide Internet governance' (Author's emphasis) (Mueller, 2007).

One way of walking through the dominant political approaches to freedom in the context of network neutrality is to organize them around their approach to the role of the ISP. The ISP is regarded as the central point through which freedom is mediated in these debates as it is the juncture at which information travelling across the Internet can be examined, privileged, discriminated against or blocked.

Pro-net neutrality view of the ISP

Those politicians in favour of network neutrality believe strongly that the ISP must be a neutral and impartial conduit for data. Many (though certainly not all) agree that network maintenance should be permitted where necessary as long as it is carried out without discrimination – that is, it is not used as a cover for privileging data for financial gain as was suggested in both of the cases documented earlier in this chapter. However, they strongly object to ISPs charging at both ends of the data flow – once for the user to connect and download data and again for the provider to have their data made accessible on a fast track. They also object to the ISP using its discretion to make certain websites or data unavailable through blocking. The fear of pro net neutrality politicians is that without adequate regulation, the ISP becomes a 'gatekeeper', able to control the flow of data across the Internet in order to privilege their own interests – commercial, political, social or religious. This, they argue, is an antithesis to 'Internet freedom' and an impediment to future innovation and growth. Senator Daniel Inouye argues that 'the Internet has become a robust engine for market innovation, economic growth, social discourse, and the free flow of ideas ... The marketplace has picked winners and losers, and not a central gatekeeper' (Inouye, 2006). [12]

Proponents of net neutrality then argue that the ISP should be disempowered in order to preserve an environment of innovation and creativity which allows small businesses or even individuals to promote the growth of the Internet economy. This is, in effect, an expression of both the way they perceive the reverse salient (the stifling of innovation) and their perception of the relevant social group (individuals and small, innovative firms with potential to grow). These factors together comprise a particular view of 'freedom on the Internet'. Senator Byron Dorgan argues for this conception of freedom in the context of ensuring that small innovators are not relegated to the 'gravel road' of the Internet by big business (Dorgan, 2007). He states very emphatically that 'I'm sympathetic to the notion of investments in network; however, I'm not sympathetic to that issue, relative to destroying what I think is basic uninhibited freedom on the Internet – freedom of content, freedom of choice' (Dorgan, 2006a, pp. 34–35). In this approach then, 'freedom on the Internet' can be understood in the broader sense of freedom of information and freedom of access.

Anti-net neutrality view of the ISP

Anti-net neutrality politicians regard the ISPs very differently – they perceive the ISP not as a 'gatekeeper' but as a 'responsible stakeholder'. In their view, the ISP is perfectly situated to be able to shape the Internet in a number of positive ways. These include helping the state to deal with intractable online crimes like piracy and the theft of intellectual property – in effect, acting in a law enforcement capacity as was discussed in Chapter 4 under the public/private partnership. In addition, the ISP is often linked to a role in upholding 'family values' by keeping offensive material off line and inaccessible to children. Finally, the ISP is seen as essential to maintaining overall QoS of the network by dealing with 'bandwidth hogs'. Although some politicians opposed to net neutrality acknowledge that there exists some capacity and motive for ISPs to engage in anti-competitive behaviour, they generally argue that if and when this happens, the market should first be allowed to correct it. Only if it fails to do so effectively should government then step in.

This is most often expressed as a liberal belief in limited government. As with the issue of private sector censorship which US politicians seem to regard as distinct from government censorship, so too do they make a distinction between limiting access to the network by public or private means. 'Now, internal organizations may want to limit what their employees are saying, but ultimately we don't want the United Nations or anybody governing the Internet. It should be the private sector and individuals. The only real role of the government is the domain-name registry... Other than that, leave it free' (Allen, 2006, p. 70). In the anti-network neutrality approach, 'freedom on the Internet' can be understood as 'freedom from government interference'.

The diagram below is a graphical representation of how these competing views of 'freedom on the Internet' play out in political debates about network neutrality.

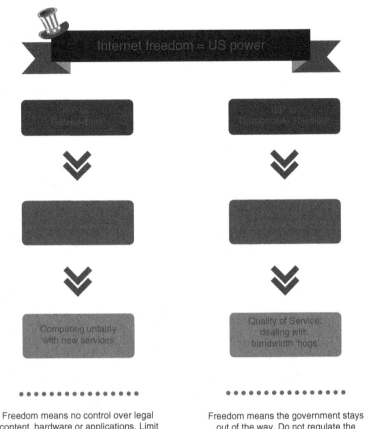

Internet freedom = US power

ISPs as Gatekeepers

ISP as 'Reasonable' Handler

Competing unfairly with new services

Quality of Service: dealing with bandwidth 'hogs'

Freedom means no control over legal content, hardware or applications. Limit the ISP's power in order to keep the Internet fair and keep the economy growing.

Freedom means the government stays out of the way. Do not regulate the Internet. Instead, let the private sector find the 'right' solution.

The analysis of these competing conceptions of freedom in the context of network neutrality reveals another layer of complexity in understanding power in these debates. Norms and values play an important role here but the case clearly demonstrates that we need to look closely at interpretations of these norms and values, including the policy implications in order to be able to comment on their relationship to power in the information age. The debate about freedom reveals two positions about US power and the Internet. The pro network neutrality view regards the internet in a determinist way as possessing a set of 'freedoms' which must be protected in order for the Internet to continue to deliver the benefits to US power that it has in the past. The anti-network neutrality view regards the Internet in an instrumental view as able to enhance US power only if 'freedom from government interference' is ensured so that the technology can continue to develop along market lines which will inevitably deliver the 'best' outcome. Significantly, though, neither of these views is accompanied by a sense of authority.

Anti-net neutrality authority: Let the market decide

The important regulatory shift which took place in 2002, when the FCC relegated Internet communications from Title II of the Communications Act to Title I, was not a decision broadly debated in politics. As demonstrated earlier in this chapter, its significance was apparent to the board of the FCC and those within the industry but network neutrality had not yet become an issue for debate in Congress. Once it had, the objective of the anti-net neutrality group became simply to prevent that decision being reversed and to prevent the passage of legislation which would further empower the FCC to enforce the four 'Internet freedoms' they articulated following the initial Comcast case.

To a large extent, politicians of this group argue not to shape or influence technology in order to address their conception of US power. Rather, they argue that their greatest responsibility is to 'stay out of the way' and to let the market shape technology – a form of market determinism. These references to the market as the appropriate mechanism through which network neutrality should be decided are common in anti-network neutrality speeches and position papers. In an open letter to Congress, Jim DeMint and Sam Brownback write that 'Opposing the heavy hand of regulation that network neutrality represents is critical if we are to maintain the Internet as an open, evolving, and market-based tool' (Brownback and DeMint, 2006). In other words, if the government would only stand clear, Internet technology (in the hands of the market) will independently evolve along a 'natural' or predetermined path which – given the newness and unpredictability of the technology – none may be able to foresee and therefore, appropriately influence. Senator Conrad Burns argues that 'my concern is that if we legislate prematurely in this area, we will not let these different approaches play out in the marketplace' (Burns, 2006, p. 3).

In contrast to the previous case study, these politicians draw on external sources of legitimacy rather than their own authority as elected public officials who might shape the technology – or the market for the technology – in order to pursue the enhancement of US power. This approach resonates not only with a liberal, market-based approach to state power but with an instrumental approach to technology. This was foreshadowed in Chapter 2 which made reference to Vig's interpretation of instrumentalism as one in which 'individuals should be free to pursue their own interests without interference from the state' (Vig, 1988, p. 13). The empirical research for this case study reveals a persistent notion on behalf of anti-network neutrality politicians that Internet technology should be developed without reference to normative expectations about how society will engage with it but rather in the framework of market drivers which are understood here as equating to a moral force.

Pro-net neutrality: The authority of technology

The pro-net neutrality position is somewhat more complex as these politicians are not simply protecting the status quo – rather they are seeking to change it. However, as with their opponents, these politicians also refrain from the claims of legitimacy for action which were common in the previous case study. Rather, they draw upon the legitimacy which they believe is vested in Internet technology itself. They do this in two ways. First, they frequently refer to a set of principles which they argue are endemic to Internet technology – the principles of network neutrality. Second, they call on the technical community of Internet pioneers – those scientists and engineers who worked on Internet technology in its infancy and who continue to be highly regarded in their field – as a kind of 'higher' authority for their claims. This approach reflects elements of technological determinism. Not only do these politicians seem to be implying that the technology has a determined path, but it is imbued with values such as equality, openness and, as previously discussed, freedom.

Congressional hearings on matters concerning the Internet often invite testimony from a number of Internet luminaries. Regular technical witnesses include Vinton Cerf (one of the engineers who worked closely on developing the IPs), Tim Berners Lee who is credited (alongside a number of colleagues) with inventing the World Wide Web (the Web) and Lawrence Lessig, a Harvard-based specialist in Internet law. In introducing testimony from the technical community at a 2006 hearing, Senator Barbara Boxer proposes that 'the voices that brought us this great revolution, I think we should really hear them, because I think at this stage we don't want to do anything to stifle them' (Boxer, 2006, p. 44).

Indeed, these witnesses generally testify strongly in favour of network neutrality principles. In his testimony before the 2006 hearing, Vinton Cerf expressed the gravity of the network neutrality debate by placing it in a historical context. 'There were key decisions made by the executive branch and by the legislative branch... that helped to commercialize the Internet. Your decisions coming up in this debate are equally important' (Cerf, 2006, p. 7). Later on, he stated that 'nothing less than the future of the Internet is at stake in these discussions' (Cerf, 2006, p. 7) and he further warned that if network neutrality is not legislated, 'we risk losing the Internet as a catalyst for consumer choice, for economic growth, for technological innovation, and for global competitiveness' (Cerf, 2006, p. 8). 'It is in our collective best interest for the United States to have the best broadband capabilities in the world, bar none. The prospects for continued American ingenuity and entrepreneurship deserve nothing less' (Cerf, 2006, p. 14). In another hearing the following year, Tim Berners Lee told the Committee that 'the Web is together technology and society... while I will do my bit as an engineer, it is very, very important that you as members of the committee should do your bit as legislators' (Berners Lee, 2007, p. 31).

Beyond the general comments above, witnesses from the technical community often reinforce the position that Internet technology is imbued with a set of principles, norms and values which should also be embodied in policy decisions about it. As was the case in the ICANN study, there is an acknowledgement of the direct links between architecture and policy in this debate. The 'bottom-up' and 'end-to-end' structures have been regarded as fundamental to the success of the Internet since commercialization and many continue to believe that preserving these is imperative to ensuring future growth.

Pro network neutrality politicians articulate this view ('the open architecture of this medium is central to our understanding of the Internet and a fundamental attribute of its success') (Cannon, 2006, p. 7), but they very often rely on the testimony of the technical community to lend weight to their position. This testimony forms a key element of the pro network neutrality position. Lawrence Lessig has testified that 'the innovation and explosive growth of the Internet is directly linked to its particular architectural design. If this Committee wants to preserve that growth and innovation, it should take steps to protect this fundamental design' (Lessig, 2006b, pp. 54–5). Vinton Cerf also argued that 'by abandoning the principles that helped foster user choice and innovation, the United States risks falling further behind in the global economy' (Cerf, 2006, p. 13). Cerf refers to a relationship between policy and the Internet architecture: 'This principle – that users pick winners and losers in the Internet marketplace, not carriers – is an architectural and policy choice critical to innovation online' (Cerf, 2006, p. 10). He further argues that 'allowing broadband carriers to control what people see and do online would fundamentally undermine the principles that have made the Internet such a success' (Cerf, 2006, p. 9).

Lawrence Lessig has argued strongly for the protection of the Internet's 'end to end' design. In a hearing in 2006, he urged the Committee to keep in view what he regards as a fundamental fact about the Internet: 'as scholars and network theorists have extensively documented, the innovation and explosive growth of the Internet is directly linked to its particular architectural design' (Lessig, 2006b, p. 54). Lessig further argues that 'if this Committee wants to preserve that growth and innovation, it should take steps to protect this fundamental design' (Lessig, 2006b, p. 54).

These statements in and of themselves are not particularly revealing. They are the testimony of witnesses who care deeply about network neutrality and believe that it is the best way forward. However, the hearing transcripts reveal that politicians hold a deep reverence for these voices and indeed, they appear to regard their views as carrying more weight than their own political perspectives do. Pro-net neutrality politicians consistently refer to these people as ultimately authoritative. Comments such as 'I think it is a great idea to have our committee go to the father of the Web and hear what he has to say before we get too much deeper into these issues' (Doyle, 2007, p. 6) and 'who better to inform us about how we should approach the task of understanding the World Wide Web and its future than its inventor' (Markey, 2007, p. 2) are representative of sentiments expressed by politicians in these hearings. This testimony is more than a supplement to political views or an opportunity to hear from those working in the technology. Rather, it is drawn upon as a source of legitimacy.

A telling exchange in one hearing demonstrates the authority which pro-network neutrality politicians vest in the opinions of the technical community. Chairman Markey makes a comment to Tim Berners Lee that if he had charged from the outset for the work he has done on the World Wide Web, he would be a very rich man. Berners Lee interjects with the reply that he firmly believes that if he had charged per click, the web would never have been taken up. Chairman Markey replies that 'it is very important for the committee to hear that sentence uttered' (Markey, 2007, pp. 30–1). In fact, it is important not only that the sentiment is uttered, but that it is uttered by

Tim Berners Lee rather than Chairman Markey himself. As the Chair of the US Subcommittee on Telecommunications and the Internet, Mr. Markey holds this opinion but he uses Berners Lee to invest it with legitimacy.

Conclusion

Marita Sturken and Douglas Thomas write that 'the meanings attributed to new technologies are some of the most important evidence we can find of the visions, both optimistic and anxious, through which modern societies cohere' (Sturken et al., 2004, p. 1). This case study on network neutrality has provided an excellent insight into the ways in which politicians attribute different meanings to the same technology. It has provided a platform from which to examine how those meanings are constructed, how they relate to conceptions of power and how they unfold in terms of policymaking which has the potential to fundamentally shape Internet technology.

While network neutrality legislation would directly affect US firms or firms operating in the United States, it is not perceived as purely a domestic issue, but rather one with significant implications for American power globally. There is unanimity in the belief amongst relevant politicians that the Internet is integral to American power. There is also a strong assumption that America, either because it was instrumental in developing network technology or because it has made so much of Internet opportunities in the past, should lead the rest of the world in this area. Network neutrality challenges these conceptions of US power because, perhaps more than any other Internet debates, it shines a light on America's trailing position in terms of Internet speed and service. This idea – that America is lagging behind in technology – is regarded as a political anathema.

Having examined these two competing approaches to network neutrality through the lenses of both the philosophy of technology and IR, it is possible to conclude the following points. First, there are a number of shared conceptions here. Both political approaches continue to regard the Internet as integral to US power for both material and social reasons. In addition, both approaches have serious concerns about the global competitiveness of the United States in terms of its information infrastructure.

Beyond these shared conceptions, these approaches differ in several important ways. They differ in the way in which they identify both the reverse salient and the relevant social group. The pro-net neutrality politicians identify the absence of net neutrality legislation as potentially stifling innovation and future economic growth on the Internet and they regard individuals and small organizations with potential for growth as the relevant social group. The anti-net neutrality politicians identify the lack of financial incentive for private sector investment in the state's information infrastructure as the reverse salient and they identify large telecommunications firms who they expect to invest in this as the relevant social group.

These groups also differ in how they conceptualize 'freedom' on the Internet – a factor which they both regard as important to US power but to which they attribute different meanings. Anti-net neutrality politicians regard freedom on the Internet as freedom from government interference. Pro-net neutrality politicians regard freedom on the Internet in terms of values like freedom of information, freedom of access and freedom of choice.

With regard to net neutrality, the debate takes place in the context of competing normative frameworks. These frameworks are a product of conceptions of power and approaches to technology. Those on either side of the debate argue that their position is best able to ensure the continued 'equality', 'innovation' and 'integrity' of the Internet. These values are regarded as desirable by every party – they simply differ on the best way to achieve the same outcome. Policymakers then are left to choose between two competing approaches to network neutrality in the pursuit of agreed ends. From the perspective of those opposed to network neutrality, a belief in market forces suggests that a 'two-lane' highway is a natural solution to heavy traffic and that those who will pay more for the tollway should be allowed to. This willingness to 'let the market decide' is understood to be inextricably linked to the 'idea of America' and consequently, its power. For those in favour of network neutrality legislation, it is the 'Ellis Island' of cyberspace. All arrive equal and progress according to their merits with no gatekeepers and no limitations but their own.

The research into political conceptions of the relationship between network neutrality and US power exposes a decided reluctance on the part of many US politicians to take the kind of initiative which characterized policy geared towards Internet governance specifically but also Internet technology more broadly in the 1980s and 1990s. While ICANN elicited strong claims about its relevance to the national interest, including the assertion that the United States had a 'special responsibility' for global governance of the Internet, network neutrality has been regarded quite differently.

Whether there is a causal relationship between the divergence in approaches and the unwillingness of politicians to claim legitimate authority to shape this technology is not clear and would require further research. However, there is certainly a distinction between the political conceptions of the previous case study and those found in this one. Politicians in the previous case study exhibited much more affinity with a social construction of technology approach. That is, they believed that they could and should work to shape Internet technology in order to address their norms and expectations. Politicians in this case study are divided with one group taking a determinist approach and the other an instrumental approach. Neither of these approaches lend themselves to a sense of political authority or legitimacy which was evident in the previous chapter.

This case study foreshadows one of the key implications of this book. Political actors who regard themselves as invested with the authority and legitimacy to shape and influence technology are able to do so. Understanding how power works in the information age may depend on understanding that societies can shape technology. Possibly, it is the knowledge that politics *can* shape technology which is a key element of power in the information age.

7
Conclusion

Albert Borgmann has written that 'living in an advanced industrial country, one is always and already implicated in technology' but because technology is so profoundly integrated into our way of being, our involvement normally remains implicit rather than self-consciously examined (Borgmann, 1984, pp. 104–5). The same could be said of our understanding of the Internet and power in international relations (IR). Understanding power in the information age *means* understanding the relationship between technology and power. And yet, as a discipline, IR has approached this problem largely without engaging deeply with technology either in an applied or theoretical sense.

This book has been oriented to the close examination of how US politicians conceptualize power in the context of Internet technology. To do so, it has been necessary to move beyond some deeply embedded assumptions about both technology and power that are held not only by politicians but by many IR scholars as well. Unpacking these individual technology issues and examining exactly which conceptions of power lead politicians to regard them as a 'problem' for US power as well as how they arrive at solutions reveal as much about power as about technology.

Integrating the philosophy of technology and international relations theory provides a means to move beyond the deeply entrenched but unexamined assumptions about technology upon which IR literature has been premised. The view that technology produces the same effects regardless of social or political context is a product of technological determinism and it has informed much of the literature that seeks to explore the relationship between new technology and power. By exposing those assumptions and demonstrating how the philosophy of technology can provide alternative approaches and a more nuanced view, this conceptual framework lays the foundation for a more useful approach to understanding power in the information age.

The analysis of the three case studies has generated a set of conclusions about the nature and exercise of US power in the context of Internet technology. It also generates conclusions about how, as IR scholars, we approach the study of global power in the information age. These conclusions can be organized around four themes. First, the book generates conclusions based on *which* conceptions of US power were detected in the case studies and *how* they have influenced the development of Internet technology. Second, the book generates conclusions about the role of authority and legitimacy in the context of power in the information age. Third, we turn to some conclusions about the future of US power in this context. Finally, some implications for understanding global power in the information age are drawn out.

Conceptions of US power and the Internet

It was anticipated at the start of this project that multiple conceptions of power would emerge in the analysis, though the preliminary research suggested that these would take shape as more or less cohesive approaches to power which could be attributed to a time (or political era) or to an administration. In fact, it was found that conceptions of power were articulated differently within the same time period and within the same administration – even with reference to a single technological issue. Conceptions of power as they relate to Internet technology are even more complex and multifaceted than anticipated and this in itself is an important finding which should prompt a re-evaluation of the relationship between power and new technology.

Complex and competing conceptions of power are not new to IR. Material power and social power considerations sometimes work together and sometimes compete in political decision making. However, finding multiple conceptions of power at work in each of the case studies is significant for three reasons. First, it highlights the complex array of implications which US politicians perceive Internet technology to have on social and material power.

Second, these conceptions of power sometimes result in conflicting policy choices. In each of the case studies, there was a tension between the policy options that privileged material power factors and the policy options that privileged social power factors. This tension provided an opportunity to examine the choices that politicians made about power through their decisions about Internet technology. These points of tension were particularly revealing and generate conclusions about the role of norms and values in information age power which will be discussed later in this chapter.

The third reason why these multiple conceptions of power are significant is because they illustrate the way that conceptions of power influence and shape technology. Politicians make choices about which factors of power they consider most important even within debates about a single issue. That matters because it means that in order to make sense of power in the information age we need to look closely at individual states, at a range of aspects of technology and over a period of time. Indeed, we could understand these processes as the 'political construction of technology.'

There are, of course, many factors that shape technology. Culture, markets and science all play a role. But when seeking to understand power in IR, it is impossible to ignore the substantial role that political decisions play. If we do, we ignore the role of choice and it is then easy to misunderstand the dynamics of the relationship between power and technology as one which is imposed rather than one which is selected or shaped.

In this book, both cyber security and Internet governance demonstrated clearly the role of political decisions in shaping Internet technology. In the cyber security case, politicians were faced with a problem, arguably of their own making. From early on, it was understood that introducing more stringent security measures on the Internet (such as attribution) would undermine important norms and values which are regarded as integral to US power. This is not to suggest that US politicians chose cyber insecurity in the 1990s, for they could not have envisaged how the Internet would be integrated into the US infrastructure. Cyber insecurity is better understood as an unintended consequence of earlier decisions. However, when faced with that problem and despite the oppressive cost in material terms, US politicians continue to promote a largely open and anonymous Internet environment.

Although they use the language of norms and values, this should not undermine the strategic reasoning behind this choice. Politicians repeatedly express the view that the most assured route to security (and the preservation of US power) is through continuing to adhere closely to the ideas and values which have been the foundation of US power in the past and that they believe will continue to be in the future. In short, in their calculation the reward of preserving these social power factors outweighs the risk which cyber insecurity poses to their material power.

In Chapter 5, politicians in the Clinton–Gore administration had a very clear vision for the Internet as a mechanism for rejuvenating US economic power. They openly set about institutionalizing a governance arrangement that was specifically intended to address those goals. In doing so, they established the United States with a degree of hegemonic power over the Internet which continues today. In large part, it is this residual control over Internet governance which sets the United States apart from other states in terms of their ability to project power over the Internet. When confronted by dissatisfaction in the international community, they chose a social power response – legitimacy. In this way, they hoped to generate enough international support to allow them to retain a level of control over Internet Corporation for Assigned Names and Numbers (ICANN) for as long as possible.

In Chapter 6, politicians were found to be in a deadlock. A politically divisive issue, network neutrality did not reveal the same clear example of technology shaped by conceptions of power as the previous two case studies did. It is, however, still able to feed into this conclusion. It demonstrates again that the Internet does not operate according to the principles of network neutrality for technical reasons and it does not perform the same way globally. Rather, it is an outcome of political conditions and decisions about power – even if they manifest in a stalemate as they do in the United States. Again, we return to political context.

Recognizing the role of choice is essential because it undermines assumptions about the universal nature of the impact of the Internet on state power. US politicians weigh up the risks and benefits of issues like cyber security policy in relation to a whole range of factors and reach a conclusion about which will best profit US power. Other states undertake the same calculations but because their conceptions of the relationship between the Internet and power are unique, their decisions differ. States which favour more restricted or supervised access to the Internet have also weighed up a range of risks and rewards and arrived at an equation that regards the risks of openness (however they may define them) to be outweighed by the rewards of state control.

The role of authority and legitimacy

'Does the state have the political and institutional capacity to control technology?' (Vig, 1988, p. 14). This is a key question posed by Norman Vig in 'Technology, Philosophy and the State' and one of the big debates which emerge from this book. The case studies would indicate that in the United States, the answer is mixed. In some circumstances, politicians have felt very strongly that the state has both the capacity and the authority to shape and control technology. In others, they have quite clearly articulated that it does not. In the cases in which they did claim authority, the effects on Internet technology have been profound. The governance system which prevails today (2015) was specifically designed to address the US economic power agenda and is perhaps the most significant example.

It is not surprising that conceptions of power which are associated with a sense of authority are the most influential in shaping technology. However, this highlights two important aspects of power in the information age. First, a belief in the authority to shape and influence technology can in itself be regarded as a form of power in the information age. (This will be discussed at more length later in this conclusion.) Second, the authority to act is not a given – even in a state such as the United States which regards itself as 'destined to lead' (a finding in the network neutrality case) and imbued with a sense of 'historic authority' (Internet governance). Despite the US history of linking innovation to national identity and also to material and social power, politicians frequently exhibit a sense that they lack the authority to shape and influence Internet technology. This raises questions about how authority and legitimacy are derived in the context of political decisions about Internet technology and US power. It also raises questions about global competition with those states that do perceive the state as imbued with authority in this context.

In Chapter 4, politicians explicitly expressed the belief that they had neither the mandate nor the capability to deal with cyber insecurity in critical infrastructure – even when it related to national security. Instead, they abdicated responsibility to the public/private partnership in an instrumental approach to technology. That is, they regarded the solution to a technical problem as more technology and they believed that it would 'naturally' emerge from the private sector.

In the Internet governance case study, pressure from the international community for the United States to relinquish its hegemonic control of ICANN was countered by an acknowledgement on the part of politicians that in order *not* to lose control they must retain legitimacy – until this was undermined by the Snowden leaks. Attaining a balance between the desire to retain control over what they had come to regard as a source of power with what they understood to be a social dimension to this power led to a series of concessions designed to best promote US power. Both of these conceptions of power were associated with a social constructivist approach to technology and both were instilled with authority to act.

In Chapter 6, neither conception of power was associated with a sense of authority. Politicians on either side of this debate deferred their political authority to an external source. Anti-net neutrality politicians adopted an instrumental approach to technology – again, expecting a solution to emerge from the private sector. They regarded themselves as without a mandate to interfere, much as was the case with the public/private partnership in Chapter 4. The pro-net neutrality politicians draw on the technology itself as a source of authority. They maintain that the Internet is built upon a set of principles which must be sustained in order for it to continue to promote US power. This is a technological determinist view which places agency in the technology rather than those who use it.

This analysis generated an unanticipated finding about the relationship between conceptions of power, approaches to technology and authority. It was found that there is a correlation between the conception of power which most significantly shaped Internet and the approach to technology which politicians associated with that conception. The most influential conception of power was always accompanied by a social constructivist approach to technology which was associated with a sense of authority and responsibility in politicians.

Understanding the causal relationship of these factors is beyond the scope of this book – given that it was unanticipated in the research design. Whether politicians adopt the language of instrumentalism or technological determinism when they perceive they lack authority or whether it is their approach to technology which determines their perception of authority is unclear but would certainly be worthy of further study. However, a correlative relationship was consistently observed in the case studies. This is a useful finding because it means that approaches to technology may be used as an indicator of political authority in studies such as this one. In addition, an awareness of the relationship between conceptions of power, approaches to technology and a sense of authority can contribute to policy formation as the question can now be asked – '*why* do politicians perceive a lack of authority in one case and not another?'

The future of US power in the information age

In his 2011 State of the Union Address, President Obama declared the United States to be facing another 'Sputnik moment'. By this, he was referring to a moment of technological challenge so significant that the government must once again claim the authority and the responsibility to assume global technological leadership in order to 'win the future' (Obama, 2011a).

This book has found that state power in the information age is linked to a belief in the agency of political actors rather than the agency of technology or the market. A willingness to claim both authority and responsibility for shaping technology was shown in these studies to be fundamental to the capacity to influence Internet technology in a way which preferences US power. US politicians have demonstrated their willingness to do this in the context of both material and social power and they have also demonstrated a determination to strive for global technological leadership – if not hegemony.

The ability to set the parameters of what is acceptable and determine which debates are legitimate was found to be central to US politicians in each of the case studies. In Chapter 4, this took the form of promoting the type of access to the Internet which US politicians believe undermines authoritarianism and repression. In the Internet governance case, establishing Internet governance in such a way as to promote a US-defined agenda and then seeking to retain control to prevent that agenda being challenged has been very important. In the context of network neutrality, politicians express a deep anxiety about the Internet infrastructure, not only for material reasons but because it undermines US 'technological leadership'.

Norms and values have played a substantial role in the analysis of the case studies but they appear to be increasingly important in US conceptions of power in the information age. The 21st Century Statecraft was specifically tailored to the task of promoting norms and values and it is worth considering carefully what implications this has for understanding both US power and power more broadly in the information age. Hillary Clinton has argued that 'we need to synchronize our technological progress with our principles' (Clinton, 2010a). More specifically, she perhaps means that the world needs to synchronize new technology with *US principles*. In a later speech, Clinton also observed that

> we all shape and are shaped by what happens [on and over the Internet]. To maintain an Internet that delivers the greatest possible benefits to the world, we need to have a serious conversation about the principles that will guide us, what rules exist and should not exist and why, what behaviors should be encouraged or discouraged and how.
>
> (Clinton, 2011)

Clinton's 21st Century Statecraft, and foreign policy thinking like it, has the potential to be the next wave of US hegemonic power expressed through the Internet. As Secretary of State, Clinton constructed a foreign policy doctrine specifically adapted to the projection of US power in the information age. While the acquisition of more material power than one's rival characterized the industrial age, 21st Century Statecraft suggested that the currency of the information age is different. Power, of course, still matters. But the projection of US power in the near future (especially if Clinton is elected president) looks set to focus much more on how norms and values which promote US power can be embedded in global expectations of Internet technology. In a Gramscian approach to hegemonic power, Clinton regards it as critical that the United States take the lead in setting the terms of debate, imbuing the agenda with favourable principles and establishing rules, boundaries and limitations.

How this happens, whose voices are heard and whose interests are privileged will have profound consequences for power in the information age. Aided by some of the methodological and conceptual tools provided in the philosophy of technology, IR should be addressing these questions and providing the analysis and theory necessary to navigate through the next chapter in global power.

Understanding global power in the information age

This book demonstrates that instrumentalism and technological determinism which have dominated IR theories about power are both inappropriate lenses through which to examine Internet technology. Adherence to this view promotes a 'black box' interpretation of technology which, when opened up as in this study, proves to be based on unstable foundations. The Internet does not possess values or norms like democracy, freedom or human rights. Nor can it be regarded as a universally applicable factor of material power – either in terms of economics or security. Rather, Internet technology is an *expression* of political decisions about power. How the Internet should develop, how it should be managed and how our use of it should be controlled fundamentally affect both the technology itself and the role it plays in our society. As scholars of IR concerned with understanding power in the information age, it is essential that we recognize not only the assumptions but the limitations of an instrumentalist/technological determinist view and begin to integrate a broader range of approaches to technology into our work.

Given that this analysis of the relationship between conceptions of power and technology in the United States alone has been so multifaceted, there can be no basis for studies that continue to assume that the Internet has universal power implications for other states. It has been shown here that US politicians make calculations about the risks and rewards of a range of Internet technologies and how they expect them to impact on multiple conceptions of power. They either try to harmonize those conceptions (as in Chapter 5) or they decide to privilege one over the other (Chapter 4).

Politicians in other states certainly go through the same process of weighing up risks and rewards of competing conceptions of power. Understanding more about the political context of power and the Internet is critical to understanding power in the information age. The United States may be proven to have made the wrong calculation about cyber security. Perhaps, upholding norms and values over imposing stricter security measures is not the surest path to security and power. Perhaps, the approach of states like China, which maintains a much tighter grip on Internet activity, will be found to be more successful. But before we can make an assessment of the success or failure of the range of global approaches to power in the information age, we need to understand what those approaches are.

There is much more comparative research needed on how state power is conceptualized in the context of Internet technology and much closer scrutiny of how these different conceptualizations play out in the relationship between power and the Internet in the information age. Having unpacked the 'black box' of power and technology, patterns may emerge, expected or unexpected – as they did in this study which found there is a relationship between conceptions of power, approaches to technology and authority. To a degree, until IR builds up a body of work which theoretically investigates these questions, we are working in the dark. If IR literature has been making assumptions about the relationship between US power and the Internet – in a state which is so comprehensively studied and which has so much openly available information – the same is almost certainly true for other more opaque or less accessible states.

Hillary Clinton has argued that 'the world's information infrastructure will become what we and others make of it'.[1] This book represents one step towards better understanding the processes by which this happens. By demonstrating how existing approaches to understanding power in the information age are flawed and by developing a conceptual framework for addressing the gaps and applying it to the study of US power and the Internet, this book helps to move beyond the confines of IR theories specifically suited to industrial technology and open new pathways for examining power in the information age.

Notes

1 Introduction

1. A recent example from September 2010 involves an online attack on an Iranian nuclear reactor. A purpose-built computer worm caused the reactor to spin too quickly resulting in system failure and lasting physical damage. While there has been some speculation that the United States and Israel were behind this attack, it has not been possible to trace its origins (Beaumont, 2010; Seltzer, 2010).
2. This debate was initiated by the Evgeny Morozov's observation that those who comment on the politics of the Internet tend to fall into 'utopian' or 'dystopian' camps. This was later articulated in the publication of Morozov's book, *The Net Delusion: The Dark Side of Internet Freedom* (2011). Clay Shirky responded arguing that despite its pitfalls, the Internet remains a 'positive force for democracy' (2009). These two views formed the poles of an ongoing debate which heightened during the events of the 'Middle East Spring'.

2 International Relations Meets Technology Theory

1. Within realist thought, there are a range of views on how power should be defined, that is, whether as a means to an end or an end in itself. This book will not provide a comprehensive catalogue of variations in realist approaches to power. Here, it is concerned only with understandings of the relationship between technology and power in IR and as such is proposing two broad conceptual approaches – the first of which – the nation-state power view – is most closely associated with a broadly realist approach.
2. Employing a Fordist approach, Alastair Buchan wrote of the decline of territory and population as a form of power with emphasis instead placed on states' technical and scientific base. In his view, 'power, influence, or prestige can now be increased by the better organization of existing domestic resources and the application of science and technology to them' (Buchan, 1972, p. 177). Richard Rosecrance also makes an argument for the declining relevance of territory in *The Rise of the Virtual State: Wealth and Power in the Coming Century* (1999).
3. In an example of US vulnerability, for at least a year during the lead up and execution of Operation Desert Storm in the Persian Gulf war, a group of Dutch hackers probed 34 different American military computer systems, gathering information on weapons systems, troop deployments and even battle orders. They amassed a significant quantity of sensitive data and then attempted to negotiate a sale to the Baathist regime. The Iraqis, taking the offer to be a hoax, did not respond but the vulnerability was clearly demonstrated (Markoff, 1991; Christensen, 1999).

4. Probably the most evolved of these is the Council of Europe's Convention on Cybercrime (also referred to as the 'Budapest Convention'), which is a multilateral treaty drafted by the Council of Europe with four observer states: Canada, the United States, Japan and South Africa. The full text can be found at http://www.coe.int/t/dc/files/themes/cybercrime/ default_en.asp.

3 A (Select) Political History of the Internet

1. For an institutional history, see *Over the Years*, on the DARPA website which is available at http://www.darpa.mil/body/overtheyears.html. For commentary, see Leslie (1993, p. 120) and Edwards (1997, p. 260).
2. Note that this is a much abbreviated version of events. There are many excellent accounts of the development of Internet technology. For further and more detailed information, see, for example, Abbate (2000). Also, there were alternatives to TCP/IP (Clark, 1988, pp. 106–14).
3. The bill would eventually be passed in 1991 as *The High Performance Computing Act of 1991* (http://www.thomas.gov/cgi-bin/query/F?c102:20:./temp/ ~ mdbsTGH4wS:e37166:). For a summary of this legislation, see the National Coordination Office for Networking and Information Technology Research and Development. Available online at http://www.nitrd.gov/congressional/laws/pl_102-194.html.
4. Hypertext refers to using a visual identifier (such as blue, underlined text) to indicate that there is more information associated with that text. Hypertext technology itself was not new when Berners Lee applied it to the Internet. Indeed it has a long and interesting history of its own but conceptually, it is generally credited to two Americans, Ted Nelson and Douglas Englebart. There was considerable activity around hypertext technology throughout the 1970s and 1980s but it was Berners Lee (with Robert Cailliau) who successfully married it to the Internet. A range of accounts can be found in Gilles and Cailliau (2000), Berners Lee (2000) and Abbate (2000).
5. In September 1993, President Clinton gave a speech to the United Nations General Assembly outlining this strategic framework which was reiterated in several subsequent speeches by senior officials including the Secretary of State and the National Security Advisor (Christopher, 1993; Clinton, 1993; Lake, 1993).
6. Although it is rarely discussed in these terms, the privatization and commercialization of the Internet was, in large part, a political development – not a technological one. Some accounts go as far as to suggest that the Internet was 'wrested' from the grip of American politics by the overwhelming force of the private sector. However, as stated above, policy documents from 10 years prior clearly state that the intention of the US government was to privatize and commercialize the network in order to maximize the potential for contributing to US economic growth and improve its international standing.
7. H.R. 775: The Y2K Dispute Resolution Act was signed into law by President Clinton on 20 July 1999. In addition, there was a House Resolution: H.R. 775 to establish certain procedures for civil actions brought for damages relating to the failure of any device or system to process or otherwise deal with the

transition from the year 1999 to the year 2000, and for other purposes. This was agreed to on 11 May 1999.

8. This communication failure is tragically ironic, given that some of the original developmental research for the Internet took place within the context of a programme aimed at establishing a secure communications system capable of withstanding a nuclear attack. Senator Ron Wyden, Chairman Subcommittee on Science, Technology and Space, *Response of the Technology Sector in Times of Crisis,* hearing before the Committee on Commerce, Science, and Transportation, US Senate, 5 December 2001, p. 20.

9. The FCC was established by the Communications Act of 1934. It is directed by five commissioners appointed by the president and confirmed by the Senate for five-year terms. In addition, the president designates one of the commissioners to serve as chairperson. Only three commissioners may be members of the same political party. None of them can have a financial interest in any commission-related business. For more information, see the FCC website at http://fcc.gov/aboutus.html.

10. The 2002 ruling applied to cable services but in 2005 this was extended to DSL services. For the complete ruling, see FCC 02–77, Declaratory Ruling and Notice of Proposed Rulemaking, *in the Matter of Inquiry Concerning High-Speed Access to the Internet Over Cable and Other Facilities/Internet Over Cable Declaratory Order Proceeding/Appropriate Regulatory Treatment for Broadband Access to the Internet Over Cable Facilities, GN Docket 00–185,* 15 March 2002, www.fcc.gov.

4 Cyber Security

1. This is distinct from the 'security dilemma'. The security dilemma suggests that if states acquire a surfeit of military capabilities, their peers will be compelled to follow suit. In this paradox, the states which have most comprehensively engaged with Internet technology do not prompt their peers to do so – although the economic benefits may attract them. Rather, those states which have not been able to develop Internet technology have also not become dependent upon an insecure system. This is the paradox. If the Internet suffered a major disruption, it might have almost no impact on many third-world states whereas it would have major consequences in the United States.

2. Her views will be elaborated on in the chapter but see this speech for a specific reference to this point (Clinton, 2011).

3. It is possible that Mandiant does not provide more substantive or compelling evidence in order to protect their practices and sources, but it is not possible to determine if this is the case or if the report really is as circumstantial as it appears.

4. Senator Robert Bennett chaired the Y2K Committee established to address the potential disruption of the global date change on computers from 1999 to 2000. It is regarded in US political circles as having been a successful intervention of an Internet security threat and is often held up as an example of what government *can* do. Partly as a consequence of the success of that operation, Senator Bennett is a highly respected voice in government approaches to cyber security. See the executive summary of Clinton (2000, p. vi).

5. Technology journalist Scott Berinato traces the use of this term back to 1991 when it was used by D. James Bidzos, the president of a computer security firm. However, the term had become common amongst policymakers by the late 1990s (Berinato, 2003).
6. This is discussed during the hearing in the context of the Presidential Decision Directive issued by President Clinton in 1998. PDD-63 ruled that federal agencies were to achieve 'reliable, interconnected, and secure information system infrastructure'. However, as Willemssen testified 'weaknesses continued to be reported in each of the 24 agencies covered by our review' (Willemssen, 2001, p. 4).
7. This bill was introduced to the 107th Congress as HR 5524. It was reintroduced as HR 48 in 2003. In addition, there was a Senate version in the 107th Congress numbered S 3093, co-sponsored by Senator Ron Wyden and Senator Jon Kyl.

5 Internet Governance

1. For example, Disneyland would want to buy Disneyland.com but if a new gTLD were released for .Travel, they would also want to buy that. Conversely, some organizations cannot obtain their preferred domain name as it may already be owned by someone else. In this instance, new gTLDs offer the opportunity for the name they need.
2. There are features of ICANN's structure which have changed over time and not all of the following details were in place at the time of this hearing. However, to avoid a full history of ICANN which is ancillary to this analysis, only key points are highlighted here. For a thorough analysis of ICANN's structure, see Mueller (2009).
3. Following years of engineering to alter the architecture of the names and number system, this was approved for four states on 22 April 2010 (ICANN, 2010).
4. Author's observation while attending this meeting. Thanks to my colleague Dr Jia Guan for explaining the language issue to me. Many Mandarin words are comprised of two characters and adding a third to comply with the current protocols on gTLDs would lead to confusion and ambiguity of meaning.
5. Representative Shimkus is referring here to Venezuelan President Hugo Chavez's controversial comments in the UN General Assembly on the previous day in which he said that 'The devil came here yesterday, and it smells of sulphur still today'. Widely reported but see CNN for an account at http://edition.cnn.com/2006/WORLD/americas/09/20/chavez.un/index.html
6. For full details on these amendments, see the ICANN website at http://www.icann.org/en/general/agreements.htm.
7. For the original document, see the ICANN website at http://www.icann.org/en/general/JPA-29sep06.pdf.

6 Network Neutrality

1. There are strong technical arguments against this which will be discussed later in this chapter. For example, built into the IP header was the field code

for prioritization. Initially, this took the form of the 'Type of Service' field superseded in 1998 by the Diffserv field in IPV4 and IPV6 headers. For a brief history of this, read section 22 in Internet Engineers Task Force (2001).

2. Most communications paths consist of a succession of links, each with its own bandwidth. If one of these is much slower than the rest, it is said to be a bandwidth bottleneck. This often happens over the 'last mile' from the Internet service provider (ISP) to the end-user – particularly in a domestic environment.

3. Voice over Internet protocol (VoIP) refers to the transmission of voice communications over the Internet. Perhaps, the most well-known proprietary VoIP application is Skype, but VoIP is increasingly penetrating traditional phone markets. For an overview of recent developments, refer to the White Paper entitled 'Voice Over Internet Protocol' on the International Engineering Consortium website at http://www.iec.org/online/tutorials/int_tele/index.asp

4. Net neutrality remains a strong norm in the technical community. Internet scholar Lawrence Lessig argues that 'as scholars and network theorists have extensively documented, the innovation and explosive growth of the Internet is directly linked to its particular architectural design' (Lessig, 2006b, p. 54).

5. Digital subscriber lines or DSL is a high-speed Internet service which uses existing copper telephone cables but is independent of a subscriber's normal telephone line. This meant that customers could connect to the Internet at a faster rate and also use their phone at the same time as opposed to earlier methods which required a modem to completely monopolize one's phone line.

6. Google was founded by Larry Page and Sergey Brin while they were students at Stanford University. Two more Stanford graduates, Jerry Yang and David Filo launched Yahoo! in 1994 and eBay was formed in 1995 by computer programmer Pierre Omidyar as part of a larger personal site.

7. The diversification of telcos to become content providers themselves has happened either by producing their own material or – more often – by sewing up exclusive deals with established content providers. For example, Verizon's V Cast which exclusively broadcasts ESPN sports coverage in mobile format. http://products.vzw.com/index.aspx?id=video

8. The 2002 ruling applied to cable services but in 2005 this was extended to DSL services. For the complete ruling, see FCC (2002).

9. In response to the complaint by Vonage, the FCC entered into a 'consent decree' with Madison River in which Madison River agreed to make a 'voluntary payment' of $15,000 and refrain from interfering with VoIP traffic in the future. Although the consent decree expressly stipulated that it did not constitute a 'legal finding regarding any compliance or noncompliance with the requirements of the Act and the Commission's orders and rules', it also stipulated that Madison River waived any rights to an appeal or review of the matter in the future. For the full text of the consent decree, see FCC (2005a).

10. These can be quite contentious as some variables favour one state or set of states over others for reasons like demography and geography. Measuring broadband penetration by a per capita rating, for example, introduces a bias against larger households as broadband is most often taken up by a

household, not an individual. In addition, what defines 'broadband speed' changes as higher speeds become expected and lower speeds are no longer considered 'broadband'. For a good overview of how some of these statistics are applied, see Benkler (2010).

11. FCC Chairman Julius Genachowski pointed out that at the time the US information and communications technology sector represented one-sixth of the US economy (Genachowski, 2009).

12. Almost the same comment is made by Olympia Snowe. 'The Internet became a robust engine of economic development by enabling anyone with a good idea to connect to consumers and compete on a level playing field for consumers' business. Anyone can send an e-mail or set up a Web site at little or no cost, and the marketplace has picked winners and losers, rather than an arbitrary gatekeeper' (Snowe, 2006).

7   Conclusion

1. Clinton, 'Remarks on Internet Freedom', 21 January 2010.

Bibliography

Abbate, Janet (2000) *Inventing the Internet,* Cambridge: The MIT Press.

Tom, Davis (2006) *A Failure of Initiative: The Final Report of the Select Bipartisan Committee to Investigate the Preparation for and Response to Hurricane Katrina,* Washington, DC: US Government Printing Office (15 February).

Akaka, Daniel (2000) Testimony at *Cyber Attack: Is the Government Safe?,* hearing before the Committee on Governmental Affairs, United States Senate (2 March).

Akaka, Daniel (2005) Statement at *Securing Cyberspace: Efforts to Protect National Information Infrastructures Continue to Face Challenges,* hearing before the Committee on Homeland Security and Governmental Affairs, Subcommittee on Federal Financial Management, Government Information, and International Security Subcommittee, United States Senate (19 July).

Akerman, Nick (2009) *Unsecured Economies: Protecting Vital Information,* Santa Clara: McAfee, http://resources.mcafee.com/content/NAUnsecuredEconomies Report.

Allen, George (2006) *Net Neutrality,* hearing before the Committee on Commerce, Science, and Transportation, United States Senate (7 February).

Applebaum, Anne (2007) 'For Estonia and NATO, A New Kind of War', *The Washington Post* (22 May), http://www.washingtonpost.com/wp-dyn/content/article/2007/05/21/AR2007052101436.html.

Aronson, Jonathon (2002) 'Global Networks and their Impact', in *Information Technologies and Global Politics: The Changing Scope of Power and Governance,* James N. Rosenau and J. P. Singh (eds.), Albany, NY: State University of New York Press.

Barnett, Michael and Raymond Duvall (2005) 'Power in International Politics', *International Organisation,* Vol. 59 (Winter).

Barney, Darin (2000) *Prometheus Wired,* Vancouver: The University of Chicago Press.

Bartels, Larry M. (1994) 'The American Public's Defense Spending Preferences in the Post-Cold War Era', *Public Opinion Quarterly,* pp. 479–508, Vol. 58, No. 3 (Autumn).

Bartholemew, Carolyn (2009) 'Report to Congress', U.S. – China Economic and Security Review Commission (November). http://www.uscc.gov/annual_report/2009/09report_chapters.php.

Beaumont, Peter (2010) 'Stuxnet Worm Heralds New Era of Global Cyberwar', *The Guardian* (30 September) http://www.guardian.co.uk/technology/2010/sep/30/stuxnet-worm-new-era-global-cyberwar.

Beckstrom, Rod (2009) 'The Affirmation of Commitments – What It Means', *ICANN web site* (30 September) http://www.icann.org/en/announcements/announcement-30sep09-en.htm.

Benkler, Yochai (2010) *Next Generation Connectivity: A Review of Broadband Internet Transitions and Policy from Around the World,* Cambridge, MA: Harvard

University; The Berkman Centre for Internet and Society.

Bennett, Robert (2000) Comments in the hearing *Cyber Attacks: The National Protection Plan and Its Privacy Implications*, before the Committee on the Judiciary, Subcommittee on Technology, Terrorism, and Government Information, United States Senate (February 1).

Berinato, Scott (2003) 'The Future of Security', *Computerworld* (30 December) http://www.computerworld.com/s/article/print/88646/The_future_of_security.

Berman, Jerry and Daniel J. Weitzner (1997) 'Technology and Democracy', *Social Research*, pp. 1313–21, Vol. 64, No. 3 (Autumn).

Berners Lee, Tim (2000) *Weaving the Web: The Original Design and Ultimate Destiny of the World Wide Web*, New York: HarperBusiness.

Berners Lee, Tim (2007) *The Digital Future of the United States*, hearing before the Committee on Energy and Commerce, Subcommittee on Telecommunications and the Internet, House of Representatives (March 1).

Bijker, Wiebe E. (1995) *Of Bicycles, Bakelites, and Bulbs: Toward a Theory of Sociotechnical Change*, Cambridge: The MIT Press.

Bijker, Wiebe E., Thomas P. Hughes and Trevor Pinch (eds.) (1989) *The Social Construction of Technological Systems: New Directions in the Sociology and History of Technology*, Cambridge: The MIT Press.

Bimber, Bruce (1990) 'Karl Marx and the Three Faces of Technological Determinism', *Social Studies of Science*, pp. 333–51, Vol. 20.

Bishop, Ann P. (1993) 'The National Information Infrastructure: Policy Trends and Issues', *ERIC Clearinghouse on Information and Technology* (December).

Blair, Dennis C. (2009) Prepared statement for *Current and Future Worldwide Threats to the National Security of the United States*, hearing before the Committee on Armed Services, United States Senate (10 March).

Borgmann, Albert (1984) *Technology and the Character of Contemporary Life: A Philosophical Inquiry*, Chicago: University of Chicago Press.

Boxer, Barbara (2006) *Net Neutrality*, hearing before the Committee on Commerce, Science, and Transportation, United States Senate (7 February).

Branscomb, Lewis M. and Richard D. Klausner (2002) *Making the Nation Safer: The Role of Science and Technology in Countering Terrorism*, Report from the Committee on Science and Technology for Countering Terrorism, National Research Council, Washington, DC: National Academy of Sciences.

Brock, Jack (1996) 'Information Security: Computer Attacks at Department of Defense Pose Increasing Risks', Washington, DC: US General Accounting Office.

Brock, Jack (2000) Testimony at *Cyber Attack: Is the Government Safe?*, hearing before the Committee on Governmental Affairs, United States Senate (2 March).

Brownback, Sam and Jim DeMint (2006) Open Letter to Congress, 'Don't Be Duped by Advocates of Network Neutrality' (16 May).

Brunn, Stanley D. (2000) 'Towards an Understanding of the Geopolitics of Cyberspace: Learning, Re-learning and Un-learning', *Geopolitics*, pp. 144–9, Vol. 5, No. 3.

Buchan, Alastair (1972) 'Technology and World Politics', in *The Aberystwyth Papers – International Politics: 1919–1969*, Brian Porter (ed.), London: Oxford University Press.

Bunge, Mario (1966) 'Technology as Applied Science', *Technology and Culture*, Vol. 7, No. 3 (Summer).

Burns, Conrad (2000) *Internet Security*, hearing before the Committee on Commerce, Science, and Transportation, Subcommittee on Communications, United States Senate (8 March).

Burns, Conrad (2002) Comments at *ICANN Governance*, hearing before the Committee on Commerce, Science, and Transportation, Subcommittee on Science, Technology, and Space, United States Senate (12 June).

Burns, Conrad (2006) *Net Neutrality*, hearing before the Committee on Commerce, Science, and Transportation, United States Senate (7 February).

Bush, President George W. (2002) *United States National Security Strategy*, Washington, DC: The White House.

Bush, President George W. (2003a) *The National Strategy to Secure Cyberspace*, Washington, DC: The White House.

Bush, President George W. (2003b) *Critical Infrastructure Identification, Prioritization and Protection: Homeland Security Presidential Directive 7*, Washington, DC: The White House (17 December).

Bush, President George W. (2003c) as quoted in 'Bush: We Will Go to War Against Iraq Without UN', *The Independent* (7 March) http://www.independent.co.uk/news/world/politics/bush-we-will-go-to-war-against-iraq-without-un-746011.html.

Bush, President George W. (2004a) *Promoting Innovation and Competitiveness: President Bush's Technology Agenda*, Washington, DC: The White House, http://www.gcrio.org/OnLnDoc/pdf/technology_agenda.pdf.

Bush, President George W. (2004b) *A New Generation of American Innovation*, Washington, DC: The White House, http://georgewbush-whitehouse.archives.gov/infocus/technology/economic_policy200404/toc.html.

Bush, President George W. (2006) *United States National Security Strategy*, Washington, DC: The White House.

Cannon, Chris (2006) *Network Neutrality: Competition, Innovation, and Nondiscriminatory Access*, hearing before the Committee on the Judiciary, Task Force on Telecom and Antitrust, US House of Representatives (25 April).

Carlin, John (1997) 'A Farewell to Arms', *Wired*, Vol. 5 (May), http://www.wired.com/wired/archive/5.05/netizen.html.

Carlson, Tucker and Paul Begala (2003) 'Gary Hart Pitches for President', *CNN Online* (28 February), http://www.cnn.com/2003/ALLPOLITICS/02/28/cf.opinion.gary.hart/.

Carr, E. H. (1964) *The Twenty Years Crisis, 1919–1939: An Introduction to the Study of International Relations*, New York: Harper and Row.

Carr, Madeline (2013) 'Internet Freedom, Human Rights and Power', *Australian Journal of International Affairs*, pp. 621–37, Vol. 67, No. 5 (November).

Cashell, Brian, William D. Jackson, Mark Jickling, and Baird Webel (2004) 'The Economic Impact of Cyber-attacks', Washington, DC: Congressional Research Service (1 April).

Castells, Manuel (2000) 'Toward a Sociology of the Network Society', *Contemporary Sociology*, Vol. 29, No. 5 (September).

Cerf, Vinton (2006) *Net Neutrality*, hearing before the Committee on Commerce, Science, and Transportation, United States Senate (7 February).

Ceruzzi, Paul E. (2000) *A History of Modern Computing*, Cambridge: The MIT Press.

Chertoff, Michael (2006) Secretary of Homeland Security, *National Infrastructure Protection Plan*, Washington, DC: Department of Homeland Security.

Chertoff, Michael (2009) Secretary of Homeland Security, *National Infrastructure Protection Plan*, Washington, DC: Department of Homeland Security.

Choate, Pat (2011) Testimony at *Communist Chinese Cyber-attacks, Cyber-espionage and Theft of American Technology*, hearing before the Committee on Foreign Affairs, Subcommittee Oversight and Investigations, US House of Representatives (15 April).

Christensen, John (1999) 'Bracing for Guerrilla Warfare in Cyberspace', *CNN Interactive* (6 April) http://edition.cnn.com/TECH/specials/hackers/cyberterror/.

Christopher, Warren (1993) 'Building Peace in the Middle East', speech at Columbia University (20 September).

Cilluffo, Frank J. (2012) *Iranian Cyber Threat to U.S. Homeland*, joint hearing before the Committee on Homeland Security, Subcommittee on Counterterrorism and Intelligence and the Subcommittee on Cybersecurity, Infrastructure Protection, and Security Technologies, US House of Representatives (26 April).

Clark, David D. (1988) 'The Design Philosophy of the DARPA Internet Protocols', *Computer Communication Review*, pp. 106–14, Vol. 18, No. 4 (August).

Clarke, Richard A. (2009) 'War from Cyberspace', *The National Interest*, pp. 31–6, No. 104 (November/December).

Clarke, Yvette (2012) *Iranian Cyber Threat to U.S. Homeland*, joint hearing before the Committee on Homeland Security, Subcommittee on Counterterrorism and Intelligence and the Subcommittee on Cybersecurity, Infrastructure Protection, and Security Technologies, US House of Representatives (26 April).

Clay, W.M. Lacy (2003) *Cyber Security: The Challenges Facing Our Nation in Critical Infrastructure Protection*, hearing before the Committee on Government Reform, Subcommittee on Technology, Information Policy, Intergovernmental Affairs and the Census, US House of Representatives (8 April).

Cleaver, Harry M. Jr. (1998) 'The Zapatista Effect: The Internet and the Rise of an Alternative Political Fabric', *Journal of International Affairs*, pp. 621–40, Vol. 51, No. 2 (Spring).

Clinton, Governor William J. (1992) remarks at Wharton School of Business, University of Pennsylvania, Philadelphia (16 April) http://www.ibiblio.org/nii/econ-posit.html.

Clinton, Hillary (n.d.) '21st Century Statecraft', *State Department web site*, http://www.state.gov/statecraft/index.htm, Accessed 15 January, 2015.

Clinton, Hillary (2010a) 'Remarks on Internet Freedom', delivered at the Newseum, Washington, DC (21 January) http://www.state.gov/secretary/rm/2010/01/135519.htm.

Clinton, Hillary (2010b) 'Remarks to the Press on the Release of Confidential Documents', *Press Release* (29 November) State Department web site, http://www.state.gov/secretary/rm/2010/11/152078.htm.

Clinton, Hillary (2010c) *The Quadrennial Diplomacy and Development Review: Leading Through Civilian Power*, Washington, DC: The State Department, http://www.state.gov/documents/organization/153142.pdf.

Clinton, Hillary (2011) 'Internet Rights and Wrongs: Choices & Challenges in a Networked World', remarks delivered at George Washington University,

Washington, DC (15 February), http://www.state.gov/secretary/rm/2011/02/156619.htm.

Clinton, President William J. (1993) Remarks to the 48th Session of the United Nations General Assembly in New York City (27 September).

Clinton, President William J. (1997) *State of the Union 1997: The Bold New World of the 21st Century*, delivered to Congress and the nation, Washington, DC (4 February).

Clinton, President William J. (1998a) *United States National Security Strategy*, Washington, DC: The White House.

Clinton, President William J. (1998b) *The Clinton Administration's Policy on Critical Infrastructure Protection: Presidential Decision Directive 63*, Washington, DC: The White House (22 May).

Clinton, President William J. (1999) *United States National Security Strategy*, Washington, DC: The White House.

Clinton, President William J. (2000) *Defending America's Cyberspace: National Plan for Information Systems Protection*, Washington, DC: The White House.

Clinton, President William J. and Vice President Albert Gore Jr. (1993) 'Technology for America's Economic Growth, A New Direction to Build Economic Strength', Washington, DC: The White House (22 February).

Clinton, President William J. and Vice President Albert Gore Jr. (1997) *The Framework for Global Electronic Commerce*, Washington, DC: The White House. http://clinton4.nara.gov/WH/New/Commerce/

Committee on Commerce, Science, and Transportation, Senate Report on S.1492: Broadband Data Improvement Act (2007) Washington, DC: US Government Printing Office.

Connolly, Kate (2009) 'Germany Accuses China of Industrial Espionage', *The Guardian* (22 July), http://www.guardian.co.uk/world/2009/jul/22/germany-china-industrial-espionage

Copps, Michael J. (2002) 'Dissenting Statement of Commissioner Michael J. Copps' in the FCC 02–77, Declaratory Ruling and Notice of Proposed Rulemaking, *in the Matter of Inquiry Concerning High-Speed Access to the Internet Over Cable and Other Facilities/Internet Over Cable Declaratory Order Proceeding/Appropriate Regulatory Treatment for Broadband Access to the Internet Over Cable Facilities, GN Docket 00–185* (15 March), www.fcc.gov.

Covault, Craig (2007) 'Chinese Test Anti-satellite Weapon', *Aviation Week and Space Technology* (17 January), http://www.spaceref.com/news/viewnews.html?id=1188.

Crandall, Robert W. (2005) *Competition and Chaos U.S. Telecommunications Since the 1996 Telecom Act*, Washington, DC: Brookings Institution Press.

David, Paul A. (1985) 'Clio and the Economics of QWERTY', *The American Economic Review*, pp. 332–7, Vol. 75, No. 2 (May).

Davis, Tom (2000) *Computer Security: Cyber Attacks – War Without Borders*, hearing before the Committee on Government Reform, Subcommittee on Government Management, Information, and Technology, US House of Representatives (26 July).

Deibert, Ronald J. (2002) 'Dark Guests and Great Firewalls: The Internet and Chinese Security Policy', *Journal of Social Issues*, pp. 143–59, Vol. 58, No. 1.

Deibert, Ronald J. (2009) 'The Geopolitics of Internet Control: Censorship, Sovereignty and Cyberspace', in *Routledge Handbook of Internet Politics*, Andrew Chadwick (ed.), New York: Routledge.

DelBianco, Steve (2006) *ICANN Internet Governance: Is It Working?*, hearing before the Committee on Energy and Commerce, Subcommittee on Communications, Technology and the Internet and Subcommittee on Commerce, Trade, and Consumer Protection, House of Representatives (21 September).

Demchak, Chris C. (2003) 'Wars of Disruption: International Competition and Information Technology-Driven Military Organizations', *Contemporary Security Policy*, pp. 75–112, Vol. 24, No. 1 (April).

DeMint, Jim (2007) 'The Federal Unbundling Commission?' (17 December). Transcript available on Senator DeMint's website at http://demint.senate. gov/public/index.cfm?FuseAction=PressReleases.Detail&PressRelease_id= ee010c53-9d44-9034-d948-a165f92ee9b1&Type=Press%20Release&Month =12&Year=2007.

Department of Commerce (n.d.) 'U.S. Principles on the Internet's Domain Name and Addressing System', US National Telecommunications and Information Administration website http://www.ntia.doc.gov/ntiahome/domainname/ USDNSprinciples_06302005.htm.

Department of Commerce (1998) 'Management of Internet Names and Addresses', National Telecommunications and Information Administration, Washington, DC (6 May), http://www.ntia.doc.gov/ntiahome/domainname/6_ 5_98dns.htm.

Department of Commerce (2012) 'Intellectual Property and the US Economy: Industries in Focus', Washington, DC (March).

Department of Commerce (2015) 'Quarterly Retail E-Commerce Sales 1st Quarter 2015', Press Release from The Census Bureau, Washington, DC (15 May), https: //www.census.gov/retail/mrts/www/data/pdf/ec_current.pdf.

Department of Justice (2014) Press Release, 'U.S. Charges Five Chinese Military Hackers for Cyber Espionage Against U.S. Corporations and a Labor Organization for Commercial Advantage' (19 May), http://www.justice.gov/ opa/pr/us-charges-five-chinese-military-hackers-cyber-espionage-against-us-corporations-and-labor.

Dingell, John (2001) *Is ICANN's New Generation of Internet Domain Name Selection Process Thwarting Competition?*, hearing before the Committee on Energy and Commerce, Subcommittee on Telecommunications and the Internet, US House of Representatives (8 February).

Dingell, John (2006) *ICANN Internet Governance: Is It Working?*, hearing before the Committee on Energy and Commerce, Subcommittee on Communications, Technology and the Internet and Subcommittee on Commerce, Trade, and Consumer Protection, House of Representatives (21 September).

Dingwerth, Klaus and Philipp Pattberg (2006) 'Global Governance as a Perspective on World Politics', *Global Governance*, pp. 185–203, Vol. 12, No. 1 (January–March).

Dorgan, Byron (2006a) *Net Neutrality*, hearing before the Committee on Commerce, Science, and Transportation, United States Senate (7 February).

Dorgan, Byron (2006b) Statement on Introduced Bills and Joint Resolutions, US Senate (19 May).

Dorgan, Byron (2007) Speech on introducing the S.215 'Internet Freedom Preservation Act' (9 January).

Doyle, Mike (2007) *The Digital Future of the United States*, hearing before the Committee on Energy and Commerce, Subcommittee on Telecommunications and the Internet, House of Representatives (1 March).

Drezner, Daniel W. and Henry Farrell (2004) 'Web of Influence', *Foreign Policy*, pp. 32–40, No. 145 (November/December).

Edwards, Paul N. (1997) *The Closed World: Computers and the Politics of Discourse in Cold War America*, Cambridge: The MIT Press.

Eggerton, John (2009) 'Comcast: FCC's BitTorrent Decision Violated Fair Notice': Cable Giant Challenges Commission's Judgment on Peer-to-peer Traffic in D.C. Federal Appeals Court', *Broadcasting & Cable* (27 October).

Ellul, Jacques (1964) *The Technological Society*, New York: Knopf.

Ensign, John (2006) *Net Neutrality*, hearing before the Committee on Commerce, Science, and Transportation, United States Senate (7 February).

Eriksson, Johan and Giampiero Giacomello (2006) 'The Information Revolution, Security and International Relations: (IR)relevant Theory?', *International Political Science Review*, pp. 221–44, Vol. 27, No. 3.

Eshoo, Anna (2007) *The Digital Future of the United States*, hearing before the Committee on Energy and Commerce, Subcommittee on Telecommunications and the Internet, House of Representatives (24 April).

Federal Communications Commission (2002) GN Docket 00–185, Declaratory Ruling and Notice of Proposed Rulemaking, *in the Matter of Inquiry Concerning High-Speed Access to the Internet Over Cable and Other Facilities/Internet Over Cable Declaratory Order Proceeding/Appropriate Regulatory Treatment for Broadband Access to the Internet Over Cable Facilities* (15 March).

Federal Communications Commission (2005a) File No. EB-05-IH-0110, *FCC Consent Decree with Madison River* (3 March), www.fcc.gov/eb/Orders/2005/DA-05-543A2.html.

Federal Communications Commission (2005b) FCC Policy Statement 05–151 (23 September), http://fjallfoss.fcc.gov/edocs_public/attachmatch/FCC-05-151A1.pdf

Federal Communications Commission (2008) File No. EB-08-IH-1518, *in the Matters of Formal Complaint of Free Press and Public Knowledge Against Comcast Corporation for Secretly Degrading Peer-to-Peer Applications Broadband Industry Practices Petition of Free Press et al. for Declaratory Ruling that Degrading an Internet Application Violates the FCC's Internet Policy Statement and Does Not Meet an Exception for 'Reasonable Network Management'*, Memorandum Opinion and Order (1 August), http://hraunfoss.fcc.gov/edocs_public/attachmatch/FCC-08-183A1.pdf.

Fingar, Thomas (2008) Comments during *Global Security Assessment*, hearing before the Committee on Armed Services, House of Representatives (13 February).

Franklin, Marianne I. (2004) *Post Colonial Politics, the Internet and Everyday Life: Pacific Traversals Online*, New York: Routledge.

Franklin, Marianne I. (2010) 'Digital Dilemmas: Transnational Politics in the Twenty-First Century', *The Brown Journal of World Affairs*, pp. 67–85, Vol. 16, No. 2 (Spring).

Genachowski, Julius (2009) 'Connecting the Nation: A National Broadband Plan', remarks delivered at the Clinton Presidential Library (24 November).

Gilles, James and Robert Cailliau (2000) *How the Web Was Born: The Story of the World Wide Web*, Oxford: Oxford University Press.

Gilpin, Robert (1981) *War and Change in World Politics*, Cambridge: Cambridge University Press.

Goldsmith, Jack and Tim Wu (2006) *Who Controls the Internet? Illusions of a Borderless World*, Oxford: Oxford University Press.

Goldstein, Fred (2005) 'Rolling, Rolling, Rolling on the (Madison) River', *Ionary.com* (October), http://www.ionary.com/ion-voipblock.html.

Gore, Senator Albert Jr. (1989a) Speech to Congress introducing the National High-Performance Computer Technology Act (the Gore Bill) (18 May), http://w2.eff.org/Infrastructure/Old/s1067_89_gore_hpc.bill.

Gore, Senator Albert Jr. (1989b) 'The Information Superhighways of Tomorrow', *Academic Computing Magazine*, Vol. 4, No. 3 (November 1989).

Gore, Vice President Albert Jr. (1993) Remarks at The National Press Club, Washington, DC (21 December).

Gore, Vice President Albert Jr. (1994) Remarks at UCLA, Royce Hall, Los Angeles, California (11 January).

Gorman, Siobhan, August Cole, and Yochi Dreazen (2009) 'Computer Spies Breach Fighter-Jet Project', *Wall Street Journal* (21 April).

Grant, Ruth W. and Robert O. Keohane (2005) 'Accountability and Abuses of Power in World Politics', *American Political Science Review*, pp. 29–43, Vol. 99, No. 1 (February).

Grove, Gregory D., Seymour E. Goodman and Stephen J. Lukasik (2000) 'Cyber-attacks and International Law', *Survival*, pp. 89–104, Vol. 42, No. 3 (Autumn).

Grow, Brian and Mark Hosenball (2011) 'In Cyberspy vs. Cyberspy, China Has the Edge', *Reuters* (14 April), http://www.reuters.com/article/2011/04/14/us-china-usa-cyberespionage-idUSTRE73D24220110414?pageNumber=1.

Habermas, Jurgen (1970) *Towards a Rational Society*, Boston: Beacon Press.

Hachigian, Nina (2002) 'The Internet and Power in One-Party East Asian States', *The Washington Quarterly*, pp. 41–58, Vol. 25, No. 3 (Summer).

Hathaway, Melissa (2009a) *Cyberspace Policy Review: Assuring a Trusted and Resilient Information and Communications Infrastructure*, Washington, DC: The White House (May).

Hathaway, Melissa (2009b) 'Strategic Advantage: Why America Should Care About Cybersecurity', Discussion Paper, Cambridge: Belfer Center for Science and International Affairs, Harvard Kennedy School.

Heilbroner, Robert (1961) 'Do Machines Make History?', *Technology and Culture*, pp. 335–345, Vol. 2 (Winter).

Holder, Eric Jr. (2000) Deputy Attorney General, US Department of Justice, prepared statement for *Internet Security*, hearing before the Committee on Commerce, Science, and Transportation, Subcommittee on Communications, United States Senate (8 March).

Hughes, Christopher R. and Gudrun Wacker (eds.) (2003) *China and the Internet: Politics of the Digital Leap Forward*, London: RoutledgeCurzon.

Hughes, Thomas P. (1989) 'The Definition of Large Technological Systems', in *The Social Construction of Technological Systems: New Directions in the Sociology and*

History of Technology, Trevor E. Pinch and Wiebe E. Bijker (eds.), Cambridge: The MIT Press.

ICANN (2006) 'New Agreement Means Greater Independence in Managing the Internet's System of Unique Identifiers', Website (29 September) http://www.icann.org/en/announcements/announcement-29sep06.htm.

ICANN (2010) 'ICANN Gives Final Approval for Four Countries to Use Non-Latin Languages in Internet Address Names: Egypt, Russian Federation, Saudi Arabia, UAE clear final hurdle', *ICANN Press Release* (22 April), http://www.icann.org/en/news/releases/release-22apr10-en.pdf.

'Improvement of Technical Management of Internet Names and Addresses: Proposed Rule' (1998) *Federal Register,* Vol. 63, No. 34 (20 February).

Inouye, Daniel (2006) Speech in support of S.2917, US Senate (19 May).

Internet Engineers Task Force (2001) Request for Comments (RFC) 3168 (September), http://tools.ietf.org/html/rfc3168#page-58.

Internet Society (2015) 'Global Internet Maps', Data collected from 2013 http://www.internetsociety.org/map/global-internet-report/?gclid=Cj0KEQjw_YKtBRC7zZjFp8bF_foBEiQAfyigc3qcdP39AI5nIZ7bBb9LFULvXoILxc3o2VKyKv3-0FMaAkjU8P8HAQ#affordability-fixed-broadband.

Jervis, Robert (1993) 'International Primacy: Is the Game Worth the Candle?', *International Security,* pp. 52–67, Vol. 17, No. 4 (Spring).

Joffe, Josef (2006) *Uberpower: The Imperial Temptation of America,* New York, NY: W.W. Norton and Company.

Juliussen, Finn-Erik (n.d.) *Worldwide PC Market,* Arlington Heights: eTForecasts, http://www.etforecasts.com/products/wwpcmkt.htm.

Kahin, Brian (1990) 'RFC1192 – Commercialization of the Internet, Summary Report', issued as a Request for Comments by the Network Working Group, Harvard (November), http://www.faqs.org/rfcs/rfc1192.html.

Kaldor, Mary (2007) *New and Old Wars: Organized Violence in a Global Era,* 2nd Edition, Stanford, CA: Stanford University Press.

Kang, Cecilia (2010) 'Court Rules for Comcast over FCC in Net Neutrality Case', *Washington Post* (7 April), http://www.washingtonpost.com/wp-dyn/content/article/2010/04/06/AR2010040600742.html.

Kapor, Mitchell (2006) 'Architecture Is Politics (and Politics Is Architecture)', *Mitch Kapor's Blog* (23 April).

Kapustka, Paul (2005) 'FCC Fines N.C. Provider $15K for Blocking Vonage', *Information Week* (3 March), http://www.informationweek.com/news/showArticle.jhtml?articleID=60405234.

Kapustka, Paul (2006) 'Verizon Says Google, Microsoft Should Pay for Internet Apps', *InformationWeek* (5 January).

Katznelson, Ira (1997) 'Liberal Maps for Technology's Powers: Six Questions', *Social Research,* pp. 1333–7, Vol. 64, No. 3 (Fall).

Kaufman, Marc and Dafna Linzer (2007) 'China Criticized for Anti-satellite Missile Test', *Washington Post* (19 January), http://www.washingtonpost.com/wp-dyn/content/article/2007/01/18/AR2007011801029.html.

Kaufman, Stephen (2010) 'Unrestricted, Secure Internet Access Critical, United States Says', *America.gov* (14 January), http://www.america.gov/st/democracy hr-english/2010/January/20100114172447esnamfuak0.2396814.html

Kellerhals, Merle David Jr (2010) 'U.S. Treasury Opens Internet Exports to Iran, Sudan, Cuba', *America.gov* (12 March), http://www.america.gov/st/

democracyhr-english/2010/March/20100312160116dmslahrellek0.7673914.
html.

Kennedy, Edward M. (2006) *Reconsidering Our Communications Law: Ensuring Competition and Innovation*, Washington, DC: US Government Printing Office (14 June).

Keohane, Robert O. and Joseph P. Nye (1998) 'Power and Interdependence in the Information Age', *Foreign Affairs*, pp. 81–94, Vol. 77, No. 5 (September/October).

Killian, James R. (1977) 'Sputnik Fever', *The Sciences*, pp. 6–9, Vol. 17, No. 6.

Kleinrock, Leonard, Cynthia H. Braddon, David D. Clark, William J. Emery, David J. Farber, A.G. Fraser, Russell D. Hensley, Lawrence H. Dandweber, Robert W. Lucky, Susan K. Nutter, Radia Perlman, Susanna Schweizer, Connie Danner Stout, Charels Ellett Taylor, Thomas W. West and Robert E. Kahn (1994) *Realizing the Information Future: The Internet and Beyond*, Washington, DC: National Academy Press.

Kraft, Michael E. and Norman J. Vig (eds.) (1988) *Technology and Politics*, Durham and London: Duke University Press.

Kristof, Nicholas D. (1993) 'The Rise of China', *Foreign Affairs*, pp. 59–74, Vol. 72, No. 5.

Kuhn, Betsy (2007) *The Race for Space: The United States and the Soviet Union Compete for the New Frontier*, Minneapolis, Twenty-First Century Books.

Lake, Anthony (1993) 'From Containment to Enlargement', speech before the Johns Hopkins University School of Advanced International Studies, Washington, DC (21 September).

Landler, Mark and John Markoff (2007) 'Digital Fears Emerge After Data Siege in Estonia', *The New York Times* (29 May).

Langman, Lauren (2005) 'From Virtual Public Spheres to Global Justice: A Critical Theory of Internetworked Social Movements', *Sociological Theory*, pp. 42–74, Vol. 23, No. 1 (March).

Larson, Rick (2008) Comments during *Global Security Assessment*, hearing before the Committee on Armed Services, House of Representatives (13 February).

Latham, Kevin (2007) 'SMS, Communication, and Citizenship in China's Information Society', *Critical Asian Studies*, pp. 295–314, Vol. 39, No. 2 (June).

Lawson, Stephen (2005) 'Vonage CEO Slams VoIP Blocking', *PCWorld* (9 March), http://www.pcworld.com/article/119919/vonage_ceo_slams_voip_blocking.html.

Layne, Christopher (2006) 'Impotent Power? Re-examining the Nature of America's Hegemonic Power', *The National Interest* (September/October), pp. 41–7.

Lebow, Richard Ned (2005) 'Power, Persuasion and Justice', *Millenium: Journal of International Studies*, pp. 551–81, Vol. 33, No. 3.

Leiner, Barry M., Vinton G. Cerf, David D. Clark, Robert E. Kahn, Leonard Kleinrock, Daniel C. Lynch, Jon Postel, Larry G. Roberts and Stephen Wolff (1997) 'A Brief History of the Internet, Part 1', *On the Internet*, The Internet Society (May/June), http://www.isoc.org/oti/articles/0597/leiner.html.

Leppard, Dave (2010) 'China Bugs and Burgles Britain', *The Sunday Times* (31 January), http://www.timesonline.co.uk/tol/news/uk/crime/article7009749.ece.

Leslie, Stuart W. (1993) *The Cold War and American Science: The Military-Industrial-Academic Complex at MIT and Stanford*, New York: Columbia University Press.

Lessig, Lawrence (2005) 'Voice-Over-IP's Unlikely Hero', *Wired* (13 May) http://www.wired.com/wired/archive/13.05/view.html?pg=4.

Lessig, Lawrence (2006a) *Code: Version 2.0*, New York: Basic Books.

Lessig, Lawrence (2006b) *Net Neutrality*, hearing before the Committee on Commerce, Science, and Transportation, United States Senate (7 February).

Lewis, James (2005) 'Computer Espionage, Titan Rain and China', published online by the Center for Strategic and International Studies (14 December), http://csis.org/publication/computer-espionage-titan-rain-and-china.

Lewis, James (2008) *Securing Cyberspace for the 44th Presidency*, Commission on Cybersecurity for the 44th Presidency, Washington, DC: Center for Strategic and International Studies (December).

Lewis, James (2009) *Cybersecurity: Assessing our Vulnerabilities and Developing an Effective Response*, hearing before the Committee on Commerce, Science, and Transportation, United States Senate (19 March).

Lewis, James (2010) testimony at *Cybersecurity: Next Steps to Protect Critical Infrastructure*, hearing before the Committee on Commerce, Science and Transportation, United States Senate (23 February).

Liang, Qiao and Wang Xiangsui (1999) *Unrestricted Warfare*, Beijing: PLA Literature and Arts Publishing House (February).

Litfin, Karen T. (2002) 'Public Eyes: Satellite Imagery, the Globalization of Transparency, and New Networks of Surveillance', in *Information Technologies and Global Politics: The Changing Scope of Power and Governance*, James N. Rosenau and J.P. Singh (eds.), Albany, NY: State University of New York Press.

Lum, Thomas (2006) 'Internet Development and Information Control in the People's Republic of China', Washington, DC: Congressional Research Service (10 February), http://www.fas.org/sgp/crs/row/RL33167.pdf.

Lungren, Daniel (2005) *SCADA Systems and the Terrorist Threat: Protecting the Nation's Critical Control Systems*, hearing before the Committee on Homeland Security, Subcommittee on Economic Security, Infrastructure Protection and Cybersecurity and the Subcommittee on Emergency Preparedness, Science and Technology, House of Representatives (18 October).

Mackenzie, Donald (1996) *Knowing Machines*, Cambridge: The MIT Press.

MacKenzie, Donald and Judy Wajcman (eds.) (1999) *The Social Shaping of Technology*, Philadelphia: Open University Press.

Mandiant (2013) *APT1: Exposing One of China's Cyber Espionage Units* (February) Available online at http://intelreport.mandiant.com/Mandiant_APT1_Report.pdf.

Maples, Michael D. (2009) Director, Defense Intelligence Agency, 'Current and Future Worldwide Threats to the National Security of the United States', prepared statement at a hearing before the Senate Committee on Armed Services (10 March).

Marcuse, Herbert (1971) *One Dimensional Man*, Boston: Beacon Press.

Markey, Edward (2001) *Is ICANN's New Generation of Internet Domain Name Selection Process Thwarting Competition?*, hearing before the Committee on Energy and Commerce, Subcommittee on Telecommunications and the Internet, US House of Representatives (8 February).

Markey, Edward (2006) *ICANN Internet Governance: Is It Working?*, hearing before the Committee on Energy and Commerce, Subcommittee on Communications,

Technology and the Internet and Subcommittee on Commerce, Trade, and Consumer Protection, House of Representatives (21 September).

Markey, Edward (2007) *The Digital Future of the United States*, hearing before the Committee on Energy and Commerce, Subcommittee on Telecommunications and the Internet, House of Representatives (1 March).

Markoff, John (1991) 'Dutch Computer Rogues Infiltrate American Systems with Impunity,' *The New York Times* (21 April).

Matalin, Mary and James Carville with Peter Knobler (1994) *All's Fair: Love, War, and Running for President*, New York: Random House.

Mayer-Schöenberger, Viktor and Gernot Brodnig (2001) 'Information Power: International Affairs in the Cyber Age', *John F. Kennedy School of Government Harvard University Faculty Research Working Papers Series* (November).

Mazanec, Brian M. (2009) 'The Art of (Cyber) War', *The Journal of International Security Affairs*, Vol. 16 (Spring).

McCullagh, Declan (2005) 'Telco Agrees to Stop Blocking VoIP Calls', *CNet.news* (3 March), http://news.cnet.com/Telco-agrees-to-stop-blocking-VoIP-calls/2100-7352_3-5598633.html.

McLoughlin, Glenn J. (2002) 'Electronic Commerce: An Introduction', Washington, DC: Congressional Research Service (1 April), http://fpc.state.gov/documents/organization/12056.pdf.

Mearsheimer, John J. (2001) *The Tragedy of Great Power Politics*, London: W.W. Norton.

Messmer, Ellen (2008) 'Cyber Espionage: A Growing Threat to Business', *PCWorld* (22 January).

Meyer, David (2009) 'Europe Calls on US to Let Go of ICANN', *ZDNet UK* (19 June) http://www.zdnet.co.uk/news/networking/2009/06/19/europe-calls-on-us-to-let-go-of-icann-39665754/.

Mills, Elinor (2009) 'Study: Cybercrime Cost Firms $1 Trillion Globally', *CNet News* (28 January) http://news.cnet.com/8301-1009_3-10152246-83.html.

Mitcham, Carl (1985) 'What Is the Philosophy of Technology?', *International Philosophical Quarterly*, pp. 73–88, Vol. 25, No. 1.

Morgenthau, Hans (1946) *Scientific Man vs Power Politics*, Chicago: University of Chicago Press (1974 Midway Reprint).

Morgenthau, Hans (1978) *Politics Among Nations: The Struggle for Power and Peace*, 5th Edition Revised, New York, NY: Alfred A. Knopf.

Morozov, Evgeny (2011) *The Net Delusion: The Dark Side of Internet Freedom*, New York, NY: PublicAffairs.

Mueller, Milton (2002) *Ruling the Root*, Cambridge: The MIT Press.

Mueller, Milton (2006) 'ICANN's New MoU: Old Wine in a New Bottle', *Internet Governance Project Blog* (30 September), http://blog.Internetgovernance.org/blog/_archives/2006/9/30/3340162.html.

Mueller, Milton (2007) *Net Neutrality as Global Principle for Internet Governance*, Syracuse, NY: Internet Governance Project (5 November).

Mueller, Milton (2009) 'ICANN, Inc.: Accountability and Participation in the Governance of Critical Internet Resources', *Internet Governance Project* (16 November), http://internetgovernance.org/pdf/ICANNInc.pdf.

Mumford, Lewis (1970) *The Myth of the Machine: The Pentagon of Power*, New York, NY: Harcourt Brace Jovanovich.

Mussington, David (1997) 'The Proliferation Challenges of Cyberspace', *Cyberspace and Outer Space: Transitional Challenges for Multilateral Verification in the 21st Century.* Proceedings of the Fourteenth Annual Ottawa NACD Verification Symposium, Ed. by J. Marshall Beier and Steven Mataija, http://www.yorku.ca/yciss/publications/cyberspace.htm

Norton-Taylor, Richard (2007) 'Titan Rain – How Chinese Hackers Targeted Whitehall', *The Guardian* (5 September), http://www.guardian.co.uk/technology/2007/sep/04/news.internet.

Nye, Joseph S. (2002) *The Paradox of American Power: Why the World's Only Superpower Can't Go It Alone,* Oxford: Oxford University Press.

Nye, Joseph S. (2004) *Soft Power: The Means to Success in World Politics,* New York, NY: PublicAffairs.

Obama, President Barack (2009a) 'Assuring a Trusted and Resilient Information and Communications Infrastructure', *Cyberspace Policy Review,* Washington, DC: The White House (29 May), http://www.whitehouse.gov/assets/documents/Cyberspace_Policy_Review_final.pdf.

Obama, President Barack (2009b) 'Remarks by the President on Securing our Nation's Cyber Infrastructure', Office of the Press Secretary, Washington, DC: The White House (29 May), http://www.whitehouse.gov/the_press_office/Remarks-by-the-President-on-Securing-Our-Nations-Cyber-Infrastructure/.

Obama, President Barack (2010) *United States National Security Strategy,* Washington, DC: The White House.

Obama, President Barack (2011a) 'State of the Union Address', Washington, DC: The White House (25 January), http://www.whitehouse.gov/the-press-office/2011/01/25/remarks-president-state-union-address.

Obama, President Barack (2011b) *A Strategy for American Innovation: Securing Our Economic Growth and Prosperity,* Washington, DC: The White House (February).

Obama, President Barack (2015) 'Net Neutrality: President Obama's Plan for a Free and Open Internet', Washington, DC: The White House (February), https://www.whitehouse.gov/net-neutrality.

O'Connell, Patricia (2005) 'Online Extra: At SBC, It's All About Scale and Scope', *Business Week* (7 November).

Overholt, William H. (1993) *China: The Next Economic Superpower,* London: Weidenfeld & Nicolson.

Paget, François (2010) 'Cybercrime and Hacktivism', Santa Clara: McAfee Labs, http://www.mcafee.com/us/resources/white-papers/wp-cybercrime-hactivism.pdf.

Palfrey, John G. (2004) 'The End of the Experiment: How ICANN'S foray into Global Internet Democracy Failed', *Harvard Journal of Law & Technology,* pp. 409–73, Vol. 17, No. 2 (Spring).

Paller, Alan (2005) Testimony at *SCADA Systems and the Terrorist Threat: Protecting the Nation's Critical Control Systems,* hearing before the Committee on Homeland Security, Subcommittee on Economic Security, Infrastructure Protection and Cybersecurity and the Subcommittee on Emergency Preparedness, Science and Technology, House of Representatives (18 October).

Pascrell, Bill (2005) *SCADA Systems and the Terrorist Threat: Protecting the Nation's Critical Control Systems,* hearing before the Committee on Homeland Security, Subcommittee on Economic Security, Infrastructure Protection and

Cybersecurity and the Subcommittee on Emergency Preparedness, Science and Technology, House of Representatives (18 October).

Pelosi, Nancy (2005) Remarks on the release of the 'Innovation Agenda' by the House Democrats (15 November), http://pelosi.house.gov/.

Pickering, Charles (2001) *Is ICANN's New Generation of Internet Domain Name Selection Process Thwarting Competition?*, hearing before the Committee on Energy and Commerce, Subcommittee on Telecommunications and the Internet, US House of Representatives (8 February).

Pinch, Trevor (1988) 'Understanding Technology: Some Possible Implications of Work in the Sociology of Science', in *Technology and Social Process,* Brian Elliott (ed.), Edinburgh: Edinburgh University Press.

Posner, Michael (2010) 'State Department Officials Brief Reporters on Internet Freedom: Officials Describe Links Between Internet Freedom, Human Rights', State Department briefing (23 January) Washington, DC: The White House, http://www.america.gov/st/texttrans-english/2010/January/20100123124856SBlebahC1.357234e-02.html.

Powell, Michael K. (2002) 'Statement of Chairman Michael K. Powell' in the FCC 02–77, Declaratory Ruling and Notice of Proposed Rulemaking, *in the Matter of Inquiry Concerning High-Speed Access to the Internet Over Cable and Other Facilities/Internet Over Cable Declaratory Order Proceeding/Appropriate Regulatory Treatment for Broadband Access to the Internet Over Cable Facilities,* Washington, DC, Federal Communications Commission (15 March).

Reinsch, William (2000) Prepared statement for *Internet Security,* hearing before the Committee on Commerce, Science, and Transportation, Subcommittee on Communications, United States Senate (8 March).

Reus-Smit, Christian (2004) *American Power and World Order,* Cambridge: Polity Press.

Ridge, Tom (2005) *Interim National Infrastructure Protection Plan,* Washington, DC: Department of Homeland Security (February).

Rockerfeller, John (2009) *Cybersecurity: Assessing our Vulnerabilities and Developing an Effective Response,* hearing before the Committee on Commerce, Science, and Transportation, United States Senate (19 March).

Rogerson, Simon and Terrell Ward Bynum (1995) 'Cyberspace: The Ethical Frontier', *The London Times* (9 June).

Rogin, Josh (2010) 'China's Expansion of Economic Espionage Boils Over', *Foreign Policy* (14 January).

Rosecrance, Richard (1999) *The Rise of the Virtual State: Wealth and Power in the Coming Century,* New York, NY: Basic Books.

Ross, Alec (2010) 'State Department Officials Brief Reporters on Internet Freedom: Officials Describe Links Between Internet Freedom, Human Rights', State Department briefing, Washington, DC: The White House (23 January), http://www.america.gov/st/texttrans-english/2010/January/20100123124856SBlebahC1.357234e-02.html.

Rothkopf, David J. (1998) 'Cyberpolitik: The Changing Nature of Power in the Information Age', *Journal of International Affairs,* pp. 325–59, Vol. 51, No. 2 (Spring).

Ruggie, John Gerard (1993) 'Territoriality and Beyond: Problematizing Modernity in International Relations', *International Organisation,* pp. 139–74, Vol. 47, No. 1 (Winter).

Russett, Bruce, Thomas Hartley and Shoon Murray (1994) 'The End of the Cold War, Attitude Change, and the Politics of Defense Spending', *PS: Political Science and Politics*, pp. 17–21, Vol. 27, No. 1 (March).

S. 1067, *National High-Performance Computing Act of 1990*, 101st Congress, 2nd Session, as marked up 3 April, 1990.

S. 2918, *National High-Performance Computing Act of 1988*, 100th Congress, 2nd Session, 19 October, 1988.

Sassen, Saskia (1999) 'The Impact of the Internet on Sovereignty: Unfounded and Real Worries', Paper presented to the *Internet and International Systems: Information Technology and American Foreign Policy Decision-Making Workshop*, Nautilus Institute, San Francisco (10 December), http://www.nautilus.org/gps/info-policy/workshop/papers/sassen.html.

Schmidt, Brian C. (2005) 'Competing Realist Conceptions of Power', *Millennium: Journal of International Studies*, pp. 523–49, Vol. 33, No. 3.

Schmitt, Michael N. (2009) *The Tallinn Manual*, NATO Cooperative Cyber Defence Centre of Excellence.

Segal, Adam (2004) 'Is America Losing Its Edge?', *Foreign Affairs*, pp. 2–8, Vol. 83, No. 6 (November–December).

Seltzer, Larry (2010) 'Who's Behind Stuxnet? The Americans? The Israelis?', Security Watch blog, *PC Magazine* (26 September), http://blogs.pcmag.com/securitywatch/2010/09/whos_behind_stuxnet_the_americ.php.

Sevastopulo, Demetri (2007) 'Chinese Hacked into Pentagon', *Financial Times* (3 September), http://www.ft.com/cms/s/0/9dba9ba2-5a3b-11dc-9bcd-0000779fd2ac.html.

Shane, Scott (2011) 'Spotlight Again Falls on Web Tools and Change', *New York Times* (29 January) http://www.nytimes.com/2011/01/30/weekinreview/30shane.html?_r=1&ref=scottshane.

Shimeall, Timothy, Phil Williams and Casey Dunlevy (2001) 'Countering Cyber War', *NATO Review*, pp. 16–28, Vol. 49, No. 4 (Winter).

Shimkus, John (2006) *ICANN Internet Governance: Is It Working?*, hearing before the Committee on Energy and Commerce, Subcommittee on Communications, Technology and the Internet and Subcommittee on Commerce, Trade, and Consumer Protection, House of Representatives (21 September).

Shirky, Clay (2009) 'The Net Advantage', *Prospect,* Iss.165 (11 December) http://www.prospectmagazine.co.uk/2009/12/the-net-advantage/.

Sifry, Micah L. (2009) 'Hillary Clinton Launches "21st Century Statecraft" Initiative by State Department', *techPresident* (13 May).

Slaughter, Anne Marie (2004) *A New World Order*, Princeton and Oxford: Princeton University Press.

Slaughter, Anne Marie (2011) 'Interests vs. Values? Misunderstanding Obama's Libya Strategy', *New York Review of Books* (30 March).

Smith, Charles R. (2003) 'U.S. Information Warriors Wrestle with New Weapons', *NewsMax.com* (13 March) http://archive.newsmax.com/archives/articles/2003/3/12/134712.shtml.

Smith, Gordon and Moises Naim (2000) *Altered States: Globalization, Sovereignty and Governance*, Ottawa: International Development Research Centre.

Snowe, Olympia (2006) Statement on Introduced Bills and Joint Resolutions, US Senate (19 May).

Spafford, Eugene H. (2009) *Cybersecurity: Assessing our Vulnerabilities and Developing an Effective Response*, hearing before the Committee on Commerce, Science, and Transportation, United States Senate (19 March).

Staudenmaier, John M. (1985) *Technologies Storytellers: Reweaving the Human Fabric*, Cambridge and London: The Society for the History of Technology and The MIT Press.

Stearns, Cliff (2006) Comments at *ICANN Internet Governance: Is It Working?*, hearing before the Committee on Energy and Commerce, Subcommittee on Communications, Technology and the Internet and Subcommittee on Commerce, Trade, and Consumer Protection, House of Representatives (21 September).

Stevens, Ted (2006) *Net Neutrality*, hearing before the Committee on Commerce, Science, and Transportation, United States Senate (7 February).

Sturken, Marita, Douglas Thomas and Sandra J. Ball-Rokeach (eds.) (2004) *Technological Visions: The Hopes and Fears That Shape New Technologies*, Philadelphia: Temple University Press.

Tanji, Michael (2007) 'Buccaneer.com: Infosec Privateering as a Solution to Cyberspace Threats', *Journal of Cyber Conflict Studies*, pp. 4–11, Vol. 1, No. 1 (December).

Tenet, George J. (2000) Director of Central Intelligence, testimony at *The Worldwide Threat in 2000: Global Realities of Our National Security*, hearing before the Committee on Armed Services, United States Senate (3 February).

Thornburgh, Nathan (2005) 'The Invasion of the Chinese Cyberspies', *Time Magazine* (29 August), http://www.time.com/time/magazine/article/0,9171,1098961,00.html.

Traynor, Ian (2007) 'Russia Accused of Unleashing Cyberwar to Disable Estonia', *Guardian Unlimited* (17 May), http://www.guardian.co.uk/russia/article/0,,2081438,00.html.

Tung, Liam (2007) 'China Accused of Cyberattacks on New Zealand', *CNet News* (13 September), http://news.cnet.com/China-accused-of-cyberattacks-on-New-Zealand/2100-7348_3-6207678.html.

Tunis Agenda for the Information Society (2005) World Summit on the Information Society, held in Tunis, Tunisia. Publication dated 15 November, http://www.itu.int/wsis/docs2/tunis/off/6rev1.pdf.

Turner, Jim (2000) *Computer Security: Cyber Attacks – War Without Borders*, hearing before the Committee on Government Reform, Subcommittee on Government Management, Information, and Technology, US House of Representatives (26 July).

Tynan, Trudy (1984) 'Dictionaries' Editors Mine a Mother Lode-Politics', in *Philadelphia Inquirer* (23 August).

UNGGE (2013) 'Group of Governmental Experts on Developments in the Field of Information and Telecommunications in the Context of International Security', United Nations General Assembly (24 June), http://www.un.org/ga/search/view_doc.asp?symbol= A/68/98.

Upton, Fred (2006) Comments at *ICANN Internet Governance: Is It Working?*, hearing before the Committee on Energy and Commerce, Subcommittee on Communications, Technology and the Internet and Subcommittee on Commerce, Trade, and Consumer Protection, House of Representatives (21 September).

Varnado, Sam (2005) Written response to questions from Representative Bennie G. Thompson at *SCADA Systems and the Terrorist Threat: Protecting the Nation's Critical Control Systems*, hearing before the Committee on Homeland

Security, Subcommittee on Economic Security, Infrastructure Protection and Cybersecurity and the Subcommittee on Emergency Preparedness, Science and Technology, House of Representatives (18 October).

Vatis, Michael (2000) Prepared statement for *Internet Security*, hearing before the Committee on Commerce, Science, and Transportation, Subcommittee on Communications, United States Senate (8 March).

Vatis, Michael (2001) *Cyber Attacks During the War on Terrorism: A Predictive Analysis*, Dartmouth: Institute for Security Technology Studies (22 September).

Victory, Nancy J. (2002) Testimony at *ICANN Governance*, hearing before the Committee on Commerce, Science, and Transportation, Subcommittee on Science, Technology, and Space, United States Senate (12 June).

Vig, Norman (1988) 'Technology, Philosophy and the State', in *Technology and Politics*, Michael E. Kraft and Norman J. Vig (eds.), Durham and London: Duke University Press.

Walt, Stephen M. (2005a) 'Taming American Power', *Foreign Affairs*, Vol. 84, No. 5 (September/October).

Walt, Stephen M. (2005b) *Taming American Power: The Global Response to U.S. Primacy*, New York: W.W. Norton and Company.

Waltz, Kenneth N. (1979) *Theory of International Politics*, Boston: McGraw Hill.

Ward, Stephen J.A. (2011) 'Social Media: Tool for Revolution or Repression?', *MediaMorals*, Center for Journalism Ethics, University of Wisconsin-Madison (31 January), http://ethics.journalism.wisc.edu/2011/01/31/social-media-tool-of-revolution-or-repression/.

Wasserman Shultz, Debbie (2008) *Net Neutrality and Free Speech on the Internet*, hearing before the Committee on the Judiciary, Task Force on Competition Policy and Antitrust Laws, US House of Representatives (11 March).

Weimann, Gabriel (2004) *Cyberterrorism: How Real Is the Threat?*, Special Report for the United States Institute of Peace, Washington, DC (December).

Weiss, Charles (2005) 'Science, Technology and International Relations', *Technology in Society*, pp. 295–313, Vol. 27, No. 3 (August).

Weiss, Thomas G. (2000) 'Governance, Good Governance and Global Governance: Conceptual and Actual Challenges', *Third World Quarterly*, pp. 795–814, Vol. 21, No. 5 (October).

Wendt, Alexander (1992) 'Anarchy Is What States Make of It: The Social Construction of Power Politics', *International Organisation*, pp. 391–425, Vol. 46, No. 2 (Spring).

Wendt, Alexander (1999) *Social Theory of International Politics*, Cambridge: Cambridge University Press.

Wheeler, Tom (2014) Prepared remarks of FCC Chairman, 'The Facts and Future of Broadband Competition', Washington, DC: September 4, 2014.

Wight, Martin (1986) *Power Politics*, Hammondsworth: Penguin Books.

Willemssen, Joel C. (1995) 'Information Superhighway: An Overview of Technology Challenges', Washington, DC: US General Accounting Office (January).

Willemssen, Joel C. (2001) Testimony at *How Safe Is Our Critical Infrastructure?*, hearing before the Governmental Affairs Committee, United States Senate (12 September).

Wilson, Clay (2003) 'Computer Attack and Cyber Terrorism: Vulnerabilities and Policy Issues for Congress', Washington, DC: Congressional Research Service (17 October).

Wilson, Clay (2006) 'Information Operations and Cyberwar: Capabilities and Related Policy Issues', Washington, DC: Congressional Research Service (14 September).

Wilson, Ernest J. and Adam Segal (2005) 'Trends in China's Transition Toward a Knowledge Economy', *Asian Survey,* pp. 886–906, Vol. 45, No. 6 (November/December).

Winner, Langdon (1977) *Autonomous Technology: Technics-Out-of-Control as a Theme in Political Thought,* Cambridge, MA: The MIT Press.

Winner, Langdon (1985) 'Do Artefacts have Politics?' in *The Social Shaping of Technology: How the Refrigerator Got Its Hum,* Donald MacKenzie and Judy Wacjman (eds.), Philadelphia: Open University Press.

Winner, Langdon (1993) 'How Technology Reweaves the Fabric of Society', *The Chronicle of Higher Education,* p. 27, Vol. 39, No. 48 (August 4).

Wyden, Ron (2001) *Response of the Technology Sector in Times of Crisis,* hearing before the Committee on Commerce, Science, and Transportation, US Senate (5 December).

Wyden, Ron (2006) *Net Neutrality,* hearing before the Committee on Commerce, Science, and Transportation, United States Senate (7 February).

Xiwei, Zhong and Yang Xiangdong (2007) 'Science and Technology Policy Reform and its Impact on China's National Innovation System', *Technology in Society,* pp. 317–325, No. 29.

Zakon, Robert (n.d.) 'Hobbes Internet Timeline', *The Internet Society,* http://www.isoc.org.

Zittrain, Jonathan (2008) *The Future of the Internet – And How to Stop it,* New Haven and London: Yale University Press.

Section 1.01 Uncredited News Reports:

BBC (2007) 'Estonia Hit by Moscow Cyber War' (17 May), http://news.bbc.co.uk/2/hi/europe/6665145.stm.

BBC (2008) 'U.S. to Shoot Down Satellite', *News* (14 February), http://news.bbc.co.uk/2/hi/americas/7245578.stm.

BBC (2010) 'Four in Five Regard Internet Access as a Fundamental Right: Global Poll', BBC World Service Poll (7 March).

CNN (2008) 'U.S. to Shoot Down Satellite Wednesday, Official Says' (19 February), http://edition.cnn.com/2008/TECH/space/02/19/satellite.shootdown/.

The Economist (2001) 'Stockmarkets Rudderless: With Markets in America Closed, the Rest of the World Drifted' (13 September), http://www.economist.com/node/780796?fsrc=rss.

The Sydney Morning Herald (2007) 'Estonia Urges Firm EU, NATO Response to New Form of Warfare: Cyber-attacks' (16 May), http://www.smh.com.au/news/Technology/Estonia-urges-firm-EU-NATO-response-to-new-form-of-warfarecyberattacks/2007/05/16/1178995207414.html.

WebSecure (2002) *'Sewage' hacker jailed* (8 May), http://www.websecure.com.au/PressRelease.asp?PR_ID=29.\

Welle, Deutsche (2007a) 'NATO Probes Cyber Attacks on Estonia' (18 May), http://www.dw-world.de/dw/article/0,,2542756,00.html?maca= en-rss-en-all-1573-rdf.

Welle, Deutsche (2007b) 'NATO Sees Recent Cyber Attacks on Estonia as Security Issue' (27 May), http://www.dw-world.de /dw/article/0,2144,2558579,00.html.

List of Hearings

2000

Cyber Attacks: The National Protection Plan and Its Privacy Implications, hearing before the Committee on the Judiciary, Subcommittee on Technology, Terrorism, and Government Information, United States Senate (1 February).

The Worldwide Threat in 2000: Global Realities of Our National Security, hearing before the Committee on Armed Services, United States Senate (3 February).

Cyber Attack: Is the Government Safe?, hearing before the Committee on Governmental Affairs, United States Senate (2 March).

Internet Security, hearing before the Committee on Commerce, Science, and Transportation, Subcommittee on Communications, United States Senate (8 March).

Computer Security: Cyber Attacks – War Without Borders, hearing before the Committee on Government Reform, Subcommittee on Government Management, Information, and Technology, US House of Representatives (26 July).

2001

Is ICANN's New Generation of Internet Domain Name Selection Process Thwarting Competition?, hearing before the Committee on Energy and Commerce, Subcommittee on Telecommunications and the Internet, US House of Representatives (8 February).

How Safe Is Our Critical Infrastructure?, hearing before the Governmental Affairs Committee, United States Senate (12 September).

Response of the Technology Sector in Times of Crisis, hearing before the Committee on Commerce, Science and Transportation, Subcommittee on Science, Technology and Space, United States Senate (5 December).

2002

ICANN Governance, hearing before the Committee on Commerce, Science, and Transportation, Subcommittee on Science, Technology, and Space, United States Senate (12 June).

2003

Cyber Security: The Challenges Facing Our Nation in Critical Infrastructure Protection, hearing before the Committee on Government Reform, Subcommittee on Technology, Information Policy, Intergovernmental Affairs and the Census, US House of Representatives (8 April).

The Invisible Battleground, hearing before the Select Committee on Homeland Security, Subcommittee on Cybersecurity, Science, and Research and Development, US House of Representatives (16 September).

2005

Securing Cyberspace: Efforts to Protect National Information Infrastructures Continue to Face Challenges, hearing before the Committee on Homeland Security and Governmental Affairs, Subcommittee on Federal Financial Management, Government Information, and International Security Subcommittee, United States Senate (19 July).

SCADA Systems and the Terrorist Threat: Protecting the Nation's Critical Control Systems, hearing before the Committee on Homeland Security, Subcommittee on Economic Security, Infrastructure Protection and Cybersecurity and the Subcommittee on Emergency Preparedness, Science and Technology, US House of Representatives (18 October).

2006

Net Neutrality, hearing before the Committee on Commerce, Science, and Transportation, United States Senate (7 February).

Network Neutrality: Competition, Innovation, and Nondiscriminatory Access, hearing before the Committee on the Judiciary, Task Force on Telecom and Antitrust, US House of Representatives (25 April).

ICANN Internet Governance: Is It Working?, hearing before the Committee on Energy and Commerce, Subcommittee on Communications, Technology and the Internet and Subcommittee on Commerce, Trade, and Consumer Protection, US House of Representatives (21 September).

2007

The Digital Future of the United States, hearing before the Committee on Energy and Commerce, Subcommittee on Telecommunications and the Internet, US House of Representatives (1, 7 March, 19, 24 April, 10 May, 2 October).

2008

Global Security Assessment, hearing before the Committee on Armed Services, US House of Representatives (13 February).

Net Neutrality and Free Speech on the Internet, hearing before the Committee on the Judiciary, Task Force on Competition Policy and Antitrust Laws, US House of Representatives (11 March).

2009

Current and Future Worldwide Threats to the National Security of the United States, hearing before the Committee on Armed Services, United States Senate (10 March).

Cybersecurity: Assessing Our Vulnerabilities and Developing an Effective Response, hearing before the Committee on Commerce, Science and Transportation, United States Senate (19 March).

Agency Response to Cyberspace Policy Review, hearing before the Committee on Science and Technology, Subcommittee on Technology and Innovation and the Subcommittee on Research and Science Education, US House of Representatives (16 June).

2010

Cybersecurity: Next Steps to Protect Critical Infrastructure, hearing before the Committee on Commerce, Science and Transportation, United States Senate (23 February).

2012

Iranian Cyber Threat to U.S. Homeland, joint hearing before the Committee on Homeland Security, Subcommittee on Counterterrorism and Intelligence and the Subcommittee on Cybersecurity, Infrastructure Protection, and Security Technologies, US House of Representatives (26 April).

2015

The Uncertain Future of the Internet, hearing before the Subcommittee on Communications and Technology, Committee on Energy and Commerce, United States House of Representatives (25 February).

Index

Andreessen, Mark, 53
ARPA (Advanced Research Projects Agency)
  ARPAnet, 48–50
  establishment of, 46–8
Atari Democrats, 12, 50, 54

Berners Lee, Tim, 52–3, 128, 176–7
Bijker, Weibe, 7
Bina, Eric, 53
Bush, George H., 55
Bush administration 2001–2009
  Homeland Security Presidential Directive 7 (HSPD-7), 68, 100
  National Strategy to Secure Cyberspace, 67, 101

Cailliau, Robert, 52–3
Cerf, Vinton, 48–9, 165, 176–8
Chehade, Fadi, 145
China
  cyber attacks, 74, 93–5
  Domain Name System (DNS), 139–40
  US indictment of PLA officials, 94
Civil liberties, see Human rights
Clarke, Richard, 63, 104, 105
Clinton administration 1993–2001
  approach to cyber security, 89–90, 103
  Clinton-Gore vision, 54–60, 124–7, 146–8
  Defending America's Cyberspace, 113
  election campaign, 55
  grand strategy, 55, 109–10
  Presidential Decision Directive 63 (PDD-63), 62–3, 77, 97, 101
  shift from military to economic power, 54–7

Clinton, Hillary
  civilian power, 75
  Internet freedom, see Internet freedom
  people to people diplomacy, 75, 110
  Quadrennial Diplomacy and Development Review, see Slaughter, Anne-Marie
  21st Century Statecraft, 75–6, 110–11, 114, 188–9
Cold War, 47–8, 54
Congressional hearings, explanation of, 10–11
Cyber security
  attribution, 85–8, 94–5, 104–5, 108–12
  concepts of, 84–5
  critical infrastructure, 60, 67–8, 84, 88–9, 100
  cyber crime, 97–8, 104–5
  cyber terrorism, 68
  cyber war, 69, 87–95
  DDoS attack, 96
  economic cost of, 89, 95–8
  and Internet development, 49–50, 85–6
  legal implications, 87–8
  National Plan for Information Systems Protection, 63
  SCADA systems, 60, 88–9
  use of proxies, 95

Domain Name System (DNS), 13
  background, 59, 121–3
  governance of, see Internet governance
  growth, 125–8
  political implications, 139
Dotcom boom, 126, 157

Ellul, Jacques, 26
Estonia, cyber attacks on, 37, 68–9, 87

Federal Communications
    Commission, 72, 159–61, 175
FEMA (Federal Emergency
    Management Agency), 66
Franklin, Marianne, 42, 152

Gore, Al, 12
    contribution to developing Internet
        technology, 50–4
    'Gore' Bill, *see* National High
        Performance Computer
        Technology Bill
    ideas about US power and
        technology, 51

Hart, Gary, 50
Hathaway, Melissa, 74, 79, 106–7
Holder, Eric, 94, 103–4
HTTP, *see* World Wide Web
Hurricane Katrina, 66–7

ICANN (Internet Corporation for
    Assigned Names and Numbers)
    Affirmation of Commitments, 144
    genesis, 59–60, 117–18, 134
    Joint Project Agreement, 145
    legitimacy, internal, 135–41
    legitimacy of US oversight, 141–5
    Memorandum of Understanding,
        145
    policy agenda, 138–41
    and the United Nations, 143–4
Internet
    Acceptable Use Policy, 58
    geopolitics, 98–9
    history, 48
    human rights, 55, 63, 109, 112–13
    and national security, 77, 91
    penetration in the US, 163–70
    privacy, 112–14
    privatization and
        commercialization, 57–60,
        125–6, 164–5
    TCP/IP, 48–50
    US investment in, 51–3, 55–6,
        79–80, 167
Internet freedom, 75–6, 109–11, 170–5

Internet governance
    Department of Commerce, 121,
        131, 133–5, 144
    Framework for Global Electronic
        Commerce, 130–1
    genesis, 59, 117–18
    Green Paper on Internet
        Governance, 131–3
    Internet Assigned Numbers
        Authority (IANA), 121, 128,
        141, 145
    National Telecommunications and
        Information Administration,
        121, 131, 133
    technology and concepts, 121–3
    White Paper on Internet
        Governance, 133–5

Kahn, Robert, 48–9
Keohane, Robert, 123–4, 129, 137

Lessig, Lawrence, 176–8
Lewis, James, 89, 106
Luce, Clare Booth, 47

MacKenzie, Donald, 20, 27–8, 42–3
Magaziner, Ira, 130
Marcuse, Herbert, 23
Mearsheimer, John, 34–5, 78
Morgenthau, Hans, 22, 34, 78, 99, 108
Mosaic browser, 53
Mueller, Milton, 118, 137–8, 145,
    171–2
Mumford, Lewis, 25–6, 49

National High Performance Computer
    Technology Bill, 51–4
National High-Performance
    Computing Act of 1990, 57–8
National Information Infrastructure
    Act of 1993, 125
National Research and Education
    Network (NREN), 51, 125
National Science Foundation, 57–8,
    128
    NSF 'backbone' 58
NATO, response to Estonian attacks,
    69, 87

Network neutrality
  anti-competitive cases,
    159–61
  background, 70–3, 154–6
  business models, 156–8
  ISP as gatekeeper, 172–3
  ISP as responsible stakeholder,
    173–5
Non-state actors, 40–1
Nye, Joseph, 123–4, 129

Obama administration 2009,
    73–6
  Cyberspace Policy Review, 74, 100,
    106–7
  National Cyber Security Review, 89
  National Infrastructure Protection
    Plan, 100

Personal computer (PC), 50, 54
Philosophy of Technology, 5–8,
    17
  approaches to technology, 6
  defining technology, 19–21
  determinism, *see* Technological
    determinism
  instrumentalism, 22, 29, 47–8, 51,
    80, 115–16, 151–2, 162
  relevant social group, 7–8, 120, 127,
    128–9
  reverse salient, 7–8
Pinch, Trevor, 20
Postel, Jon, 122, 128, 134
Power
  asymmetry, 91–3
  civilian, 75
  conceptions of, 5–8, 14, 114–16,
    183–5
  geopolitics and, 98–9
  hegemonic, 118, 129, 141, 169
  material, 33–8, 80–4, 89–91, 103,
    114–16, 150–3, 163–8
  relationship to technology, 12,
    32–44, 115, 126, 142–3, 146–8,
    165–7
  social, 38–43, 54, 80–4, 115–16,
    150–3
  US conceptions post Cold War,
    51–2, 54–5, 92, 124–6, 129

PRISM project, 114
Public private partnership, 62–3, 67–8,
    80, 100–7
  assessing the effectiveness, 105–7
  private sector approach, 103–5
  US government approach, 102–3

Reus Smit, Christian, 40
Ross, Alec, 111

Sassen, Saskia, 42
SCADA systems, *see* Cyber security
September 11 attacks, 66–8, 99
Slaughter, Anne-Marie, 111
Social construction of technology, 7,
    28–32, 49
Sovereignty, *see* Technology, effects on
    sovereignty
Snowden, Edward, *see* PRISM project
Sputnik, 35, 47
Stuxnet, 88–9

TCP/IP, *see* Internet, TCP/IP
Technological determinism, 23–8,
    29–30
  hard determinism, 24–5
  'lock-in', 25, 49
  'megamachine', 25, 49
  norm-based approach, 26–7
  and policy making, 27–8, 51–2,
    151–2
  and social power, 39
Technology
  disruptive qualities, 37, 56, 64–70
  effects on sovereignty, 39, 42, 98–9
  effects on state power, 41
  and material power, 35–8, 103,
    114–16, 150–3, 163–8
  and national character, 108
  nuclear, 37–8, 48
  social/political shaping of, 28–32,
    57, 64–5, 130–3, 188–9
  and social power, 38–43
  as a source of power, 52, 55–6, 95,
    119, 179
  undermining power, 64–70, 90, 95
Telecommunications
  competition, 72
  law, 70–3

Tenet, George, 90, 92, 94–5
21st Century Statecraft, *see* Clinton, Hillary

United Nations
  Declaration of Human Rights, 111
  Group of Governmental Experts, 41
  International Telecommunications Union, 142, 144
  World Conference on International Telecommunications (WCIT), 144
  World Summit on the Information Society (WSIS), 124, 171–2
United States
  primacy, 46–7, 51–2, 55–6, 62, 165–7

technological leadership, 51–2, 54, 74, 107, 150–2, 168–70
Vanguard satellite, 47

Vatis, Michael, 92, 94–5, 103, 113
Vig, Norman, 22–3

Wacjman, Judy, 42–3
Waltz, Kenneth, 34–5, 78
Wikileaks, 40, 76
Winner, Langdon, 27, 146
World Wide Web (the Web), 52–3
  browser history, 53
  HTTP (Hypertext Transfer Protocol), 53

Y2K bug, 64–5